100
PHILOSOPHERS

100 PHILOSOPHERS

A Guide To The World's

Greatest Thinkers

PETER J. KING

CHARTWELL
BOOKS, INC.

CONTENTS

A QUARTO BOOK

This edition published in 2013 by
Chartwell Books, Inc.
A division of Book Sales, Inc.
276 Fifth Avenue, Suite 206
New York, New York 10001
USA

ISBN: 978-0-7858-3022-1

QUAR.FPS

Conceived, designed, and produced by
Quarto Publishing plc
The Old Brewery
6 Blundell Street
London N7 9BH

Project Editor Paula McMahon
Senior Art Editor Penny Cobb
Copy Editor Carol Baker
Designer Julie Francis
Picture researcher Claudia Tate
Photographer Paul Forester
Illustrators Kuo Kang Chen, Coral Mula
Proof reader Jo Fisher
Indexer Geraldine Beare

Art Director Moira Clinch
Publisher Piers Spence

Printed in China

78 EARLY MODERN

116 NINETEENTH CENTURY

136 TWENTIETH CENTURY

INTRODUCTION

The word "philosophy" comes from the Greek, meaning "love of wisdom." As is usually the case with etymology, though, that doesn't get us very far. Even leaving aside the tricky question of what "wisdom" means, simply loving it doesn't seem either very useful or much like what philosophers actually do. Perhaps we could interpret it as meaning something more: like the attempt to gain knowledge and understanding. But how does philosophy differ from other human activities that have the same purpose?

The question is complicated by the fact that the scope of philosophy has changed over the centuries. For a very long time it included almost every intellectual endeavor, from theology to physics, from psychology to logic. This lasted until the end of the medieval period, when the situation began to fragment. The first split was between theology and philosophy; though preceded by a number of writers who had laid the groundwork, **Descartes** marks the beginning of the new age. He makes use of the notion of god, and even offers two arguments for god's existence, but he does so in the service of his attempt to provide secure foundations for human knowledge. The second split was between the empirical and the nonempirical: what we now think of as the physical sciences gradually took on identities of their own, becoming physics, chemistry, and biology. Disciplines such as psychology and sociology split off later, often in a deliberate attempt to move them into the empirical, scientific arena.

Part of the problem of defining philosophy, then, is that it's everything that's left—and unsurprisingly, it's impossible to give a neat definition that includes and excludes everything that should be included and excluded. The best approach is to look at some examples of what goes on in philosophy. We can start by asking what the difference is between, for example, the philosophy of religion and the psychology or sociology of religion. The psychologist is typically concerned with the role that religion and religious practices and beliefs play in the individual psyche, as well as the role of psychological phenomena in the nature and development of religion. Similarly, the sociologist is typically concerned with the role of religion and religious practices in society, and with religions as social structures. Neither is concerned with the *truth* of religious claims, or with whether religious beliefs and practices make sense; that's the concern of philosophy.

This distinction sheds *some* light on the nature of philosophy, but we need more detail. Let's take a question from the philosophy of religion. What, for example, is the relationship between morality and god (or the gods)? In his dialogue *Euthyphro*, **Plato** poses a problem to the believer that has been debated by philosophers and theologians ever since—a problem known as the Euthyphro dilemma: are pious things pious because the gods love them, or do the gods love them because they're pious? The same dilemma can be raised for morality, in terms of monotheism: are moral actions good because god commands them, or does god command them because they're good?

Alexandria is often described as the world's first great center of learning. The library housed works by the greatest thinkers of the ancient world. It was at the library that Euclid discovered the rules of geometry, Ptolemy wrote the Almagest, Eratosthenes measured the diameter of the Earth, and Archimedes invented the screw-shaped water pump that is still used today. Works by Plato, Socrates, and many others were destroyed by the fire which razed it to the ground.

Throughout history, philosophy has sought to assess and explain basic concepts such as morality and god, and to analyze the relationships between them.

Neither horn of this dilemma is very attractive to the believer. If god's commands create morality, (this is known as Divine Command Theory), then he could have commanded very differently—for example, that murder is good and charity evil—and our moral values would have been reversed; if on the other hand, god commanded that murder is evil because it is evil, then morality is independent of god's will, so he hasn't created everything (and is subject to morality just like the rest of us). Responses include accepting or trying to minimize the problems associated with one horn or the other, arguing for a combined approach in which some moral values are created and some not, and rejecting the link between morality and god.

We're not concerned here with what different religions have said about what is moral and what isn't, nor with what they've said about god's commands, or his relationship with morality. We're working at a higher level of abstraction, examining the basic concepts of morality and god, and analyzing and assessing their relationship. Philosophy is a way of carrying out this sort of examination rigorously, dispassionately, and disinterestedly. Just as science is a determined effort to overcome human subjectivity in the investigation of the empirical aspects of the world, so philosophy is the effort to do the same thing in the investigation of the nonempirical. Its subject matter includes our concepts, methods, and assumptions, so that philosophy investigates not only its own distinctive subject matter, such as the nature of the mind and consciousness, morality, logic, and so on, but also other disciplines such as the sciences, history, mathematics, and others.

THE MAIN DIVISIONS

Traditionally philosophy has been divided into a small number of core areas; this hasn't really changed much over the centuries, though the questions and approaches often have. These four fundamental areas are common to every philosophical tradition, though different traditions at different times have emphasized some and neglected others.

Metaphysics is the hardest category to explain, partly because of the origins of the term. In the traditional ordering of **Aristotle's** works, the *Metaphysics* was the book that came after the *Physics* ("*meta ta phusika*": "after the Physics"); thus metaphysics concerned the topics dealt with in that book—primarily the nature of being, substance, causation, and the existence of god. Aristotle himself referred to such fundamental issues as *First Philosophy*. The main category of metaphysics is *ontology*; this concerns the question of how many fundamentally distinct sorts of entity there are (material bodies, minds, numbers, and so on). Other metaphysical questions concern the nature of causation, possibility and necessity, and the nature of space and time.

The twentieth century saw a number of movements hostile to metaphysics, such as logical positivism, though they all make unexamined metaphysical assumptions (such as that everything that exists is observable). However, writers such as **Strawson**, **Kripke**, and **Lewis** have brought metaphysics back into the mainstream philosophical arena.

Some people misuse the word "metaphysical" to refer to things like ghosts, magic, and the like; this makes little sense. "Material substance" is as much a metaphysical notion as "immaterial substance"; that everything that exists is physical is as much a metaphysical claim as that

Christiaan Huygens and Salomon Coster admiring their first pendulum clock. Science is rooted in philosophy; Indeed, many philosophers engaged in both philosophical and scientific inquiry as they sought to explain the world. It was, in fact, Mersenne who suggested the use of a pendulum as a timing device to Huygens.

there are nonphysical things such as minds. Indeed, the concept of the world is itself a metaphysical concept, not a scientific one.

Epistemology deals with the notions of knowledge and belief. The main questions concern the nature of knowledge (how, for example, is it to be distinguished from mere true belief?), the possibility of knowledge in general, and the possibility of specific kinds of knowledge (such as knowledge of the past, knowledge through the senses, or knowledge derived from inductive reasoning).

One of the main disagreements has traditionally been between what are called *Rationalists* and *Empiricists*. The two extreme positions are that genuine knowledge (as opposed to merely true beliefs) can come only through our use of reason, not through the senses (Plato in his dialogues *Meno* and *Republic* provides an example of this position), and that genuine knowledge can come only through our use of the senses (the logical positivists, such as the early **Carnap** and the early **Ayer**, come closest to this). In fact, most philosophers lie somewhere between the two extremes.

Logic is the science of valid reasoning and argument; it concerns the relationships between propositions, ideas, or beliefs. The first great logician was Aristotle. In a valid *deductive* argument, the premises and the conclusion are related in such a way that to affirm the former and deny the latter is to contradict yourself. In a valid *inductive* argument (one that moves from a set of singular premises to a general conclusion) this isn't the case, and exactly what such arguments do is an important question for the philosophy of science, epistemology, and philosophical logic. A *sound* argument of either type is a valid argument whose premises are true. In *formal* (or *mathematical* or *symbolic*) logic, whose first great propounder was **Frege** (building on the work of the mathematicians George Boole and Augustus de Morgan), logical structures are put in symbolic form, and the scope of logic is much greater.

Philosophical logic (or the philosophy of logic) started as an investigation of the concepts, terms, and methods of logic, but expanded in scope during the twentieth century, partly as a response to the developments in formal logic, but partly to fill the gap left by the (temporary) discarding of metaphysics. A typical example of this is the question of existence: in metaphysics one might ask whether existence is a genuine property, whereas in philosophical logic one would ask whether "exists" is a predicate.

Moral Philosophy is, for many nonphilosophers, philosophy's central concern—and, indeed, the investigation of the nature of morality and of how we should live our lives has been a key concern of philosophers in all traditions. It has also, however, been seen as being outside the core of philosophy, because it relies upon more fundamental theories in metaphysics and epistemology. The two main divisions of moral philosophy (see Overview page 181 for a more detailed account) are Metaethics and Normative Ethics.

Metaethics deals with the most basic questions of morality, such as whether moral values are objective, whether moral statements can be true or false, and the relationship between morality and the concept of free will.

Normative ethics typically deals with more practical questions, such as whether abortion, suicide, and euthanasia are intrinsically wrong, wrong in certain circumstances, or never wrong. In the twentieth century specialized areas grew up around the application of moral thinking to specific areas of human activity—for example medical ethics, business ethics, and environmental ethics.

THIS BOOK

It should now be clear that philosophy (like the sciences) is a process, not a product—a way of thinking and arguing about a certain kind of subject matter, not a set of beliefs. Strictly speaking, in fact, there's no such thing as a philosophical belief, because what counts isn't where you get to but how you get there; the key is to have good reasons for your beliefs, in the form of arguments for your position and defenses against criticisms. Someone might hold that nothing exists apart from matter and its arrangements. This may be because she's thought about it, examined the arguments for and against, and come down (albeit with an open mind) on one side of the debate. She may subscribe to a particular belief because that's what she's been told, or it's what all her friends think, or it's what sounds intellectual and daring in the cafeteria. Only the first case counts as philosophy.

This imposes a number of constraints on what follows. Most importantly, there have been many people throughout history who have produced important systems of beliefs. Many are often referred to as philosophers, but they haven't let us know the reasoning that got them to their conclusions—Gautama Buddha and Jesus, for example, fall more or less into that category. This book generally covers thinkers who pass on not only their conclusions but their reasoning, too. Occasionally exceptions have been made for thinkers whose arguments have been lost, but who have had a significant effect on the philosophical tradition, or those who haven't presented their reasoning but whose followers have been prompted to supply relevant arguments and counterarguments. This explains the inclusion of **Thalēs of Miletos** and **Lao-zi**, for example.

The philosophers are presented chronologically, by year of birth. However, philosophy isn't—despite its popular image—a solitary pursuit; it develops through dialogue, through the interchange of ideas, and especially through responses to criticism. It's in trying to meet and overcome the objections of other philosophers that much important development occurs. Thus lists of those who influenced and who were influenced by each philosopher have been included.

There are many philosophers—especially in the modern period—who are as deserving of entry as the 100 listed here—and if this book had been longer, or written by another philosopher, or at a different time, it would have included some or all of the following: Protagoras of Abdera, Strato of Lampsacus, Philo, Abraham ben David Hallevi ibn Daud, Madhva, Levi ben Gershom, Julien Offroy de la Mettrie, Sir William Hamilton, Auguste Comte, Herbert Spencer, Henry Sidgwick, Ernst Mach, Alexius von Meinong, Henri Bergson, Pierre Duhem, Alfred North Whitehead, John McTaggart, Nishida Kitaro, Moritz Schlick, Otto Neurath, L. Susan Stebbing, C. D. Broad, Gilbert Ryle, J. L. Austin, J. L. Mackie, Philippa Foot, J. J. C. Smart, David Armstrong, Bernard Williams, Ronald Dworkin, Kwame Gyekye, Alvin Plantinga, John Searle, Robert Nozick, John McDowell, and Kwame Anthony Appiah.

Philosophy is a way of thinking, it is concerned with having good reasons for your beliefs and not about the beliefs themselves.

The origins of philosophy are hard to pinpoint; its development was gradual, a slow change in the way that people thought. Things are complicated by the fact that there are different ways of defining philosophy, of distinguishing it from non-philosophy. We might look for the record of a certain way of arguing, but then we'd have to omit thinkers who clearly did think in such ways, but who omitted to write anything except their conclusions. We'd also have to omit writers whose works have formed the

625 B.C.E.

551 B.C.E.

510 B.C.E.

570 B.C.E.

subject matter for generations of philosophical thinkers.

Thalēs of Miletos, for example, left no writings, but is a significant figure because of the way that he thought, and the sorts of explanation that he thought were satisfactory. K'ung fu-zi, on the other hand, left us the *Analects*, but we do not know the structure of his thought, or the sorts of argument that he used to reach and defend his views. What makes him significant are the views themselves, and the way that future generations of thinkers philosophized about what he said.

1125 B.C.E.   Zhou dynasty in China

776 B.C.E.   First Olympiad in Greece

508 B.C.E.   Democratic constitution in Athens

490 B.C.E.   Battle of Marathon

ANCIENT
700 B.C.E.—400 C.E.

480 B.C.E.   The Buddha dies. Battles of Thermopylæ; and Salamis

461 B.C.E.   Accession of Pericles in Athens

447 B.C.E.   Parthenon begun

431 B.C.E.   Outbreak of Peloponnesian War

404 B.C.E.   Athens surrenders to Sparta

403 B.C.E.   Start of Period of Warring States in China

338 B.C.E.   Philip II of Macedon defeats Greek city-states

428 B.C.E.

336 B.C.E.   Philip II assassinated; accession of Alexander the Great

334 B.C.E.   Alexander invades Persia

332 B.C.E.   Alexander occupies Egypt

326 B.C.E.   Alexander conquers the Punjab

470 B.C.E.

323 B.C.E.   Alexander dies; breakup of his empire

322 B.C.E.   Demosthenes dies

321 B.C.E.   Maurya dynasty unifies northern India

275 B.C.E.   Rome dominates all of Italy

273 B.C.E.   Accession of Asoka in India

221 B.C.E.	Qin dynasty in China
213 B.C.E.	Purge of non-Legalist Chinese philosophy by Emperor Shi Huangdi
212 B.C.E.	Archimedes dies
206 B.C.E.	Earlier Han dynasty in China
160 B.C.E.	Judas Maccabaeus dies
73 B.C.E.	Third slave revolt, under Spartacus
55–54 B.C.E.	Julius Caesar's two expeditions to Britain
49 B.C.E.	Caesar crosses the Rubicon
44 B.C.E.	Caesar assassinated
42 B.C.E.	Battle of Philippi
6 B.C.E.	Birth of Jesus (?)
9 C.E.	Xin dynasty in China
17 C.E.	Livy dies
18 C.E.	Ovid dies
25 C.E.	Later Han dynasty in China
29 C.E.	Crucifixion of Jesus (?)
43 C.E.	Roman invasion of Britain
60 C.E.	Revolt of Boudicca (Boadicea)
79 C.E.	Destruction of Pompeii and Herculaneum
122 C.E.	Hadrian's Wall begun
220 C.E.	Han dynasty ends; Period of Disunion begins
306 C.E.	Constantine the Great proclaimed emperor
320 C.E.	Gupta dynasty unites India
410 C.E.	Sack of Rome by Alaric the Goth

EAST AND WEST

The traditions of East and West differ in other ways too. Just as it is a fair generalization to say that the Chinese were uninterested in science but made great technological advances, so we can say that they were largely uninterested in abstract philosophical thought as it is understood in the West, preferring practical matters of politics and ethics. One of the main things that distinguishes Thalēs from the Babylonians and Egyptians is his interest in astronomy and math for their own sakes, not for the purely practical purposes of calendar reform or ziggurat and pyramid building. The defining feature of Western philosophy was set

371 B.C.E.   334 B.C.E.

during this period: the search for truth through questioning and argument. The defining feature of Eastern thought was also set: the search for the best way to live (individually and socially). When we talk about *philosophy* in these different traditions, then, we're using rather different definitions of the word—or, at least, emphasizing very different aspects of the concept.

Of course it's always possible to describe things so as to bring them closer together (or to move them further apart). For example, we might point out

that the pre-Socratic Greeks' interest in cosmology wasn't completely removed from the Chinese interest in ethics (the Greek word "*kosmos*" could also be used to mean "good order," which had ethical connotations), and the Greek interest in abstract reasoning was in addition to their interest in solving practical problems in science, ethics, politics, and so on. Moreover, we can find many parallels between the thoughts that the philosophers in each tradition developed and the attitudes that they expressed about human beings,

341 B.C.E.   280 B.C.E.   150 C.E.   354 C.E.

society, the world, and the role of philosophy—as for example, the notions of *dao* and *logos*, or the willingness to question ordinary, common-sense beliefs. It's possible, though, to be misled by surface similarities, and to take two concepts or doctrines to be alike when they're simply equally obscure.

SOCRATES

Socrates is the turning point in ancient philosophy, and those philosophers who lived before him are known collectively as the pre-Socratics. They divide into a number of schools, of which the most important are the Milesians, the Pythagoreans, the Eleatics, and the Atomists. But it's Plato and Aristotle who form the center and the main focus of interest in ancient philosophy; that's not only because we have large bodies of accessible work from them both, rather than the scattered fragments of most of their predecessors, but because they're formidable philosophers who between them set the philosophical agenda for the next two millennia, in terms both of methodology and of topics of interest.

THALĒS OF MILETOS

BORN c.625 B.C.E., Miletos	DIED c.545 B.C.E.

MAIN INTERESTS   Science, cosmology

INFLUENCES   Egyptian geometry, Mesopotamian astronomy

INFLUENCED   Pythagoras; science and philosophy

The elements of earth, air, fire, and water weren't what we'd mean by those terms; rather, they represented types of substance. Moreover, the types of substance represented by each term would often be surprising to modern readers—for example, "water" included metals (presumably because they can melt).

Thalēs came from the Greek colony of Miletos on the western coast of Asia Minor, and is generally considered to have been the first genuine scientist, in that he developed a rational, nonsuperstitious account of the natural world. Little is known for sure about his life; the only definite date we have is 585 B.C.E., because he's said to have successfully predicted an eclipse on May 28 of that year.

Thalēs is supposed to have been a merchant who traveled widely and encountered many other cultures and ideas, which he took back to Greece. In particular, he's supposed to have introduced geometry to the Greeks, and to have been the first to prove that a circle is bisected by its diameter. His cosmology, which was probably influenced by Egyptian and Babylonian creation myths, held that the Earth is a cylinder or disc, with water below and above it—it floats on the former and is rained upon by the latter. Water, moreover, is the basic principle or constituent of the universe.

We know little else for certain about his beliefs; none of his writings survive, so that all we have are various legends and an account in Aristotle's *Metaphysics*, written some two hundred years after his death. He may have held some version of panpsychism.

Thalēs was the first of an important line of Milesian thinkers. These included Anaximander (c.611–547 B.C.E.), who is credited with introducing a basic cosmology

In a nutshell:
The world can be explained without appealing to gods of the gaps.

that lasted for two thousand years, until the Copernican revolution: the Earth is at the center of the universe, the Sun, Moon, and stars being arranged in circles around it. He developed a theory of evolution, according to which living things arose from elemental water acted upon by the Sun, then higher animals from the lower (human beings evolving from fish). He held that the world must originate from some substance (*the Boundless*) that underlay the four elements.

Anaximenes (c.550–475 B.C.E.), on the other hand, held that air (or mist) was the primordial element. In the case of each thinker, what's important is not the theory itself (though they're not as crude as they might seem), but the general approach. Though the Egyptians and Babylonians held that water is the primordial element, they appealed to divine action to explain the creation and nature of the world; the Milesians, on the other hand, offered naturalistic explanations. For example, Thalēs explained earthquakes, not by appealing to the actions of some sea god, but by suggesting the occurrence of tremors in the water upon which the Earth floats.

PYTHAGORAS OF SAMOS

BORN	c.570 B.C.E., Samos	DIED	c.500 B.C.E., Metapontum

MAIN INTERESTS Mathematics, science

INFLUENCES Thalēs, Anaximander, Anaximenes

INFLUENCED Heraclitus, Parmenides, Socrates, Plato, Aristotle

The fact that the Earth is roughly spherical, not flat, has been known since the time of Pythagoras, and was familiar to generations of philosophers and scientists. The idea that people thought that the Earth was flat until Columbus showed otherwise is now almost universally believed, and seems to derive from a 19th-century German novel about Columbus (a best seller in its day, but now forgotten).

Pythagoras was born on Samos, but fled the island to escape the reign of its tyrant, Polycrates, and settled in the Greek colony of Croton in southern Italy. There he founded a religious community, which followed strict dietary rules (vegetarianism, plus other taboos, including beans) and other forms of self-discipline. We know his teachings only through his students, many of whom were women, including his own wife (Theano of Crotona) and daughters. He seems to have taught that there is a cycle of reincarnation, and that through study and right living one can reach a state where the soul escapes the cycle and joins the world soul.

In mathematics he probably discovered the *proof* of the theorem that bears his name (the *fact* had been known through experience for centuries); in astronomy he is traditionally credited with discovering that Hesperus and Phosphorus (the Evening Star and the Morning Star) are the same thing (now known as the planet Venus); and in acoustics he established the mathematical ratios that relate to the intervals of the musical scale.

This last discovery is perhaps the most important, for it led Pythagoras to the view that the Universe as a whole could be explained in mathematical terms. This was an important step forward from the Milesians; instead of looking for some hypothetical primal matter—whether fire or water or the Boundless—the Pythagoreans concentrated on explaining the world mathematically. This set the course for science in general, and influenced a succession of later scientists and philosophers, most notably **Plato** and Galileo.

It must be admitted that the Pythagoreans often came up with pretty far-fetched accounts of numerical relationships, based on mystical presuppositions rather than observation or logic. Some of Pythagoras' later followers went even further, making actual numbers the building blocks out of which the Universe is built. On the credit side, they were the first to develop a cosmology in which the Earth was a sphere like the Moon and other heavenly bodies, all of which orbited an invisible central hearth, *Hestia* (unfortunately they made the Sun orbit Hestia too). Even here, though, their number-mysticism interfered; because ten is the perfect number, there had to be ten bodies orbiting Hestia, so they invented a "counter-Earth" to make up the numbers. The Pythagoreans, then, offered an uneasy mixture of groundbreaking thought, which established a foundation for modern science, and fuzzy mumbo-jumbo, establishing a foundation for centuries of numerology and other pseudo-sciences.

In a nutshell:
The structure of the world must be understood through numbers.

K'UNG FU-ZI (CONFUCIUS)

| BORN | 551 B.C.E., Ch'ufu, Lu | DIED | 479 B.C.E., Lu |

| MAIN INTERESTS | Ethics, politics |

| INFLUENCES | Unknown |

| INFLUENCED | Everyone who came after him |

MAJOR WORKS
Analects

*"Is there any one word,"
asked Tzu-Kung, "which
could be adopted as a
lifelong rule of conduct?"
The Master replied: "Is
not Sympathy the word?
Do not do to others what
you would not like
yourself."*

Analects XV, xxii

*If the ruler is virtuous,
the people will also be
virtuous[...]*

Analects i

K'ung fu-zi (Confucius) was born illegitimate in the small kingdom of Lu (now Shandong province). His father died when he was three, leaving the family in poverty. He received an excellent education, however, both from the state and through private study, though he had to go to work early to support his mother. After his mother died, in 527 B.C.E., he turned the family home into a school, where he taught history, poetry, and *li* (the rules of proper conduct). Teaching made him very little money, so he was forced to supplement his income with various jobs.

When he first traveled in neighboring states, he found himself unwelcome, probably because of his questioning and forthrightness. After a brief period of study in the capital, he returned to Lu and continued teaching, as well as acting as adviser to various rulers. K'ung fu-zi himself never achieved high office, though some of his followers did. There are a host of apocryphal stories, in which he undergoes a variety of trials and tribulations on his travels. What is certain is that he taught a number of students, who traveled around the country with him.

Living at a time when China was in a state of social and moral decline, K'ung fu-zi taught the need to follow the *dao* (the way or path) of the ancients, emphasizing the ancient cardinal virtues, claiming that the old social hierarchies reflected the moral order of the world, but stressing the need for

Note:
The suffix "-zi" is an honorific, often translated "Master," and "fu" means "great" or "venerable."

virtue and human sympathy at every level of society. His political theory was paternalistic, stressing the need for all members of society to know their places, and to fulfill their position in the social (and domestic) hierarchy to the best of their abilities. He doesn't simply argue for the maintenance of the status quo, however; if rulers are unjust, or in any other significant way fail to fulfill their proper role, the people have the right to rebel against them.

K'ung fu-zi's naturalistic moral and political teachings themselves have reached us through the *Analects* (*Lun-Yu*)—a set of conversations, sayings, and events collected by two of his followers. His teachings had a huge effect on future Chinese thought. His thinking has gone in and out of fashion, but it has never been neglected (though sometimes it's been harshly criticized, as in the People's Republic of China during the 1970s, after a period of equally vehement defense in the 1960s). Its lowest point was probably in the fourth century B.C.E., when it had so degenerated that K'ung fu-zi was worshipped as divine, and Confucianism was declared the state religion of China.

OVERVIEW
CHINESE
PHILOSOPHY

The history of Chinese philosophy is normally divided into three eras: the classical, which lasted from about the sixth to the second century B.C.E. (the last four centuries of the Zhou dynasty), the medieval, which lasted until the eleventh century C.E. (covering the Qin and Han dynasties, the Six-Dynasties Period, the Sui and Tang dynasties, the Five-Dynasty Period, and the beginning of the Song dynasty), and the modern era, from then until the present (covering the major part of the Song dynasty, the Yuan, Ming, and Manchu dynasties, and modern nondynastic China).

The classical era was a time of turbulence, as the Zhou dynasty went through its long, slow, and often violent collapse; it saw the lives of **K'ung fu-zi**, **Mo-zi**, **Meng-zi**, **Han Fei-zi**, and, if he was a real person, **Lao-zi**. The four great systems of Chinese thought originated during this period. K'ung fu-zi (or Confucius) gave us the moral and political system, *Confucianism*, and nearly two hundred years later, Meng-zi developed it further, spending his life attempting to establish Confucianism at the heart of Chinese government. Around the same time, the more mystical (though still essentially naturalistic) system of *Daoism* (or Taoism) appeared, attributed to the probably mythical philosopher Lao-zi (or Lao-tzu); however, the book that bears his name wasn't in fact written until about 300 B.C.E. This system was elaborated and established on a firmer footing by Zhuang-zi, whose book of the same name offers a mixture of argument and anecdote in defense of the Daoist position that what is natural is best, and the less government the better (and that presents K'ung fu-zi as if he'd been a Daoist). Mo-zi developed the notion that universal love and mutual benefit was the only way to save society; he founded a community on these *Mohist* lines, which became economically self-sufficient and militarily prepared to fight just wars.

Finally, at the beginning of the fourth century B.C.E. a new system of thought arose, which rejected the generally rosy view of human nature that in different ways underlay the other schools; this was *Legalism*, and

its greatest exponent was the third-century philosopher Han Fei-zi. Legalism regarded human beings as intrinsically evil, held in check only by a strict system of laws and punishments. The result is a political theory that comes close to totalitarianism and had a great influence on Chinese politics for centuries.

VIRTUE VERSUS LAW

Put very simply, then, Confucianism and Mohism argue for rule by virtue (humanity and righteousness), Legalism argues for rule by law and its enforcement, whereas Daoism is largely unconcerned with ruling, and sometimes even argues for a withdrawal from society.

Though, as is clear from the above, Chinese philosophy mostly centered on social, moral, and political issues, there were many thinkers who grappled with other concerns, including logicians (Mohists in particular developed logic to a high level, though their work was largely neglected by other philosophers), and metaphysicians (though this was always more than slightly tinged with mystical and semi-religious assumptions, as with the Pythagoreans of Ancient Greece).

Two lesser, though still interesting and important, schools should also be mentioned here. The Yin-Yang school offered a cosmology and philosophy of history founded upon the *Five-Powers* theory of the world, which appealed to the five "elements" or powers of water, fire, wood, metal, and earth, together with the Yin-Yang approach developed in the classic Chinese text the *Yi Jing*. The School of Names was centrally concerned with language, but few of its writings have survived, and it has generally been neglected by other philosophers.

The history of philosophy in China after the classical era is almost entirely one of consolidation and development of the great schools (especially Confucianism) and of foreign systems of thought, rather than of new, original thinking. That is not to say that a great deal of interesting and important work wasn't done—for example, see the entries on the medieval philosopher **Wang Chong**, and the modern philosophers **Zhu Xi** and **Wang fu-zi**.

LAO-ZI (LAO-TZU)

LIVED c.570–490 B.C.E.?	**DIED** Unknown

MAIN INTERESTS   Ethics, politics, metaphysics

INFLUENCES   Unknown

INFLUENCED   Everyone who came after him

MAJOR WORKS
Lao-zi (Dao De Jing)

Though originally a philosophical system, Daoism had become a religion by 440 C.E.; Lao-zi was treated as a divinity, and the Daoists vied with the Buddhists and Confucians for favor at Court.

Like the Greek bard Homer, it is not clear who Lao-zi (Lao-tzu) was, or even if he existed. "Lao-zi" is a title, meaning "Old Master," which may have been given to any one of a number of philosophers, or may simply stand for "whoever wrote the book called *Lao-zi*." Even the time at which he lived is uncertain, with different accounts placing him anywhere from the thirteenth to the fourth century B.C.E. The following is a more likely account than most.

Lao-zi was born to a farming family in Henan around 570 B.C.E. He held the post of imperial historian of the State Archives at the court of Zhou. It was a time of political and social instability, and Lao-zi resolved to become a hermit. He set out for the mountains, but was stopped at the border. The customs official allowed him to pass, on condition that he leave some record of his wisdom; Lao-zi wrote a short book, mounted his ox, and left China forever. The book became known as the *Lao-zi*, otherwise called the *Dao De Jing*—the founding text of Daoism. (It seems actually to have been written some time in the third century B.C.E.)

The book is in two parts: the *De Jing* (the Book of Virtue), followed by the *Dao Jing* (the Book of the Way). (The discovery of the oldest surviving copy, the Silk Manuscript, in 1973, gave us this ordering.) The first deals with social, political, and moral matters, the second with metaphysics. At the heart of Daoism is a belief in the natural unity of

In their own words:

Humans model themselves on Earth,/ Earth on Heaven,/ Heaven on the Way,/ And the Way on that which is naturally so.

Dao De Jing §251

humankind and the world. When that unity is in place, people live in simplicity and harmony; when its unity is disrupted, the result is desire, selfishness, and competition. Morality and politics are called upon in the absence of the unity, but they only make things worse. The aim of the Daoist is to return to unity by rejecting social conventions, accepted morality, and worldly desires. So long as unity isn't achieved, governments will be formed. Governments should make it possible for people to live their lives naturally, but not impose any code of conduct. Ideally, the philosopher, or sage, is so filled with the *de* (virtue, or power) of the *dao* that the people will recognize and respond to it, making him their ruler.

The Daoist notion of the *dao* is not the Confucian *dao*; it's eternal, unchanging, both transcendent and immanent, the source of everything, yet uncreative and empty. This union of opposites is an integral part of Daoism. Unsurprisingly, it lent itself to mysticism, and became bound up with alchemy, and the search for immortality.

HERACLITUS OF EPHESOS

BORN c.535 B.C.E., Ephesos	DIED After 480 B.C.E.

MAIN INTERESTS Metaphysics, cosmology

INFLUENCES The Milesians, Pythagoras

INFLUENCED Parmenides, Socrates, Plato, Aristotle, Zeno of Kition

MAJOR WORKS
[Fragments]

As a single, unified thing there exists in us both life and death, waking and sleeping, youth and old age, because the former things having changed are now the latter, and when those latter things change, they become the former.

Quoted in pseudo-Plutarch,
Consolation to Apollo

Born in the Greek city of Ephesos, in what is now Turkey, Heraclitus was considered by the Ancient Greeks to have been one of the most important philosophers, yet he's now a rather obscure figure. Little is known of his life (ancient biographies being fanciful at best), and though he wrote at least one book, *On Nature*, his writings reached us in fragments preserved in the work of other authors. From these fragments, a more-or-less coherent reconstruction of his thought has been developed, though there's considerable disagreement over most of the details. Contemporary accounts agree that his written style was obscure—some say deliberately so, in order to restrict its readership to the educated élite. It's unsurprising, then, that with only the scattered remains to go on, his work is difficult to follow.

Heraclitus seems to have had little time for ordinary people. When asked to help produce a written constitution for Ephesos, he refused, on the grounds that the city was too corrupt. Ordinary people lacked understanding, and he had no interest in them. He had a similar attitude toward other philosophers, especially those from nearby Miletos, against whose work he reacted. His political views seem to have been authoritarian, with an emphasis on the law.

The most important part of Heraclitus' thought, though, is his account of the nature of the world. At the heart of his system is change; either everything in the world, or the world as a whole (it isn't clear from what survives of his writings), is in a constant state of flux, or becoming, and this underlies the nature of everything. For that reason, he took the element of fire to be the primordial substance, and held a view reminiscent of the Pythagoreans, whereby the fire of virtuous human souls will become one with the cosmic fire.

What balances the shifting nature of the world is the *logos*. Like Daoism's notion of the *dao* (with which it is sometimes, misleadingly, equated), the notion of *logos* is complex and difficult to understand. The normal translation would be "word," "speech," "thought," or "reason," depending on the context, though in Heraclitus it plays more the role of universal, cosmic law or principle. The *logos* has the function of reconciling or unifying opposites, of creating and maintaining order. Though it permeates everything, the ordinary person has no understanding of it. There's more than a hint, here and elsewhere in Heraclitus' thought, of **Plato's** doctrine of the Forms, and **Plotinus'** notion of the One.

Note:
In later thought, the notion of logos would pass via the Stoics to the Christian use of the term to refer to god.

PARMENIDES OF ELEA

| BORN   c.510 B.C.E. | DIED   Unknown |

MAIN INTERESTS   Metaphysics, epistemology

INFLUENCES   The Milesians, Pythagoras, Heraclitus, Xenophanes

INFLUENCED   Everyone who came after him

MAJOR WORKS
On Nature

One of Plato's most important dialogues about epistemology, the Parmenides, is based on a meeting between Parmenides, his student Zeno, and Socrates, and Plato is unusually careful to make Parmenides more than just a foil for Socrates' wisdom.

Parmenides' life is a little hazy. The year of his birth is calculated from **Plato's** dialogues, and we don't know when he died. He came from the Greek colony of Elea in southern Italy, which gave its name to the school of which he was the chief figure, the Eleatics. He was involved in the drafting of the laws of Elea, and every year the citizens had to swear an oath to maintain what Parmenides had created. More of his writings survive than of the other pre-Socratics: over a hundred lines of his philosophical poem *On Nature* and fragments of the rest.

In *On Nature*, Parmenides presents theories derived from **Pythagoras** and **Heraclitus**. However, his work is more recognizably philosophical than that of his predecessors: his arguments are clearer, more rigorously deductive, and more abstract. Many of his ideas have continued to shape philosophical thought up to modern times.

Parmenides distinguishes between the world as it is in itself—necessary, unchanging, atemporal—and as it appears to us—contingent, constantly changing, temporal. Unlike **Kant's** noumenal and phenomenal worlds, though, Parmenides argues that the world as it is, Reality, is unperceivable but knowable (via the Way of Truth), whereas the world as it appears is perceivable but unintelligible (the Way of Seeming). Some of his arguments anticpate **Descartes**: we can't doubt that there is thinking, but thinking must have an existing object—therefore we

In a nutshell:
The senses deceive us, but reason reveals the truth.

can be certain that something exists. Moreover, the nonexistent can't be the object of coherent thought, and any theory that refers to what doesn't exist must be incoherent. Whatever exists can be conceived, so whatever can't be conceived can't exist. Also (and this is what seems most peculiar to us), whatever can be conceived must exist, for nothing can't exist.

One conclusion that he draws is the essential unchangingness of the world; coming into being and passing away are both ruled out. Our empirical theories about the world can be convincing and well constructed, and even useful in our everyday lives, but they are unprovable so cannot constitute genuine knowledge. Sense experience is essentially related to change, to coming to be and passing away, yet change is impossible—so sense experience is essentially misleading. Reason alone can lead us to the truth.

For about a century, philosophy was molded by Parmenides. Some, such as **Zeno of Elea**, accepted his position, others, such as Empedocles of Acragus, rejected it, but no one could ignore it.

ZENO OF ELEA

| **BORN** c.490 B.C.E., Elea | **DIED** c.425 B.C.E., Elea |

MAIN INTERESTS Logic, metaphysics, epistemology

INFLUENCES Parmenides

INFLUENCED Plato, Aristotle, Plotinus

MAJOR WORKS
[Fragments]

Zeno's reductio ad absurdum paradoxes have kept philosophers busy over many centuries.

Little is known about Zeno's early life, except that he was the favorite student of his compatriot, **Parmenides**, with whom he traveled to Athens in about 450 B.C.E. Zeno seems to have stayed in Athens for a time, making a living as a teacher (two of his students were Pericles and Callias), before returning to Elea. There he became involved in resistance to the tyrant Nearchos; this story varies, however, with little agreement on the details or, indeed, on whether Zeno survived or died under torture, though his courage is always cited.

He wrote at least one treatise, of which only fragments have survived; we know his work mainly through references in the work of **Plato** and **Aristotle**. Zeno's philosophical position was essentially that of Parmenides; he accepted that Reality was simple and unchanging, and held that sense experience is misleading. What made him famous were his arguments against those who, like the Pythagoreans, emphasized the role of the senses in gaining knowledge, and who proposed accounts of the world involving plurality, motion and change, and spatial structure. He's especially known for his paradoxes, and for his style of reasoning.

His famous arguments are two against the possibility of motion, and the paradox of the heap. Each is a *reductio ad absurdum*.

The arrow: Assume that time is a series of instants, like points on a line. Now, if an arrow is flying through the air, what can we say about it at any instant? Is it moving or at rest? It can't move *in* an instant, because an instant has no duration; therefore it must be at rest. But then it can't be moving at all.

Achilles and the tortoise: Two runners—say, the warrior Achilles and a tortoise—have a race, and Achilles gives the tortoise a ten yard headstart. By the time Achilles has run ten yards to where the tortoise started, the tortoise will have moved some distance farther. By the time Achilles has run that distance, the tortoise will have moved a (shorter) distance farther. By the time Achilles has run that distance, the tortoise will have moved a (yet-shorter) distance farther ... and so *ad infinitum*. So Achilles can never catch up with the tortoise.

The heap: One grain of wheat isn't a heap, and you can't make a nonheap into a heap by adding a single grain. But then, if you start with one grain, and add another, you don't have a heap; and if you add another, you don't have a heap; and if you add another, you don't have a heap ... and so on *ad infinitum*. So it's impossible to make a heap by adding grains.

In a nutshell:
Change and motion and space and time are all in the mind.

MO-ZI (MO-TZU)

BORN	479 B.C.E., Lu	DIED	438 B.C.E.

MAIN INTERESTS Ethics, politics, epistemology

INFLUENCES K'ung fu-zi, Lao-zi

INFLUENCED Later Mohists

MAJOR WORKS
Mo Jing

Mohism was attacked, with the other non-Legalist schools of thought, at the end of the third century B.C.E. by Shi Huangdi, the first Qin emperor. Because it wasn't as well established or as popular as the other major schools, which survived the burning of books and murders of philosophers, Mohism disappeared until modern times, when it began to be investigated by scholars.

Mo-zi (Mo-tzu or Mo-di) was born in the kingdom Lu, though he spent his life traveling. He seems to have started out as a Confucian, and certainly shared **K'ung fu-zi's** love of learning and history; however, he turned against the Confucian acceptance of ceremony and ostentation, and developed his own distinctive theories.

Where Confucianism put great stock in family ties and social hierarchies, Mo-zi widened the scope, arguing that universal love had to be the foundation of individual and political life. Love that discriminates leads to disaster—people who love only their own homes will happily become burglars, rulers who love only their own countries and people will happily go to war. If we love others as we love ourselves, we will not be inclined to harm them. Though he spent his life traveling from one state to another, attempting to influence their rulers, he had relatively little success, universal love being unattractive to politicians, who prefer emotions that are easier to manipulate.

While K'ung fu-zi thought of Heaven (*tian*) as impersonal, Mo-zi personalized it, the will of Heaven providing a sort of moral measure against which to gauge human actions. He made a great deal of the existence of spirits who, he said, saw everything that human beings did, however secretly they tried to act. He rejected fatalism as pernicious, weakening belief in Heaven and the spirits, and endangering the empire.

Consider this:
If a man steals a pig, they call him wrong; but if a state is stolen, they call it just.

Despite this side to his thought, Mo-zi's approach was much more rationalistic than that of either K'ung fu-zi or **Lao-zi**. He refused simply to follow what was found in the past, but offered logical arguments for his positions. Later Mohists, in the third century B.C.E., developed informal logic to its highest level in Chinese philosophy; their interest was always practical, in line with Mo-zi's aims—to determine what is true, what is morally right, what is best for the people in a state. It is perhaps not too far-fetched to see in Mohism an anticipation of **J. S. Mill's** utilitarianism.

Mo-zi's most important methodological tool was the *san biao*—three criteria for judging the truth of a belief: "tracing its source, examining its situation, and testing its practicality." The first involves examining what history tells us, the second involves examining the experiences of ordinary people, and the third involves applying the belief to the law or to politics to see if it fits with what is best for the country and the people.

SOCRATES

| BORN | c.470 B.C.E., Athens | DIED | 399 B.C.E., Athens |

MAIN INTERESTS   Ethics, epistemology

INFLUENCES   The Milesians, Pythagoras, Heraclitus, Parmenides

INFLUENCED   Everyone who came after him

Athens at the time was home to a large number of sophists—teachers of a wide range of subjects and skills, but especially of rhetoric and argument. Some were philosophically acute thinkers, but many simply peddled the age-old political skills of glib dishonesty. Socrates was often lumped in with them by the Athenians; understandably, he rejected this.

The son of a sculptor and a midwife, Socrates was born into the golden age of Athens—the time of Pericles, Aeschylus, Sophocles, Euripides, and Aristophanes. His early life and education are obscure; he started life as a sculptor and stonemason, and is said to have worked on the Acropolis. He married Xanthippe, whose acid and quarrelsome temperament became proverbial; they had several children together, and he went on to have two more children with a second wife, Myrto.

Socrates played a full part in the Athenian state, serving with distinction in the heavy-foot (*hoplites*) against Sparta during the Peloponnesian War; he took part in the running of the city, being at one time president of the *prytaneis* (a committee chosen by lot from all the citizens). His main concern, however, was to act as a questioner, trying to irritate the Athenians into thought. Despite his forthright opposition to them, he survived the reign of the Thirty Tyrants (backed by the Spartans after their defeat of Athens). Four years after the revolt in 403 B.C.E., which saw the reestablishment of democracy, Socrates was charged with corrupting the youth of Athens, neglecting the gods, and introducing new gods (the last charge is obscure, but possibly a reference to the *dæmonion*, or divine inner voice, to which he sometimes appealed). Socrates was found guilty and sentenced to the traditional death penalty—poison. Although he could easily have escaped from Athens, he chose to submit to the penalty, drank the hemlock, and died a painful and prolonged death.

Socrates wrote nothing, and we know of him and his methods and ideas through the work of his contemporaries—primarily **Plato**, but also the historian and soldier Xenophon and the playwright Aristophanes. In his play *The Clouds*, Aristophanes portrays Socrates as a sophistical clown; in his writings, Xenophon paints a reverential picture of a "wise old man," dispensing advice and preaching simplistic morality. In Plato's dialogues, we're faced with an acute, rigorous, rational, questioning mind, given to sarcasm and extravagant modesty, and constantly questioning people's fundamental beliefs. This is the Socrates who changed the nature of philosophy, one of the most innovative and influential thinkers of all time.

One of his main weapons was the method of *elenchus*, or cross-examination, known as the Socratic Method; it consists in asking questions and of bringing out the hidden confusions and absurdities of people's positions. Rather than teaching, Plato's Socrates sees himself as like his mother the midwife, helping people to give birth to the truth by their own efforts.

In their own words:
The unexamined life is not worth living.

Plato's **Apology**, *38 A*

PLATO

BORN c.428 B.C.E.		**DIED** c.348 B.C.E.	

MAIN INTERESTS   Epistemology, metaphysics, ethics, politics

INFLUENCES   Pythagoras, Parmenides, Socrates

INFLUENCED   Everyone who came after him

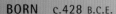

MAJOR WORKS
The dialogues

Aristotle was a student of Plato's. He recognized Plato's genius, but rejected his idea of the world of Forms. As depicted here, Plato points to higher realms, while Aristotle gestures that we should keep our feet on the ground, basing philosophy in what we can really know through observation, rather than what we can attain through pure reason.

Born toward the end of Athens' golden age, Plato was a member of a well-established aristocratic family; his real name is said to have been Aristocles, "Plato" being a nickname (meaning "the broad one"). Little is known of his early life; his father probably died when he was young, leaving him to be brought up by his mother and stepfather. Aristotle tells us that Plato was a student of Cratylus, who himself had studied under **Heraclitus**. He certainly became a student of **Socrates**, who remained a friend and teacher until his execution (when Plato was about thirty years old). We don't know whether he started writing his dialogues before or after Socrates' death; indeed, the general chronology and ordering of Plato's dialogues remains a matter for debate.

After Socrates' trial and execution Plato left Athens in disgust, but where exactly he traveled is unclear (legend has him spending time in Egypt); in 387 B.C.E. he ended up in Megara in Sicily, where he met the last living member of the Pythagorean school, and made important contacts in Syracuse. From Megara he returned to Athens, and some

In a nutshell:
Philosophy is the only route to genuine knowledge—knowledge of the Forms—so the philosopher should rule the state.

time afterward cofounded (with Theætetus, a mathematician) a school in the suburbs of Athens. It stood in a garden that he'd inherited, in an area called the Academia, and so became known as the Academy. A wide variety of subjects was taught there, from mathematics to biology, from philosophy to astronomy, and it's not too far-fetched to call it the first European university. In his quest to bring philosophical thought and understanding to politics, Plato twice went back to Sicily as tutor to Dionysius the Younger, the new tyrant, but the attempts ended in disaster. He spent the rest of his life writing and teaching.

Plato's writings are almost all in dialogue form, the exceptions being thirteen letters, whose authenticity remains unestablished, and the *Apology* (Socrates' speeches at his trial). Most of them feature Socrates as the central character, and present him in discussion and debate with a range of people, many, if not most, of them real (for example, Theætetus, the Eleatic philosophers **Parmenides** and **Zeno**, and Plato's brothers, Glaucon and Adeimantus). They vary enormously in length and complexity, but

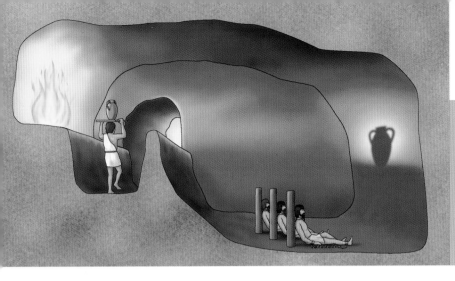

scarcely at all in readability and philosophical interest.

Scholars divide the dialogues into three groups: early, middle, and late. Most of them are easily placed in that scheme, but there are debates about where certain dialogues should go. Nevertheless, a picture builds up of the development of Plato's thought (and of the move from a reasonably accurate representation of Socrates, to the use of Socrates as a mouthpiece for his own views).

EPISTEMOLOGY

In discussing Plato's thought, it's best to start with his account of knowledge and belief. Knowledge, he argues, can only be of eternal and unchanging truths; of everyday, temporary matters we can have true beliefs (and very useful they can be), but not knowledge. Genuine knowledge isn't learned, but recollected; our souls go through a cycle of reincarnation, but birth is so traumatic that it makes us forget everything we know, and the teacher's task is to help us to regain that knowledge (in the manner of Socrates' midwife).

METAPHYSICS

The objects of knowledge aren't to be found in the world as we perceive it, for that's essentially changing, relative, and impermanent. Indeed, to understand what we experience through the senses, we must have some knowledge of the eternal and changeless. For example, what is beautiful

varies from person to person, and for the same person over time; how could we gain and apply the concept "beautiful" if there's nothing that we can point to and agree is beautiful? To fill the gap, Plato appeals to the Forms; these are the perfect and unchanging ideals of which things in the world are the faint and distorted shadows. When we see something as beautiful, we're seeing that it partakes in the Form of Beauty. The world of Forms can be experienced, but only through reason—only by the philosopher. The highest of the Forms is that of the Good, through which all other Forms gain their existence, and through which we can come to know them.

POLITICS

This line of thinking leads directly to Plato's political theory: if only the philosopher can experience genuine reality, then only the philosopher is in a position to rule. Plato's account of the ideal state, developed in his dialogue *Republic*, introduces the notion of the philosopher-ruler, male or female (he rejected the notion of the sexes having different capacities), who is trained from birth to fill that position. In the same way, the other functions in society are performed by people who have been trained in the relevant area.

Plato's writings remain among the richest and most fascinating in all philosophy; without him, we'd be living in a very different world.

The ideal society we have described can never grow into a reality or see the light of day, and there will be no end to the troubles of states, or indeed of humanity itself, till philosophers become kings in this world, or till those we now call kings and rulers really and truly become philosophers.

Republic, 473c10

ARISTOTLE

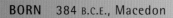

BORN 384 B.C.E., Macedon	DIED 322 B.C.E., Chalcis, Euboea

MAIN INTERESTS Metaphysics, ethics, politics, science, cosmology

INFLUENCES Pythagoras, Heraclitus, Parmenides, Socrates, Plato

INFLUENCED Everyone who came after him

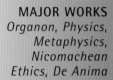

MAJOR WORKS
*Organon, Physics,
Metaphysics,
Nicomachean
Ethics, De Anima*

Aristotle was the son of a court physician to King Amyntas of Macedon. His father died when he was young, so he was brought up and educated by a guardian, who sent him at the age of seventeen to the center of intellectual and artistic life, Athens. There he entered **Plato's** Academy, where he stayed for about twenty years, first as student, then as teacher.

When Plato died, the story becomes a little obscure. Aristotle left Athens, but it's not clear exactly why. It might have been because he was passed over as head of the Academy, or because of his philosophical differences with the new head, Speusippus, or because of his Macedonian antecedents. Macedon was unpopular at that time, because the new king, Philip, was rapidly expanding the borders of his kingdom, and Athenians felt threatened. Aristotle was a childhood friend of Philip, and had retained his connections with the family.

Whatever the reason, Aristotle sailed for Assos in Asia Minor, where he lived for three years, developed his interest in anatomy and biology, and began work on his book, *Politics*. However, the Persians attacked and overran Assos in 345 B.C.E., killing the king, and Aristotle left with his circle of philosophers, staying for a year in Mytilene on Lesbos before moving to Macedon, where he became tutor to Philip's son, Alexander.

THE LYCEUM
When Philip died and Alexander succeeded him, Aristotle returned to Athens. The Academy was flourishing under its new head, Xenocrates, and Aristotle founded his own school outside Athens, in a place called the Lyceum. He taught there for thirteen years, giving both public and private lectures. The Lyceum had a broader curriculum than the Academy, and a stronger emphasis on natural philosophy. With Alexander the Great's death in 323 B.C.E. came a change in the government of Athens, and a wave of anti-Macedonian feeling. Aristotle left Athens to live in a family house in Chalcis, where he died the following year.

Aristotle's writings formed a huge and varied corpus, including dialogues, popular treatises, and serious works of scholarship; most of these have been lost, as has the vast collection of scientific and historical observational data that he built up himself and through his correspondents. What remains falls mainly into two (unclearly differentiated) categories: lecture notes worked up and published after his death, and work by later members of his school. It's

*Aristotle, the third in a
succession of great intellects,
passed on his knowledge to
Alexander the Great, who
later conquered the known
world, establishing a vast
empire of Greek
administrative centers.*

The schools of Athens, such as the Academy and the Lyceum, educated their students through debate and discussion, rather than blind acceptance of the teacher's views.

emphasized the role of reason, but Plato held that the most important truths must be attained through reason alone, whereas Aristotle took observation to be crucial; he held that both the world and the human mind were so structured as to make understanding possible. His scientific work was hugely important for the development of our knowledge of the world. His project of a systematic investigation into natural phenomena—especially the living world—marks the birth of empirical science.

His concern with empirical observation wasn't restricted to sciences such as biology and astronomy, but extended to history, psychology, language, ethics, and politics. Ironically, though, his influence on medieval philosophy was so great that it somewhat stifled empirical investigation (though not completely). It could be said that people lived in an Aristotelian world for nineteen centuries after his death. Not only were Arab philosophers deeply influenced by him (and it's largely through them that his work survived the collapse of the Roman Empire), but Christian theology from the end of the twelfth century, and especially in the work of **Thomas Aquinas** and his successors, spent much time trying to adjust Christian teaching to fit with Aristotelian theories.

for this reason that most of what we know of Aristotle's work is very unlike the golden prose so admired by his contemporaries. The content, however, makes up for the style.

The surviving works fall into five main categories, usually ordered as they were in the first edition of Aristotle's work by his follower Andronicus of Rhodes (fl. 1st century B.C.E.): the six logical works, which together are known as the *Organon* ("tool"); the three works on the physical sciences (including the *Physics* itself); the work devoted to "first philosophy," the most fundamental and abstract of studies, now known as the *Metaphysics* ("*meta ta phusika*": "after the physics"); six works in politics, ethics, and esthetics, including most importantly the *Nicomachean Ethics* (named for his son, Nicomachus); and a large number of works on psychology and natural history, including *De Anima* (On the Soul).

EPISTEMOLOGY

Aristotle was the first to divide the subjects in the way that we still do nearly 2,500 years later, as well as the first to treat them systematically and rationally. The major difference between him and Plato lay in their epistemology. Both valued and

Both Plato and Aristotle played such a central role in medieval theology that they were dubbed "Christians before Christ," and sometimes even given haloes in paintings.

A likely impossibility is always preferable to an unconvincing possibility [...]

Poetics 1460a

In a nutshell:
Experience is the source of knowledge, and logic is its structure.

OVERVIEW
HUMAN
NATURE

It might be thought that human nature is the concern of the empirical sciences, not of philosophy. After all, how can we decide how humans are naturally, except by going out and looking at them? The trouble with this is that it's impossible to find the natural human beings whom such a study demands, for every human being we might examine lives in, and is the product of, some society or other, and that includes all the human beings of whom there are written records.

Philosophers might take an interest in this question for its own sake, but in fact they usually have an ulterior motive: most (perhaps all) political and ethical theories depend upon some account of the origins of good and evil, of chaos and order, and that means that they have to decide whether humans are naturally good or evil, naturally social or solitary, and so on. The history of philosophy reveals many different approaches to this question.

One example is the Chinese tradition, where we find two followers of **K'ung fu-zi**—Xun-zi and **Meng-zi**—in disagreement; the former argues that people are intrinsically evil and selfish, needing education and social pressure to make them good, whereas the latter argues that, on the contrary, people are essentially good, and are merely made evil by bad education and corrupt society. Similarly, in the Western political tradition, Hobbes holds that in the presocial state of nature, people would be constantly waging war against each other, so that a social contract between them is needed for their protection, each against the other; Locke, on the other hand, denies the inherent evil of human beings, and thinks that the social contract is needed only to smooth the "inconveniencies" of the natural state. Thus, for Hobbes, the nasty, brutish state of nature is always around the corner, waiting to pop out if society breaks down, whereas for Locke the state of nature is in the distant past.

Rousseau brings out what's wrong with both these views, and perhaps with those of Xun-zi and Meng-zi too: as I started by saying, we have only the experience of socialized, unnatural human beings to go on. Hobbes and Locke don't show us genuinely natural people, but modern, political people whom the philosophers have placed into a natural state of affairs. (In fact, Rousseau goes on to argue that people are indeed naturally morally good.)

The introduction of modern biology—whether evolution or genetic theory—doesn't help, as it gives us (at best) *ex post facto* explanations of how we got here from there—and the whole problem is that we don't know where "there" *is* (nor, in fact, where exactly "here" is either). Moreover, though biology sets out to explain the physical, causal facts, we're also concerned here with the mental, rational facts. That is, the moral side of human nature is mainly bound up with the *reasons* rather than the *causes* of our actions.

Are humans naturally good or evil? This issue is at the heart of many philosophers' interests and has been the subject of much debate throughout the ages.

MENG-ZI (MENCIUS)

| BORN c.371 B.C.E. | DIED c.289 B.C.E. |

MAIN INTERESTS Ethics, politics

INFLUENCES K'ung fu-zi, Mo-zi

INFLUENCED Zhu Xi

MAJOR WORKS
Meng-zi

The Book of Mencius became one of the Confucian Four Books chosen by Zhu Xi, which were the set texts for the Imperial examinations.

The life of Meng-zi (Mencius) is scantily documented, despite his position as the second-greatest Confucian philosopher. He was born either in Zou or Lu, and studied Confucianism with a disciple of K'ung fu-zi's grandson. Having developed his ideas, and living at a time of disruption and political fragmentation, he traveled around the various states of China in the attempt to influence their rulers; he was respectfully received, but had little practical effect. He therefore withdrew from public life, and spent his remaining years working, with his disciples, on the records of his travels and his teachings, which they arranged and edited into the *Meng-zi* (Book of Mencius).

Meng-zi argued that human beings are naturally good, and naturally act morally. They have compassion and the ability to tell right from wrong, and thus evil is the result of external influences. The aim of all learning should be to regain our natural state, which is latent within us. This isn't easy, though, and it's important to *work* at wisdom—real wisdom concerns how we live with and treat others. It's not that everyone could become the equal of **K'ung fu-zi**, but we all have the capacity to become sages if we work at it and are helped by the correct teaching. It's important, though, not to *try* to become a sage, for then we will certainly fail. We have to behave well for its own sake, and cultivate our minds and hearts, and the "supreme spiritual force" will inevitably rise within us.

Meng-zi opposed rule by force and tyranny, but supported sovereign rule. His position was a version of the European notion of the divine right of kings; Heaven (*tian*) was the source of a sovereign's legitimacy, and Heaven would act if the sovereign tyrannized his people. If the ruler let down the people, their loyalty to him was weakened, and in extreme cases they might have the right to revolt. In the hierarchy of importance, the people came first and the sovereign last, for the sovereign's power was justified purely in order to ensure that the people lived in peace and comfort. This material happiness was important not only for its own sake, but because without it we can't become sages.

Meng-zi comes very close to the teachings of **Mo-zi**, but he objects to Mo-zi's doctrine of universal love. For him, there must be a hierarchy of degrees of love, dependent on relationships of kinship and the social order. One should love things, but not as much as one loves people; one should love people, but not as much as one loves one's family.

In their own words:
All who speak about the natures of things, have in fact only their phenomena to reason from, and the value of a phenomenon is in its being natural.

Meng-zi, Li Lau *xxvi, 1*

ZENO OF KITION

| BORN c.334 B.C.E., Kition, Cyprus | DIED 262 B.C.E., Athens |

MAIN INTERESTS Ethics, politics, logic, metaphysics

INFLUENCES Heraclitus, Antisthenes, Plato, Aristotle, Diogenes

INFLUENCED Chrysippus, Plotinus, Cicero, Seneca, Marcus Aurelius, Epictetus

MAJOR WORKS
Republic [lost]

The Stoic school of Zeno and Chrysippus is known as the Old Stoa, that of the 2nd century B.C.E. as the Middle Stoa, and the later Roman development as the Late Stoa.

Different writers interpret the Stoic position according to their own predilections, seeing it as anything from a sort of proto-Christianity to pantheism, and there is probably some truth in each of these approaches.

Zeno was born in Kition (or Citium, near modern Larnaca) in southern Cyprus, but was nicknamed "the Phoenician," so he may have possessed some Phoenician blood. He initially followed his father's profession and became a merchant. When in Athens, he discovered philosophy and became a student of the cynic, Crates of Thebes He also attended Xenocrates' lectures at the Academy.

Having developed his own philosophical ideas, Zeno began to take students. He taught in a public *stoa* (colonnaded walk) called the *Stoa Poikilē* or "Painted Stoa," and so the school that grew out of his teaching became known as the Stoics. He taught in Athens for about fifty years, and aroused a mixture of scorn for his nonconformist ways and admiration for his moral uprightness and frugal life-style. He was given the keys to the city, and was buried in a handsome tomb at public expense, but never took Athenian citizenship (possibly as part of his rejection of artificial social norms and strictures).

None of Zeno's writings has survived, but we know from other writers that his chief work was an alternative to **Plato's** ideal state, also called *Republic*. This presented the ideal Stoic society of rational people—a society of sexual equality and freedom, lacking the structure of law and convention, but morally upright. Stoics believed in living and working within society rather than withdrawing from it; the aim was to achieve the Stoic ideal through education and example.

In a nutshell:
The structure of logic is the structure of Nature; our aim should be to live in accordance with Nature.

Stoic ethical and social theories are grounded in an account of the world that is essentially materialistic, yet adopts **Heraclitus'** notion of the *logos*—a complex notion involving reason, nature, and fate that animates the world, and that serves to link the human soul with that of the universe. Our nature is to seek order and understanding, and to live together in the Stoic way. This metaphysical theory was linked to a physical theory that included the notion of a cyclic life of the universe, with regular cleansing conflagrations.

Perhaps the most significant part of Stoic thought was the development of logic, which prefigured much later work such as that of **Frege**, and formed an integral part of their complex system of thought. This was largely set in motion by Chrysippus (c.280–207 B.C.E.), who also tempered Zeno's fatalism with a compatibilist theory of free will. Many Roman writers took up Stoicism and developed it further, developing the important notion of natural law, and emphasizing the easing of the soul to be gained through submission to providence.

EPICURUS OF SAMOS

BORN 341 B.C.E., Samos	**DIED** 270 B.C.E.

MAIN INTERESTS Ethics, logic, metaphysics

INFLUENCES Plato, Aristotle, Democritus

INFLUENCED Lucretius, Gassendi, Bentham, J. S. Mill

MAJOR WORKS
On Nature (lost)

Epicurus' parents were *klirouchs*—Athenian poor who had been allotted land in overseas territories. His father, a schoolteacher, first educated his son at home; later, Epicurus was taught by a Platonist philosopher, Amphilus. While he was in Athens, doing his statutory military service, his family were forced to move to the mainland city of Colophon, where Epicurus joined them.

For some years he lived and studied in that region. His first experience of teaching was in Mytilene on Lesbos, but his unorthodox views led to his abrupt departure to Lampsacus on the mainland, where he founded his own school. Finally, in 306 B.C.E., he traveled to Athens and founded a second school, teaching in the garden of his house (hence the school's name, the Garden).

This school—or, more accurately, community—became famous and popular (though it was also the target of gossip, as it accepted both male and female students, and even slaves). Epicurus organized it as a sort of campaign center, sending out letters around the civilized world, and building up Epicureanism as a secular movement; one of Epicurus' main concerns was to free people from the tyranny of superstition and religion. It was organized in a nonauthoritarian and informal way, in accordance with Epicurus' principles. His school continued to flourish after his death, with new centers being created all over the Greek-speaking, and later the Latin-speaking, world.

Epicurus was one of the most prolific ancient philosophers, publishing at least forty works, some of them enormous (like his masterpiece *On Nature*, comprising thirty-seven books). Perhaps as a result of later Christian hostility toward Epicureanism (which also led to a severe distortion of the theory in black propaganda), only a few fragments survive, in other writers' work.

Like the Stoics, the Epicureans divided philosophy into three parts—ethics, logic, and physics. They also held that ethics was the most important. Epicurus argues that subjects such as astronomy are important only insofar as they relieve us of puzzlement about heavenly phenomena and demonstrate the falsity of religious doctrines. What is important is happiness, meaning living well rather than living a life of shallow pleasure seeking. We should cultivate the right sort of desires, leading to the right kind of happiness, including health, friendship, lack of fear of death, and wisdom.

The difference in ancient Athens between a klirouchia *and a colony was that the inhabitants of the former remained Athenian citizens rather than becoming citizens of a new state.*

In their own words:

When we say that pleasure is the goal we do not mean the pleasures of the dissipated and those which consist in the process of enjoyment [...] but freedom from pain in the body and from disturbance in the mind.

Letter to Menœceus

HAN FEI-ZI

BORN 280 B.C.E.	DIED 233 B.C.E.

MAIN INTERESTS   Ethics, politics

INFLUENCES   K'ung fu-zi, Xun-zi, Shang Yang, Shen Buhai, Shen Dao

INFLUENCED   Li Si

MAJOR WORKS
Han Fei-zi

The past should not be used as a pattern for the present: the wise man does not seek to follow the ways of the ancients, nor to establish any fixed standard for all time, but examines his own age and prepares to deal with its problems.

Han Fei-zi 49

In the reign of Shi Hunagdi, at the urging of Li Si, nonapproved books were burnt and philosophers murdered.

Born a prince of the ruling family of Han, Han Fei-zi was educated at the Chi-Xia academy, where he was taught by the Confucian Xun-zi. He soon rejected key elements of Confucian beliefs and submitted his advice and arguments to the king of Han, but he was effectively ignored. His writing came to the attention of the king of Qin, Shi Huangdi, who was pleased to meet him. However, Han Fei-zi's former fellow student, Li Si, was chief minister of Qin, and poisoned the king's mind against him. Han Fei-zi was imprisoned, and refused an audience with the king. Instead, he sent him messages, including advice about the policies and territorial ambitions of Qin. Li Si opposed these ideas, and secretly sent poison to Han Fei-zi, who, in despair, drank it.

Han Fei-zi's writings gave birth to a new school of Chinese thought known as *Legalism*, or the School of the Law. He followed the version of Confucianism of his teacher, Xun-zi, which opposed the position of **Meng-zi**, arguing that human beings are naturally evil, and need education and political pressures to make them good. He added the emphasis on law from the writings of Shang Yang, together with the need for management skills and the right position and situation. The result is a political theory that plays down philosophical speculation in favor of empirical observation, and rejects the Confucian emphasis on the past in favor of a sweeping away of old laws and customs in order to make way for the new.

In a nutshell:

Rather than following the ways of the past, one should examine the present and work out how best to deal with it.

Han Fei-zi's position isn't wholly materialist and positivist. He favored Daoist metaphysics, which he developed to support his emphasis on law and control. His political theory retained a link with what had gone before: he held that the ruler should also act within the law, and that the imposition of strict order was ultimately for the benefit of the people. Later Legalists (including Li Si) abandoned this aspect of his thought, and taught a complete disregard by the ruler for anything but personal power and security. The early collapse of the Qin dynasty after a popular revolt had the effect of discrediting Legalist teachings, though the Han dynasty that followed it adopted much the same approach.

Han Fei-zi is often compared with **Machiavelli**, and dubbed as a devious, even immoral, writer. Such a description would better fit his fellow student Li Si, and one should remember that the overwhelming desire for stability and order that characterizes Legalism must in part derive from the turmoil of the long Period of Warring States at the end of which Han Fei-zi lived.

WANG CHONG

BORN 27 C.E., K'uei-chi	**DIED** 97 C.E., K'uei-chi

MAIN INTERESTS Ethics, politics, metaphysics, epistemology

INFLUENCES K'ung fu-zi, Lao-zi

INFLUENCED Neo-Daoists

MAJOR WORKS
Lun-Heng

People say that spirits are the souls of dead men. That being the case, spirits should always appear naked, for surely it is not contended that clothes have souls as well as men.

Lun-Hen

Human beings don't become ghosts at death. Why should they have ghosts and not other animals? Animals share the same principle of vitality. And, given how many people have died since the beginning of the world, the ghosts would outnumber the living, and we'd be surrounded by them.

Wang Chong was so poor that when studying in the capital, Luoyang, he did his reading standing at bookstalls. Unusually, he belonged to no school or tradition. He nevertheless developed a wide knowledge of literature, and achieved the rank of secretary of a district, though his argumentative, nonconformist, and forthright nature lost him the job. His work came to the attention of the emperor though, who invited him to court, but Wang Chong was too ill to go.

The work for which he is known is the *Lun-Heng*, variously translated as *Balanced Enquiries*, *Fair Discussions*, or just *Critical Essays*. Confucianism had become the state religion in 136 B.C.E., rapidly degenerating into a mass of superstition (the same fate had befallen Daoism long before). K'ung fu-zi was worshipped as a god alongside Lao-zi, prodigies and omens were constantly being seen and acted upon, ghosts and spirits were said to walk the Earth, and people had begun to order their lives according to *feng shui*. Wang Chong rejected all of this with undisguised scorn, and argued for a rational, naturalistic, mechanistic account of the natural world and the human place in it.

His central claim was that Heaven is spontaneous; that is, it's not purposeful, and so doesn't act for or against human beings. Those who insist that Heaven provides us with food and clothing are saying that Heaven becomes a farmer or a weaver for the sake of human beings, which is absurd:

"Man holds a place in the universe like that of a flea or a louse under a jacket or robe," so how can we think that we can bring about changes in the universe, or that it orders itself for our benefit?"

Wang Chong's epistemology was equally straightforward: beliefs need evidence, just as actions need results. It's all too easy to rattle off whatever nonsense comes into one's head, and the right sort of audience will believe it, especially if it's dressed up in the right sort of clothes of superstition. What's needed is reason and experience.

Wang Chong's arguments are rational, but he suffered from the lack of any real tradition of science in China, which meant that his attempts at a naturalistic account of the world often strike us as only a little less peculiar than the views he argued against. Nevertheless, his ideas became well known, especially after his death, and had an influence on a new form of Daoism, sometimes called "neo-Daoism," which developed a more rational, naturalistic metaphysics, free from most of the mysticism and superstition that had infected Daoist thought for so long.

In a nutshell:
We should understand the world through the use of experience and reason, not foolish superstition.

OVERVIEW
SKEPTICISM

The term "skeptic" derives from the Greek term *skeptikos*, which originally meant "inquirer." The first ancient skeptic is thought to be Pyrrho of Elis (c.360–230 B.C.E.), who tried not to commit himself to any claims about the nature of reality, and instead suspended judgment about how things *really* are in themselves, independently of our perceptions, so aiming to attain *ataraxia*, or peace of mind. But skepticism as a philosophical doctrine was first formulated by the heirs of Plato's Academy around the third century B.C.E., who rejected Plato's metaphysical theories, and instead accepted the Socratic dictum that "All I know is that I know nothing."

At the beginning of the sixteenth century, skeptical arguments were used to attack the Scholastics' conception of the cosmos. New astronomical theories and discoveries showed many of the scholastic claims about the nature of the cosmos to be wrong. As a result, many thinkers became doubtful about our certainty with regard to what we claim to know. At the beginning of the seventeenth century we see perhaps the most forceful form of skepticism put forward by **Pierre Gassendi**, who challenged almost every aspect of the Aristotelian view of the cosmos.

QUESTIONING BELIEF

Philosophical skepticism isn't concerned with ordinary everyday life (the skeptic also has to live in the world). Rather, it's interested in what evidence we have for our beliefs, and whether this evidence is adequate to convert our beliefs into knowledge. It tries to find an adequate and consistent account of knowledge about the world, and concludes that, given that things appear differently to different people at different times and in different cultures, these conflicting appearances cannot all be equally true of a single objective world—that is, of how things really are in themselves. The skeptic is searching for a criterion or a set of criteria of truth that would determine which of the conflicting views should be accepted, but concludes that there is no intellectually satisfying criterion. In its extreme form, skepticism results in a complete suspension of judgment. The conclusion that we can't know anything about the world around us is called skepticism about the external world. The pattern of this skeptical argument extends (especially in the modern period) to skeptical arguments about our knowledge of other people's minds (that is, I know that I have a mind, but I have no certainty that anyone else has a mind), our knowledge of the past, and our knowledge of the theoretical entities postulated by scientific theories.

PYRRHO'S LEGACY

Our inquisitive nature, however, keeps the quest for knowledge of the ultimate nature of reality going, whereas the skeptic poses a challenge to every claim to such knowledge. But perhaps without skepticism we wouldn't be able to differentiate between propaganda, prejudice, dogmatism, and superstition, on the one hand, and any form of meaningful belief on the other. A friend of **David Hume** said: "The wise of every age conclude what Pyrrho taught and Hume renewed, that dogmatists are fools."

It's argued that **Descartes'** formulation of the problem of skepticism in its complete, general form is new in philosophy, and that nothing exactly similar appears before that time. What it is important to get clear, and what Descartes' method demands, is to doubt what one has good reason to doubt. For example, Descartes has no good reason to doubt his ability to reason and think logically. This isn't because he doesn't want to, but because it's logically impossible to do so, since there's no other tool that he can use to cast doubt on his ability to reason other than reason itself. The problem about the nature of reality arose for Descartes in his concerns about the nature of certainty and truth. He thus casts the problem, not epistemologically, not in terms of evidence or justification about our claims to knowledge, but metaphysically. That is, for Descartes the problem is the nature of knowledge, and it's prompted by the question "Is knowledge possible, and if so, how?" In other words, the latter question cannot be answered until one answers the question "What is knowledge?" Unlike Pyrrhonist skepticism, which aimed at overcoming the desire to find certainty, Descartes uses skepticism to do exactly that. The difference between Descartes and the skeptic is that Descartes uses skepticism as a route to certainty and truth, and to demonstrate that knowledge is possible, unlike the skeptic, who uses it as a route to uncertainty.

SEXTUS EMPIRICUS

LIVED 2nd century C.E.	DIED Unknown

MAIN INTERESTS   Ethics, epistemology

INFLUENCES   Plato, Pyrrho of Elis

INFLUENCED   Montaigne, Descartes, Hume

MAJOR WORKS
*Outlines of Pyrrhonism,
Against the Dogmatists,
Against the Professors*

Sextus advocated that human beings live in accordance with natural and social rules—not because such rules could be proved to be true or justified, but because so doing makes it possible for us to live undisturbed lives.

A medical doctor, Sextus Empiricus lived in Alexandria and Athens, and possibly Rome. He was taught by Menodotus of Nicomedia, and was the head of a philosophical school, in which he was succeeded by Saturninus. Little more is known about him. He was probably Greek, judging by his use of language, and "Empiricus" may be a nickname referring (albeit inaccurately) to his views on medicine.

Among the many medical sects of that time, three of the most important were the Dogmatists, the Empiricists, and the Methodists. Dogmatists held that one must discover the hidden causes of disease to cure them; this was to be achieved through experience and reasoning. Empiricists held that it was impossible to learn about what isn't visible; the doctor's job is to cure the patient, and a doctor should limit him- or herself to examining and dealing with the symptoms in each individual case. The Methodists disagreed with both, agreeing that uncovering hidden causes was no part of the doctor's job, but arguing that to assert that such knowledge was impossible, that it was as dogmatic as to assert that it were possible. Sextus' views, despite his name, were Methodist rather than Empiricist.

Sextus Empiricus wrote nothing of any great originality, nor was his style anything more than plain and clear. His importance lies in the fact that through him comes most of what we know of Greek skepticism, and especially the oral teaching of Pyrrho of Elis, though his responses to, and arguments about, the various positions are also sometimes of interest.

The main motivation of Pyrrhonist skepticism wasn't so much epistemological as ethical and practical; on the one hand it concerned the search for happiness, here meaning freedom from mental disturbance (*ataraxia*), and on the other, it involved the avoidance of mental paralysis. Put simply, *ataraxia* resulted from *epoche* (the suspension of judgment), through the recognition that there was no point worrying about what couldn't even in principle be known. This clearly applies only to what genuinely can't be known, to what is beyond our experience. We shouldn't allow ourselves to fall into skepticism about what we see and hear, or about what we can legitimately infer from what we experience. Thus, as a doctor Sextus would refuse to speculate about the hidden mechanisms that caused diseases, but would (albeit tentatively) make prognoses based upon a patient's symptoms, and prescribe treatment on that basis.

In their own words:
[...] by scepticism [...] we arrive first at suspension of judgement, and secondly at freedom from disturbance [...]

Outlines of Pyrrhonism

NĀGĀRJUNA

BORN c.150 C.E., Andhra Pradesh	**DIED** c.230 C.E.

MAIN INTERESTS Metaphysics, epistemology, ethics

INFLUENCES Mahāyāna Buddhism

INFLUENCED Middle-Way Buddhism

MAJOR WORKS
Madhyamakakārikās

Nothing exists purely in itself, everything exists in relation to other things, such as its causes and effects, or its opposite.

Nāgārjuna's life is almost completely undocumented (there are detailed accounts, but these were written long after he died, and are largely mythologized); the birth and death dates given above should be taken as approximations. He was born into a Hindu, perhaps a Brahmin (priestly), family.

At some stage, he converted to Buddhism, and went to study at the ancient University of Nalanda in Bihar. Buddhism had started as a religious breakaway from Hinduism in the fifth century B.C.E., focusing almost wholly on ethics, but within a couple of centuries it had begun to develop a broader range of philosophical concerns. Sometime during the first or second centuries C.E. a new school emerged, known as Mahāyāna ("great vehicle") Buddhism. Mahāyāna Buddhism distinguished itself from existing schools, lumping them together as Hānayāna ("lesser vehicle") Buddhism, of which the main surviving school is Theravāda Buddhism.

Mahāyāna Buddhism sought to move away from what it saw as the rigid dogmatism of the older schools, and to soften the selfish striving for personal enlightenment by the introduction, for example, of *bodhisattvas*, who make the moral choice to postpone their passage to *nirvāna* to help others toward that goal. Where Buddhist writing had become more academically philosophical, Mahāyāna Buddhism claimed to return to the original core of Buddhist practice. Nāgārjuna's achievement was to

In a nutshell:
Everything is relative, and nothing should be either affirmed or denied.

inject into the Mahāyāna school intellectual rigor and analysis. He was influenced by the general philosophical climate of the time, in both the Buddhist and Hindu schools, with a new interest in logical, metaphysical, and epistemological debate. He founded one of the three Mahāyāna schools, the Mādhyamika ("Middle Way") school, which set out to teach no system of thought, only to reject the claims and denials of other systems; his main tool was the *reductio ad absurdum* of all the other schools of Buddhist and Hindu thought.

Nāgārjuna's approach emphasizes the interconnectedness and essential emptiness of all things. Everything is connected to and conditions everything else, and this is what underlies and makes possible the cycle of rebirth, for there are no unchanging essences of things; the world of experience is one of constant change, so that the notion of an unchanging essence is absurd. Though at the level of experience the world is real, at a deeper level it is empty, a void, zero, *sūnyatā*; things are real at one level, unreal at another. Things neither exist nor don't exist—hence the Middle Way.

PLOTINUS

BORN c.205 C.E., Egypt	**DIED** 270 C.E.

MAIN INTERESTS   Metaphysics, ethics

INFLUENCES   Plato, Aristotle, Zeno of Elea, Zeno of Kition, Ammonius Saccas

INFLUENCED   Porphyry, Augustine, Hypatia, Conway

MAJOR WORKS
Enneads

Plotinus' style is elliptical, the subject matter obscure, and even his handwriting is difficult to read. The first two problems, at least, he was fully aware of, explaining that he was trying to put into words what can't truly be expressed.

Plotinus was probably born in Lykopolis (now Asyā) in Upper (southern) Egypt, and was either Greek or Hellenized Egyptian. Our first definite knowledge of him is that in 232 C.E. he studied philosophy in Alexandria, then the capital of Egypt and the center of the intellectual world. It was here that he met Ammonius Saccas, a Platonist and teacher of the Christian writer Origen.

Plotinus studied with Ammonius for eleven years before joining the emperor Gordian's expedition to Persia and India. The expedition was cut short by the murder of Gordian in Mesopotamia. Plotinus escaped to Antioch, and then traveled to Rome, where he set up a school and taught philosophy. With the help of his most prominent pupil, Porphyry (c.232–305 C.E.), he produced what is now known as the *Enneads*: six volumes of nine treatises each, drawing together his writings and lecture materials.

Toward the end of his life he hoped to set up a philosophical community along the lines of **Plato's** *Republic*, but the project foundered on the opposition of the emperor's counselors. He died after a long illness.

Plotinus was essentially a Platonist, though his views were influenced by other writers, such as Aristotle, the Pythagoreans, and the Stoics. He didn't merely pass on the positions and arguments of others; he produced a strikingly original philosophical system of his own, which became known as neo-Platonism

and had a great influence on early Christian theologians, and on the seventeenth-century Cambridge Platonists.

At the center of Plotinus' system is the Platonic notion of the Form of the Good, called by Plotinus "the One" or "the Good." This is the first principle, the source of all being, the highest of the *hypostases* (essences, incorporeal substances, or realities), the others being Noūs, Mind or Soul, and Nature. The One is beyond everything, including description; using language we can only hope to gesture toward it (or *him*, as Plotinus would say). As with the Platonic scheme, the One is in principle present to all, open to our experience of him—but Plotinus thought that in practice this was possible only for a very few. Noūs is the realm of concepts or ideas, Minds or Souls are incorporeal substances that can be incarnated in a cycle of death and rebirth, and Nature (really the lower part of the realm of Soul) is the realm of the material. Our task is to leave the cycle of rebirth, first to attain existence at the level of Noūs, and finally to achieve union with the One. Evil arises only as a result of the lowest *hypostasis*, the material.

In their own words:
We stand towards the Supreme when we hold Noūs pure [...]

Enneads V, 3.14

AUGUSTINE OF HIPPO

| BORN | 354 C.E., Tagaste, Numidia | DIED | 430 C.E., Hippo, Numidia |

MAIN INTERESTS Metaphysics, language, ethics

INFLUENCES Plato, Plotinus, Cicero

INFLUENCED Boethius, Anselm, Aquinas, Mersenne, Arnauld Wittgenstein

MAJOR WORKS
Confessions,
The City of God,
Retractions

Manicheism was a curious mixture of Zoroastrianism, Buddhism, Christianity, and Gnosticism, which had at its heart a strong dualism between good and evil. Human beings arose as a result of the actions of Satan, who invaded the realm of light, god's realm; as a result, human beings are partly good (the mental) and partly evil (the body), and reflect in themselves the greater struggle between god and evil.

Born of a Christian mother and pagan (later Christian) father in what is now Souk-Ahras in Algeria, Aurelius Augustinus was educated in rhetoric in the North African cities Tagaste, Madaura, and Carthage, being especially inspired to philosophical inquiry by a work of Cicero's (now lost), the *Hortensius.* While young he rejected Christianity, put off by the crudeness of its doctrines and of the written style of its scriptures; he switched his allegiance instead to Manicheism, a religion founded by Mani (c.216–c.276 C.E.). Augustine stayed with the Manicheans for nine years, during which he returned to Tagaste and opened a school there, before returning to Carthage to teach rhetoric.

In 383 C.E. he turned away from Manicheism to the skepticism of the later Academy. Traveling to Rome in the same year, he used contacts to secure a post teaching rhetoric in Milan, where he took up neo-Platonism. While in Milan, however, he became acquainted with the bishop, Ambrose, whose Platonistic approach to Christianity attracted Augustine; he was baptized in 387 C.E.

He returned to North Africa, to Hippo Regius, where he was ordained a priest in 391 C.E., and became a bishop four years later. The times were turbulent, both in the secular world (Rome was sacked by Alaric the Goth in 410 C.E., and barbarian tribes were seizing Roman territory throughout the empire), and in the Christian church, which was racked within by competing sects, and

In a nutshell:

Faith comes first, and is made clear and supported by reason.

threatened from without by popular religions such as Augustine's old faith Manicheism.

Augustine spent the next thirty-four years battling all comers, and in doing so produced a number of books of philosophy and theology that changed the face of Christianity and the philosophical world. His most important works are the *Confessions,* an autobiographical work written in about 400 C.E., *The City of God,* a huge work of philosophical theology and church history written between 413 and 426 C.E., and the *Retractions,* a reconsideration of his earlier works, written in 428 C.E. He died in 430 C.E. during the siege of Hippo by the Vandals.

THEOLOGY

Much of Augustine's work, though philosophically sophisticated, is purely theological in content, the later writings being mostly polemical in nature. He took philosophy to be the search for truth, and Christianity was the truth. Any non-Christian philosophy was by definition misguided, and therefore a target for refutation. Though he interpreted Christian thought against a background of Platonism and neo-Platonism,

For Augustine, man was not inherently evil, because he was part of god's plan. Evil existed as part of the free will that god gave to man.

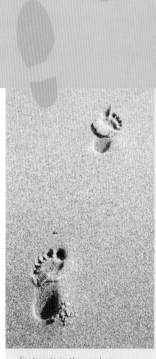

Footprints in the sand are signa naturalia, *they are an indication that someone has passed that way. The picture of footprints is* signa data, *it could signify a public pathway.*

he was not an **Aquinas**, for whom the Bible had to be interpreted to bring it into line with science and philosophy; for Augustine, when philosophers diverged from the Bible, the Bible took precedence.

He rejected the notion that matter and the body are inherently evil. For Augustine, the body was at the heart of god's plan; the existence of evil in a world created by a good, omnipotent, omniscient creator was explained in terms of the free will of human beings, which both explained the immediate origin of much evil, and justified god's use of evil as punishment (this position gradually changed, as he came to believe, first, that human beings couldn't follow the divine commands without god's help, and then to suggest that such help, if offered, couldn't be resisted by human beings).

Thanks to **Wittgenstein's** *Philosophical Investigations*, Augustine is known (outside of theology and classical scholarship) as having written on the philosophy of time and of language. The former was part of his response to challenges to the Christian account of creation, for it was asked why, if god had always existed, he should have chosen to create the world when he did. Augustine's response was to argue that god created time, and so was himself eternal. Time, then, is a function of the human mind rather than something real in the world.

LANGUAGE

His approach to language is more standard for the period, involving the thought that human languages do two things: they serve to represent ideas and thought, and they represent the structure of thoughts, as though there are "inner words," themselves in no language, that are made public by our linguistic utterances. He distinguishes between two kinds of sign: *signa naturalia* are like symptoms (for example, smoke is a sign of fire); *signa data* are symbols, involving the intention to signify (for example, the weather forecaster's little cloud is used to signify rain). Language, of course, consists of the latter kind of sign, which is wholly conventional in nature. What exactly is going on in the mind, however, changes in the course of Augustine's thinking, and is not at all easy to determine.

Augustine is of central importance in the early development of Christian thought, and he represents a key stage in the transition from ancient to medieval, from pagan to Christian philosophical thought.

What is time? If no one asks me, I know; if they ask and I try to explain, I do not know.

Confessions *11, 14, xvii*

OVERVIEW
WOMEN IN PHILOSOPHY

Uncovering the historical role of women in philosophy isn't straightforward. It is complicated by two things: the differences between cultures, which is relatively straightforward, and the process of historical recording, which isn't.

With regard to cultures, we are concerned here almost solely with the Western tradition. Though the Tang dynasty (618–907 C.E.) saw female writers producing works for women's education, these were not philosophical books by any stretch of the imagination. Ancient Indian philosophy doesn't even boast this sort of work. To find women involved in philosophy before modern times, we must start with Greece.

ANCIENT GREECE

It's impossible to generalize about the place of women in ancient Greece, as different city-states and colonies had very different customs and attitudes. All we can say is that women's status was undeniably lower than that of men, even in those Greek societies that adopted a more enlightened approach. There are frequent references in modern feminist literature to the women from whom most male philosophers are supposed to have gotten their ideas—mothers, priestesses, mistresses, wives, and so on. Even leaving aside the vagueness and sometimes obvious fictionality of such accounts, we've seen that philosophers such as Thalēs count as *philosophical* originals even if they were heavily influenced by the ideas of others.

Such elaborations are unnecessary, however, for there's an impressive list of genuine women philosophers, going right back to the beginnings of philosophy. Pythagoras' school, for

example, certainly included women, including his own family, and fragments of some of their writings survive. Aspasia, the wife of Pericles, is said by Plutarch to have been visited by Socrates and his pupils. Perictione, who may have been Plato's mother, wrote at least two philosophical treatises, and the Garden of Epicurus was open to both male and female students. By the Hellenistic period, **Hypatia** was the most prominent of a small number of women philosophers, including Asclepigenia of Athens (with whom Hypatia might have studied), and Macrina of Caesarea Mazaca, sister of Basil the Great.

None of this should be allowed to disguise the fact that women faced significant barriers, first to their education, and then to their success in the intellectual world. Compared with the next thousand years, however, ancient women had it easy. Their position in the ancient world was the result of social and cultural conventions, but during the medieval period it tended to be treated as a matter of religious doctrine. Similarly, though there have been far more women philosophers through post-Ancient history (and they have, in their times, been more highly regarded than is now realized), their numbers have been tiny compared with their male counterparts, and their achievements have been acquired in the face of considerable social, religious, and academic obstacles.

Although it was dependent upon social status, women in Ancient Greece had far more intellectual freedom than those in the medieval period.

HYPATIA

| **BORN**   c.370 C.E. Alexandria | **DIED**   415 C.E. Alexandria |

MAIN INTERESTS   Mathematics, logic, science

INFLUENCES   Plato, Plotinus, Iamblichus, Theon

INFLUENCED   *Synesius of Cyrene*

The great library at Alexandria was founded by Ptolemy I at the end of the fourth century B.C.E. It was said to be the largest collection of books in the ancient world (more than half a million volumes on some accounts), and it acted as a copying center, sending books out all over the known world. It was damaged by fire on a number of occasions, before finally being destroyed in 643 C.E. by Caliph Omar I.

Hypatia was born in Alexandria in the fourth century C.E. (there's disagreement about her age at death, so that different scholars put her year of birth at either c.370 or c.355 C.E.). Her father, Theon, was a mathematician and philosopher who taught at the University of Alexandria, and seems to have been responsible for her education, though she might also have been taught by Plutarch the Younger in Athens. She helped her father with his books on mathematics, astronomy, and philosophy, and became a teacher at his school, eventually becoming its head.

As a teacher Hypatia was extremely well known and respected (it's said that letters addressed simply to "The Philosopher" were delivered to her). She taught from a neo-Platonist standpoint, influenced in particular by **Plotinus** and the Syrian philosopher Iamblichus of Chalcis (c.250–c.327 C.E.), but mainly as applied to mathematics and natural philosophy. None of her works survive; we know only their titles, from which it appears that they were commentaries on earlier writers. Most of what we know about her work and life comes from letters preserved by one of her students, Synesius of Cyrene, together with various later romanticized or politicized accounts of her life.

Hypatia's Alexandria was certainly turbulent. Christianity was becoming dominant, and religious riots began to be common during the 390s. Things became worse when Cyril of Alexandria became patriarch in 412 C.E. He instituted a zealous and violent assault on non-Christians and members of other Christian groups; heretical Christian sects had their churches closed and looted, and Jews were attacked on the streets and in their homes, and driven out of the city. Hypatia, as a person of education, was a natural target (Christians tended to see learning as evidence of diabolism, and saw little distinction between science and magic); in addition she was a friend of Orestes, the civil governor of Alexandria and an opponent of Cyril. In 415 C.E. she was attacked by a Christian mob (possibly Nitrian monks), who stripped her and horribly murdered her. Cyril was later canonized as a saint, and declared a Doctor of the Church.

Hypatia is important for a number of reasons. Apart from her role as a popular and charismatic teacher, and as a preserver of ancient thought, she stands as a symbol of the light of learning in a world too often dark with superstition and ignorance, and as a symbol of the ability of women even in the most unlikely places and periods of history to overcome the social and cultural barriers to their intellectual success.

In a nutshell:
This world is an imperfect copy of the Real, which as philosophers we must strive to know and understand.

For philosophical purposes, the term "medieval" is vague, but here, this era covers the period until to the end of the sixteenth century. This includes the Renaissance and takes us to the big change that arrived with Descartes. The term "philosophy" was applied throughout this period to what would now be considered very diverse subjects—from astronomy to zoology. This section extends itself to thinkers who were primarily or at least largely philosophers in the narrower modern sense.

480

801

870

980

The four main sources of medieval philosophy in the West were Classical philosophy and the three major religions of the time: Christianity, Judaism, and Islam. Though neo-Platonism was influential, especially for early Muslim philosophers, **Plato** was a much less important figure than **Aristotle**. And though, by the beginning of this period most of Aristotle's works had been lost to Europe, many were regained during the twelfth century thanks to the Arabs, who had come into contact with Greek philosophy in the course of their conquests, and had studied and preserved it.

570	Birth of Muhammed
589	Reunification of China under Sui dynasty
618	Tang dynasty in China
622	Hejira—flight of Muhammed from Mecca to Medina

MEDIEVAL
500-1599

632	Muhammed dies; Abu Bakr first caliph
637	Jerusalem taken by Caliph Omar I
643	Alexandria taken and the great library destroyed
711	Spain invaded by Tariq ibn Ziyad
751	Carolingian dynasty in Europe
786	Accession of Haroun-al-Rashid in Baghdad
793	Viking raids on Britain begin
800	Death of Charlemagne
868	First printed book in China
960	Song dynasty in China
965	Harold Bluetooth converts to Christianity
968	Start of Fatimid rule in Egypt
1066	Norman Conquest of England
1095	First Crusade begins
1099	Godfrey of Bouillon takes Jerusalem
1135	Civil war in England: Stephen and Matilda

PHILOSOPHY AND RELIGIOUS BELIEF

A central feature of especially the early part of this period was the relationship between philosophical argument and religious belief. That there was, at least potentially, a clash could hardly be denied, and the ways in which the different philosophers (and groups of philosophers) dealt with the issue had a huge effect—not only on themselves, but on the course and even existence of philosophy itself. The philosophical work of Jewish writers (who mainly lived in Muslim countries and wrote in Arabic)—including **Moses ben Maimon**, Moses Nahmanides, Yehuda Hallevi, and Solomon ben Yehuda ibn Gabirol—as well as that of Muslim

1130 1135

writers—such as **al-Kindī**, **ibn Rushd**, **ibn Sīnā**, and **al-Fārābi**—suffered a theological backlash because of conflicts between religious beliefs and, especially, new metaphysical speculations; thus, only the Christian tradition survived to the end of the medieval period. This was partly because Christian philosophers were less bold than their Jewish and Muslim counterparts in bringing out the conflicts between reason and religion (with the occasional exception such as **Eriguena**). Later Jewish and Muslim philosophers (such as **Spinoza** and **Iqbal**) were primarily part of the philosophical tradition that grew out of the medieval tradition as developed by Christian philosophers.

The point of medieval philosophy wasn't to build grand systems, nor to develop world views (in this respect, at least, it resembled twentieth-century philosophy). The medieval philosopher had a world view already in place: the religious one. Indeed, the dominant theme of the period can be viewed as being the attempt by thinkers from the three religions to come to terms with Classical philosophical ideals. In the process, a clear and separate philosophical tradition emerged during the thirteenth century, helped by the creation

originality of thought, but there was a gradual move toward more speculative thinking. Issues that had importance, not only at the time but for later philosophy, included the debate between realists and nominalists, the relationship between faith and reason, and the development of a philosophical-technical vocabulary that could deal with metaphysical and logical speculation.

The slow development of medieval philosophy was finally overtaken in the fifteenth and sixteenth centuries by much quicker developments in the field of politics and later the physical sciences—a development commonly called the Renaissance,

1214   1266   1469   1548

and growth of universities such as those in Bologna, Paris, and Oxford. Especially in the Christian context, that philosophical tradition became known as scholasticism—the philosophy of the Schools and Schoolmen.

ARISTOTLE AND THEOLOGY
Much of the work of the period consisted in, or arose out of, the study of Aristotle, and various attempts to apply his thinking to and reconcile it with revealed religion (the most prominent example being **Aquinas**). Little emphasis was placed upon

typified in philosophy by the work of **Nicholas of Cusa**, **Machiavelli**, and **Suárez**. There was also a move away from Aristotelianism and toward neo-Platonism, inspired in large part by the fall of Constantinople, which resulted in a flood of refugees, carrying with them ancient works hitherto unknown in Western Europe. However, in general it would be fair to say that philosophy made scant progress during the Renaissance, which can be seen with only a little exaggeration as being little more than a period of transition between the medievals and the moderns.

ANICIUS MANLIUS SEVERINUS BOETHIUS

BORN c.480, Rome	DIED 524, Pavia

MAIN INTERESTS   Logic, ethics, metaphysics

INFLUENCES   Plato, Aristotle, Porphyry, Augustine

INFLUENCED   Eriguena, Anselm, Abelard, Aquinas, Nicholas Kryfts

MAJOR WORKS
The Consolation of Philosophy

Arians were Christians who denied that Jesus was god. Arianism was declared a heresy in 325, and finally rejected by the Roman Empire (which it had dominated) by 381.

Boethius was the last of the ancient philosophers and the first of the medievals. He was born to a high-ranking Christian family. His father, a consul, died when Boethius was about seven, and he was brought up and educated by Symmachus, an ex-consul whose daughter he married. The details of Boethius' education aren't clear, though his great learning must have resulted from study at one of the chief centers of philosophy, either Athens or Alexandria.

At this time Rome was ruled by the Ostrogoth king Theodoric. Boethius became consul in 510 and was entrusted with many diplomatic missions. However, Theodoric began to suspect his minister of engaging in treasonable negotiations with the Byzantine emperor, Justin I, and though these suspicions were probably baseless, Boethius was imprisoned in Pavia. He was held for some time, being regularly tortured, and was finally executed in 524.

Boethius is important for his Latin translations of and commentaries on ancient writers such as Aristotle and Porphyry; he was the last philosopher to have direct acquaintance with their works in the original Greek, and for a long time his translations provided the only access to Aristotle. He also wrote a number of treatises on mathematics, music, astronomy, and logic, and in discussing Plato, Aristotle, and Porphyry he set off the great eleventh-century controversy about universals.

In their own words:
What kind of happiness can there be in the blindness of ignorance?

The Consolation of Philosophy *ii, i*

The work for which he is most respected, among non-philosophers and philosophers alike, was his *De Consolatione Philosophiæ* (The Consolation of Philosophy), which he wrote in prison between bouts of torture. The book arose from the way his situation tested his Christian faith; how could a good god allow the good to suffer and the bad to prosper? Despite this, he didn't produce a work of Christian theology but one of philosophy, dealing especially with the issue of free will and the problem of evil. Though the nature and role of god is at the heart of much of what he says, this god is more like the neo-Platonists' "One" than the Christian personal god, and the consolation that he develops has its roots in both neo-Platonism and Stoicism.

The book is a dialogue between Boethius (in prose) and the personification of Philosophy (in verse). Its most influential philosophical passage is probably that about god's temporal status. Boethius argues that god is *eternal* (that is, exists outside time), whereas the world is *sempiternal* (that is, exists without beginning or end, but within time).

ITALIEN

ADI SAMKARA

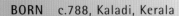

BORN	c.788, Kaladi, Kerala	DIED	c.820, Kedarnath, Himalayas

MAIN INTERESTS   Metaphysics, epistemology

INFLUENCES   Bādārayana, Gaudapāda

INFLUENCED   Rāmānuja, Radhakrishnan, Vivekānanda

MAJOR WORKS
*Viveka cūdāmani,
Upadesasāhasrī,
Brahmasūtrabhāṣya*

Brahman *is not
absolutely beyond
apprehension, because
it is apprehended as
the content of the
concept "I" [...]*

Brahmasūtrabhāṣya *3*

The early life of Samkara (Saṅkarācārya, Shankara) is obscure, though there are the usual culture-hero myths of his birth and childhood exploits. He was born into a Brahmin family and his father died when he was young. He was a pupil of Govindapāda, who had been a pupil of Gaudapāda—the thinker—who, in approaching *vedānta* Hinduism from a background of Buddhist thought, introduced the *advaita* (non-dualist) position that Samkara established as a major Hindu philosophical school. Samkara's life was short, but he produced a very large number of writings, and traveled all over India, debating with Hindu and Buddhist thinkers and religious leaders, and founding Hindu monasteries. His place and manner of death are as obscure as his birth, and the subject of many conflicting accounts; he seems, though, to have died in a Himalayan village.

At the heart of Samkara's system is his rejection of two orthodox schools of Hindu thought: Vai sesika, founded by Kanāda in the second century B.C.E., and Sāmkhya, which had existed since the seventh century B.C.E. The former holds that there are seven *padārthas* (categories of being), some material, some immaterial, each subdivided into basic components of the world, for example, atoms. The latter is dualistic, distinguishing between two kinds of being: *puruśas* ("knowers," or individuals whose essence is consciousness) and *prakṛti* (nonconscious "nature" or "matter").

Samkara accepts that the world appears to be dualistic, but argues that this is simply an appearance, for everything is *Brahman*. *Brahman* is a difficult concept, and can be compared (but not identified) with **Heraclitus'** *logos*, **Lao-zi's** *dao*, **Plotinus'** One, and **Spinoza's** Substance; it's the unchanging, indivisible, eternal reality, which we experience in terms of time and space, plurality and change. Experience (and inference from experience) can give us no knowledge of *Brahman*, though we have some direct awareness of it, for we each have direct awareness of our own consciousness, which is identical with *Brahman*. For understanding we need to go to the *Upaniṣads*, which embody the result of *philosophical* (not *religious*) meditation, and demand similar meditation from us. Genuine knowledge of *Brahman* comes in our understanding that we are in fact simply part of it, not genuine individuals.

Samkara is often presented as the Hindu **Kant**. If such comparisons are useful at all he would be better compared with **Parmenides**, who argued that we can know the unperceived world-as-it-really-is, as Samkara stressed that we can have knowledge of *Brahman*. Kant held, however, the noumenal world to be necessarily unknowable.

Note:
*Samkara's advaita (non-dualist) vedānta
Hinduism became the most influential
of all Hindu philosophical schools.*

ABŪ-YŪSUF YA'QŪB IBN ISHŪQ AL-KINDĪ

BORN c.801, Kufah, Iraq	**DIED** c.873, Baghdad

MAIN INTERESTS Epistemology, metaphysics

INFLUENCES Plato, Aristotle, Plotinus, John Philoponus

INFLUENCED Roger Bacon

MAJOR WORKS
*On First Philosophy
(Fī'l-Falsafa al-Ūlā)*

Not only did Islamic philosophers at this time read Aristotle from a neo-Platonist viewpoint, but matters were further confused by the popularity of a book known as **The Theology of Aristotle,** *which was in fact a collection of extracts from Plotinus.*

Al-Kindī (Alkindus) was born into a prominent family in Kufah; according to some accounts his father was governor there. He was educated in Kufah and Basrah, and completed his studies in Baghdad. Word of his scholarship spread, and the caliph (al-Ma'mun) appointed him to the newly established "House of Wisdom" in Baghdad—a center for the translation of Greek philosophical and scientific texts.

When al-Ma'mun died, his brother (al-Mu'tasim) became caliph, and al-Kindī continued in his post, as well as tutoring al-Mu'tasim's son. However, on the accession of al-Wathiq, and especially of al-Mutawakkil, al-Kindī's star waned. Some accounts blame rivalries among the scholars at the House of Wisdom; others blame al-Mutawakkil's often violent persecution of non-Muslims and unorthodox Muslims. Al-Kindī was at one stage beaten, and his library confiscated, though it was later returned to him.

During his lifetime, and for a century or so, he was held to be the greatest Islamic philosopher, eventually being outshone by such thinkers as **al-Fārābi** and **ibn Sīnā** (he remained, however, the only major philosopher of Arab descent, and so continued to be known as "the Arab philosopher"). He wrote prolifically, though many of his books have been lost; a few of them were translated into Latin, and there have been discoveries of Arabic manuscripts of others (most importantly in

In their own words:

We do not believe that [a philosopher] could give an answer which matched in conciseness and clarity and directness and grasp of what was required than that given by the blessed Prophet [...]

Rasā'il al-Kindī al-Falsafiyya I, 373

the mid-twentieth century of twenty-four of his lost works). He produced original work in the fields of chemistry, music, medicine, geometry, astronomy, and logic.

The main concern of much of his work was to show the compatibility of philosophy and natural theology with both revealed and speculative theology (*kalām*). Nevertheless, he held that revelation was a superior source of knowledge, and that it guaranteed certain matters of faith that were unattainable by reason (he rejected speculative theology though). The position from which he argued was a combination of Aristotelian and especially neo-Platonist thought, and he added little that was original. His main importance lies in the role he played in introducing and popularizing Greek philosophy in the Muslim intellectual world. He also introduced much of what became standard Arabic philosophical vocabulary. Without al-Kindī, the work of al-Fārābi, ibn Sīnā, and **al-Ghazālī** might not have existed.

JOHN SCOTUS ERIGUENA

BORN c.810, Ireland	DIED c.877, unknown

MAIN INTERESTS Metaphysics

INFLUENCES Pseudo-Dionysius, Gregory of Nyssa, Augustine, Boethius

INFLUENCED Amalric of Bene, Aquinas, Nicolas Kryfts

MAJOR WORKS
*On
Predestination,
On the Division
of Nature*

The pseudo-Dionysius
was an anonymous
early-sixth-century neo-
Platonist Christian writer
from Syria, whose works
were until the fifteenth
century attributed to
Dionysius the Areopagite,
an Athenian converted by
St. Paul.

The Holy Roman Empire
lasted from 800 until
1806. Originally called
"the Western Empire,"
and later "the Roman
Empire," "Holy" was
added in the thirteenth
century. Voltaire
famously wrote that it
was neither holy, nor
Roman, nor an empire.

"Scotus" and "Eriguena" both indicate that the philosopher was born in Ireland, though his parents were probably Scottish. Ireland was at the time one of the last centers of classical learning in Europe; Eriguena's knowledge of Greek was probably gained during his education at an Irish monastery. In about 840 he went to France, and by 850 had been appointed to the Palatine school in the court of King Charles I (who became Emperor Charles II). He seems to have lived in France for the rest of his life, though in about 858 the Byzantine emperor commissioned him to produce translations from the Greek into Latin, which led to his influential translation of pseudo-Dionysius. After surviving a number of religious attacks on his very heterodox writings, he is thought to have died at about the same time as his patron, the Emperor Charles, in 877.

Throughout his writings Eriguena clearly takes there to be two authorities: the Bible and (neo-Platonist) philosophy. He set the agenda for much of the rest of the medieval period by insisting that the two couldn't be in opposition, and trying to reconcile them by interpreting revealed religion in line with the findings of reason. In doing this, he tackled internal inconsistencies in Christian doctrine as well as the apparent inconsistencies between Christianity and reason. Unsurprisingly, the result was viewed by many orthodox Christian thinkers as suspect, the most common criticism being that Eriguena was a pantheist.

One of Eriguena's first forays into philosophy was his book *On Predestination*, which he wrote at the request of one of the participants in the debate. His book failed to find favor with either side, and was in danger of being declared heretical (it was in fact eventually condemned in 855). Eriguena wisely moved on to other issues.

His masterpiece was the dialogue *On the Division of Nature*, in which he develops the first original medieval philosophical system. He defines "Nature" as everything that exists, and divides it into four categories: uncreated Nature that creates, created Nature that creates, created Nature that doesn't create, and uncreated Nature that doesn't create. God is uncreated Nature that creates, and he produces the *Logos*, the Divine Word, and in this the eternal divine ideas, which are created Nature that creates; these ideas are like Platonic Forms, the archetypes of the finite things that make up the world of our experience—created Nature that doesn't create. The fourth category, uncreated Nature that doesn't create, is the final stage, when everything returns to god, and god is everything.

In their own words:
Nature is the general name [...] of all things which are and which are not [...]

On the Division of Nature *I*

ABŪ NASR MUHAMMAD IBN AL-FARAKH AL-FĀRĀBI

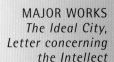

BORN c.870, Wasij, near Farab	**DIED** 950, Damascus, Syria

MAIN INTERESTS   Epistemology, metaphysics

INFLUENCES   Plato, Aristotle

INFLUENCED   ibn Sīnā, al-Gazalī, ibn Rushd, ben Maimon, Aquinas

MAJOR WORKS
*The Ideal City,
Letter concerning
the Intellect*

*The false philosopher is
he who acquires the
theoretical sciences
without achieving the
utmost perfection so as
to be able to introduce
others to what he
knows in so far as their
capacity permits.*

The Attainment of
Happiness *iv: 61*

Of Persian stock, al-Fārābi (Alfarabius, Abunaser) was born in Turkestan. He traveled extensively throughout his life, though he spent much of his time in Baghdad, where his main teacher was Abū Bishr Mattā ibn Yūnus, a Christian Aristotelian from Syria; it was in Baghdad that he studied Arabic. At one stage he is said to have been a *qādī* (judge), and to have been caretaker of a garden; he certainly spent much of his life teaching and writing. He produced introductions to philosophy, original works of scholarship on logic, music, medicine, and the sciences, and commentaries on **Aristotle**, though he was influenced by the misattributed *Theology of Aristotle* (see **al-Kindī**), and read Aristotle through neo-Platonist eyes. His own written style was not terribly clear.

While visiting Halab (now Aleppo) in Syria, he gained the patronage of the local ruler, Sayf al-Dawla, and it was during his time there that his fame spread throughout the Muslim world. He was dubbed *the Second Teacher*, Aristotle having been the first. Details of his death are even vaguer than those of his life, and he is variously said to have died peacefully in Damascus and to have been killed by bandits.

Al-Fārābi's view of philosophy was very different from that of al-Kindī (and more typical of Muslim philosophers): philosophy was the supreme product of the human mind, and the only path to genuine

In a nutshell:
Only through philosophy can knowledge be gained, so those who can philosophize have a religious duty to do so.

knowledge. For non-philosophers, some access to the truth was possible, but only through the distorting lens of symbols, which are different for different societies. Thus, philosophy is universal, but other accounts of the truth—most significantly, religious accounts—are culturally relative. He accepted the Koran's status as revealed truth, but its status was limited to its own cultural context; Islam couldn't be exported to other cultures, which had their own symbolic expressions of truth.

IMMORTALITY OF THE PHILOSOPHERS
Philosophy is not only the highest possible human activity, but is demanded by god of those who are capable of it. Moreover, though al-Fārābi generally takes the Aristotelian position against the immortality of the soul (the Koran's talk of Paradise is an example of the symbolic expression of truth, designed to be understood by non-philosophers), he seems to make an exception in the case of the few who manage to raise themselves above the lowest level of human intellect (merely potential intellect).

Situated halfway between the Euphrates and the coast, pilgrims and traders from the north passed through the ancient city of Aleppo on their way to Damascus. Legend has it that the prophet Abraham, on his way to Canaan, stopped at Aleppo to milk his cow on the citadel hill. The city's Arabic name is Halab, derived from the word for milk (halib).

THE NATURE OF THINGS

Metaphysically, al-Fārābi identified god (Allah) with the neo-Platonists' One, which is highest in the hierarchy of intellect, and from which (through a process of self-contemplation) comes a succession of emanations, down to the lowest level of self-existent intellect, the "active" or "agent" intellect, which acts as intermediary between the human mind and the realm of intellect. The human mind is itself analyzed into many levels of intellect, and al-Fārābi carefully explains the relationship between the different levels, and the means of moving from one to the next. Where he differs from most other Muslim philosophers is in his argument that, though god is the creator, the created world is eternal.

THE STATE

Al-Fārābi took more of an interest in political philosophy than most other Muslim philosophers; he was very much influenced by **Plato's** *Republic*, and produced his own version, *Fī Ārā' Ahl al-Madīnah al-Fādilah*, variously translated as *On the Principles of the Views* (or *On the Opinions*) *of the People/Citizens of the Virtuous/Excellent/ Ideal/Perfect City/State*. This presents an Islamicized version of Plato's views, with a philosopher-prophet rather than Plato's philosopher-king (his discussion of prophethood was itself important and influential). Al-Fārābi thought that such a combination was unlikely, though, so that after the initial founding of the state,

philosophers and statesmen would have to collaborate in order to ensure its correct running. At the heart of the virtuous state is the physical and spiritual happiness of its citizens. He also offers an analysis of four kinds of non-virtuous state.

Al-Farabi believed religious accounts of truth to be culturally relative. The Koran was the revealed truth for Islam, but other religions had their own expressions of truth.

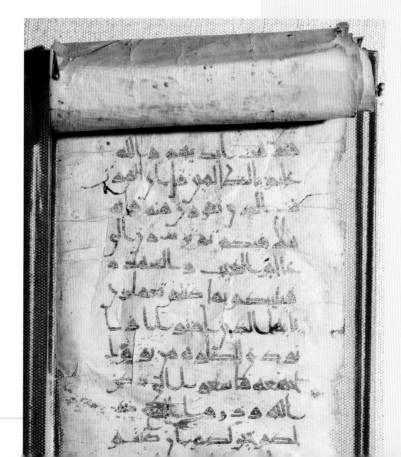

ABŪ ALĪ AL-HUSSAIN IBN ABDALLAH IBN SINĀ

| BORN | 980, Afshana, Bukhāra | DIED | 1037, Hamadan |

MAIN INTERESTS Metaphysics

INFLUENCES Plato, Aristotle, Plotinus, al-Fārābi

INFLUENCED ibn Rushd, Roger Bacon, Aquinas, Duns Scotus, Spinoza

MAJOR WORKS
Al-Shifā
(Sufficientiæ),
*Book of Healing
of the Soul*

Brought up and receiving his early education in Bukhāra (now Uzbekistan), ibn Sīnā (Avicenna) was something of a child prodigy, soon outstripping his teachers in logic, and educating himself in a wide range of subjects, including poetry, theology, the sciences, mathematics, and philosophy. He taught himself medicine well enough not only to treat patients but also to teach practicing doctors; his book *al-Qanun* (The Canon of Medicine) was used as a textbook for centuries, both in the Middle East and in Europe. One story has him, aged seventeen, curing the King of Bukhāra, for which his chosen reward was access to the extensive royal library.

However, he struggled with metaphysics, and claimed he did not understand **Aristotle's** *Metaphysics* until he came across a book by **al-Fārābi** that made everything clear. He was certainly influenced by al-Fārābi, whom he went on to displace as the preeminent Muslim philosopher—a position he retained for centuries, though he was eventually joined in equal place by **ibn Rushd**.

Ibn Sīnā's life wasn't always easy; the need to make a living after the death of his father, together with the political instability of the period, meant that he was forced to travel extensively, being employed by various rulers, sometimes as vizier (chief minister), sometimes as court physician. Nevertheless he managed to write more than a hundred books, many of which have survived. Most of

In a nutshell:
God is necessary, one, and outside time; everything emanates from god, so everything is necessarily the way it is.

his writing was in the usual philosophical language of Arabic, though he wrote at least two books in his native language, Farsi. One significant advantage he had over al-Fārābi was the clarity of his writing.

His philosophical position was, inevitably, grounded in Plato, Aristotle, and neo-Platonism, and as we've seen, he himself made much of his debt to al-Fārābi. In fact, in many areas of his work, such as natural philosophy and his account of the mind, he was important simply because he provided a clear account of Aristotle's thought, not for any originality of his own thought or argument. Where he differed from the strict rationalism of al-Fārābi was in returning to the rather more mystical predilections of the neo-Platonists. For example, where al-Fārābi had rejected Plotinus' notion of eventual union with the One (or, in the Muslim philosophers' account, god), ibn Sīnā returned to it, though he argued that such union was possible only for a few souls. On the other hand, he held that *all* human souls are immortal, as against al-Fārābi's position that restricted immortality to only philosophers.

[...] the soul comes into existence whenever a body does so fit to be used by it. The body which thus comes into being is the kingdom and instrument of the soul.

al-Najāt xii

that god is a person, however, and there's a tension between these two claims that he seems not to have noticed (much that is essential to being a person is concerned with time and change). More important for the development of Muslim philosophy, the notions that god is atemporal and that the world emanates from god by virtue of the necessity of god's nature don't sit well with the Koranic account of god and creation.

Nor, indeed, does a consequence of his discussion of the existence of god: the universe is seen as wholly deterministic (every event has a cause), and ultimately depending upon the uncaused cause, god—who is himself necessary, his essence being bound up with his existence. That means that there is no room for freedom, or even for contingency, in ibn Sīnā's universe. This is a problem that faces any philosopher who tries to reconcile the metaphysical with the ethical claims of religion (most explicitly, **Spinoza** and **Leibniz**). Ibn Sīnā also shares with Spinoza the label "pantheist," which is implicit in much of his work, though a book in which he was supposed to have offered an explicit defense of pantheism has been lost, and might not have been by him at all (ibn Sīnā is thought to have been the genuine author of only about half of the books attributed to him).

THE COSMOLOGICAL ARGUMENT

Ibn Sīnā's main argument for the existence of god, was a version of the cosmological argument that is found in many of the medieval Muslim philosophers, and which is in consequence often now referred to as the *kalām* cosmological argument. It rests upon the distinction, drawn in al-Fārābi and elaborated by ibn Sīnā between *possible* and *necessary* beings. At least some of the things that we experience in the world are possible beings—they exist, but they might not have done; their essences are distinct from their existence. But if a thing might or might not exist, then there must be some cause of its existence. That cause might itself have a cause, but there can't be an infinite regress of causes. We must therefore eventually reach an uncaused cause, a necessary being, and that is what we call god.

CREATION AND TIME

Ibn Sīnā takes the same line as **Augustine**, and argues that god is unchanging and outside time, and thus is a *metaphysical* cause of the world (unlike a *physical* cause, a true metaphysical cause isn't prior to, but is simultaneous with, its effect). He also holds

The notion of cause used by ibn Sīnā is Aristotle's, and continued in use until the 18th century. Four kinds of cause exist, as illustrated using the example of a bronze statue of Hermes.

1. *The efficient cause: what brings the statue into being (the sculpting)—this is generally what we now mean by "cause";*

2. *The formal cause: the form of the statue—the relationship between its parts;*

3. *The material cause: the matter of which it's made—the bronze;*

4. *The final cause: the reason for which it was made, its purpose.*

ANSELM OF CANTERBURY

BORN 1033, Aosta	**DIED** 1109, Canterbury

MAIN INTERESTS   Metaphysics, epistemology

INFLUENCES   Aristotle, Augustine, Boethius

INFLUENCED   Aquinas, Nicolas Kryfts, Descartes, Anscombe

MAJOR WORKS
Monologion,
Proslogion

I do not seek to understand so that I may believe, but I believe so that I may understand [...]

Proslogion

Anselm was born in Aosta, at that time part of Burgundian Piedmont (now Italian Piemonte). He wanted to become a monk when very young, but was prevented by his father. When he was able to leave home, in his early twenties, he went on his travels, eventually settling at the Benedictine Abbey at Bec, Normandy. After some years of study under its prior, Lanfranc, he joined the order, and when in 1063 Lanfranc left to become abbot of the new monastery of St. Stephen at Caen (and later in 1070, archbishop of Canterbury) Anselm took over from him, going on to become abbot of Bec in 1078.

It was at Bec that, at the urging of the monks, he wrote down his teachings in two books: the *Monologion* or "soliloquy" (1077) and his masterpiece, the *Proslogion* or "discourse" (1078), as well as a number of works on language, truth, and freedom. In 1093, however, he was appointed to succeed his old teacher Lanfranc as archbishop of Canterbury. He rather reluctantly took up this position, and so left the tranquillity of Bec for the turmoil of England, where he entered into a period of constant battle, first with William II, then with Henry I.

During this time he was bounced back and forth between England and virtual exile in Rome, as he fought with the crown over the independence of the church and the use of church funds. Though generally on friendly terms with Henry, who held him in high regard, Anselm was faced with numerous

In a nutshell:
Reason brings knowledge, so religious knowledge must be grounded in valid arguments.

conflicts. Finally, in 1107, they were able to come to a compromise settlement, and Anselm lived peacefully in Canterbury until his death at the age of seventy-six.

Anselm's philosophical position is realist (as against medieval nominalism), and the familiar mixture of **Aristotle** plus neo-Platonism, applied to Christian beliefs. He also acknowledged a debt to **Augustine**, whose work he tried not to question, so gaining the title "the second Augustine" (though inevitably, as an original thinker, he departed from Augustinian ideas). He rejected the idea that faith should be somehow extra-logical, and stressed the importance of reason, offering arguments for the major tenets of Christianity, including the incarnation and the trinity. His best-known arguments, however, are those for the existence of god, and especially the argument developed in the *Proslogion*, now known by **Kant's** name for it: the *ontological argument*. This was criticized by his contemporaries, and most influentially by **Aquinas**, but was resurrected by many early modern philosophers, most notably **Descartes**.

After Lanfranc's death in 1089, the post of archbishop of Canterbury was left empty for four years. By refusing to recognize a new archbishop, William II prevented anyone from having moral governance over England or its king. However, in 1093, while Anselm was visiting England, William fell ill, and, thinking that he may go to Hell if he died without an archbishop of Canterbury, he and his bishops forced Anselm to accept the post. Once recovered, the king repudiated his repentance and a difficult relationship between church and state ensued until William's death.

THE ONTOLOGICAL ARGUMENT

The argument attempts to show that the existence of god follows logically from the concept of "god"; that is, it's a contradiction to deny that god exists. Anselm argues roughly as follows:

1. We can conceive of a being than which no greater being can be conceived (call it "god").
2. God exists either only in our minds or in the world (he's either imaginary or real).
3. But it's greater to be real than to be imaginary.
4. If god existed only in our minds, we could conceive of a greater being—one that exists in the real world.
5. But then that would be a being greater than a being than which no greater being can be conceived, which is a contradiction.
6. *Therefore* god really exists.

In other words, once one has understood the concept of "god," then to deny god's existence is to talk nonsense.

GAUNILO'S OBJECTION

The argument is deceptively simple, and most people feel immediately that it can't work— but more thought reveals that it's difficult to see *why* it doesn't work. A contemporary of Anselm and fellow Benedictine, the monk Gaunilo, offered what has become known as an *overload objection*. Rather than showing how the argument failed, he argued that it must be faulty, because if it were sound,

then so would be a vast number of other arguments of the same form, so overloading the universe with things whose existence we have good reason to doubt. He takes the idea of an island than which no greater island can be conceived, and claims that we can use Anselm's argument to prove that such an island exists—and so on, replacing "island" with anything you want.

The trouble is that Gaunilo's argument doesn't work, because there's no such thing as *the* concept of an island than which no greater can be conceived; we each have a different notion of the greatest possible island (some may want it to have plenty of fruit and vegetables, and not too much heat; others will want tropical sun and plenty of fish). If Gaunilo responds that he means not an island that's perfect for anyone, but just the greatest island *as an island*, then we reply that all islands are perfect in that sense, for they're all perfectly islands (something is either an island or it's not). The concept of "god" is unique, because it's the concept of something that's maximally great—not for me or for you, not as one kind of thing or as another, not for this purpose or that, but just great, full stop.

Despite long periods of neglect (especially after Aquinas attacked it), the ontological argument became one of the main arguments for the existence of god, especially among philosophers. It doesn't work, in fact, but that's another story.

OVERVIEW
INDIAN PHILOSOPHY

Whereas ancient Greek philosophy mainly developed out of scientific and metaphysical concerns, gradually extending to moral, political, epistemological, and logical questions, ancient Indian philosophy mainly developed out of religious and theological writings, and extended to other areas. This generalization is potentially misleading, however; the work that constitutes the earliest evidence of Indian philosophical thinking, and out of which later philosophy grew, was the Veda (*Knowledge*), originally, three ancient collections (*samhitas*) of writings: the *Rig-veda* (a collection of 1,028 hymns), the *Sama-veda* (a rearrangement of part of the *Rig-veda*), and the *Yajur-veda* (material for the use of sacrificing priests). To these was later added the *Atharva-veda*, a collection of popular material such as spells, charms, and so on. The oldest parts of the Veda date back as far as the fourteenth century B.C.E., though the current (written) form first appeared about the end of the third century B.C.E.

Though the Veda is certainly a religious scripture, it differs markedly from, say, the Judeo-Christian Bible; where the latter has a primarily historical nature, tracing the story of a certain Semitic tribe from mythological origins through its many tribulations, the Veda—and especially the *Rig-veda* and *Sama-veda*—is primarily metaphysical. This doesn't mean simply that it makes statements about the nature of the world; it also poses questions, and implies a developed, probably mainly oral, tradition of philosophical investigation and questioning.

Nevertheless, the Veda's religious status makes itself felt in many ways, not least through the traditional division of the nine main schools of thought into two unequal parts: six orthodox and three unorthodox schools, see below.

A number of these (especially Vedānta and Materialism) are in fact collections of related schools, and sometimes these subschools move very far from each other. The most striking example of this is the Vedānta school.

VEDĀNTA
Vedānta arises out of study of the later Veda, especially of the *Upaniṣads*. These are works by different authors, written at different (widely separated) times (of the more than two hundred *Upaniṣads*, fewer than twenty are considered to be ancient, the rest being later imitations). As with much of Indian philosophy, little is known about the *Upaniṣad* authors; this is why few Indian philosophers appear in this book—the individual thinker is not as prominent in the Indian as in the Chinese and Western philosophical traditions. The first and main Vedānta texts were the Brahma-sūtras, and these were so elusive that they needed interpretation—hence the development of different Vedānta schools, of which the most important was **Saṁkara's** *advaita* (non-dualist) *vedānta*.

The many schools that are collected under the heading "Materialism," on the other hand, are the result more of an historical fragmentation; Materialist philosophy was usually strenuously opposed by the more religious—and especially the orthodox—schools, and so tended not to last long. Nevertheless, they had considerable influence on many other facets of Indian thought.

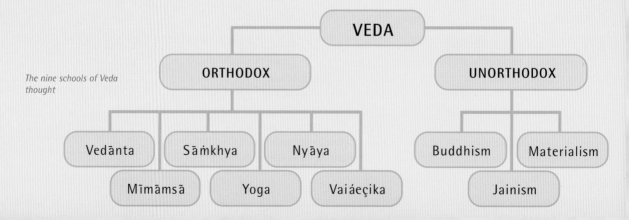

The nine schools of Veda thought

RĀMĀNUJA

BORN 1017, Sriperumbudār	**DIED** 1137, Srīrangam

MAIN INTERESTS   Metaphysics, epistemology

INFLUENCES   Saṁkara

INFLUENCED   Radhakrishnan

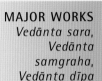

MAJOR WORKS
Vedānta sara,
Vedānta
samgraha,
Vedānta dīpa

A sannyāin is someone who renounces the world to seek mokśa—release or liberation from the cycle of birth and death (saś māra). Thus a sannyāsin is essentially an ascetic religious wanderer.

Born near Madras in South India, and named Ilaya Perumal, Rāmānuja came from a Brahmin family. His father died when he was young, and he started studying the Vedas with the Vedānta scholar Yadava Prakasha in nearby Kanchipuram. He was a precocious student, and soon came to disagree with his teacher about the correct interpretation of the texts. They eventually parted company acrimoniously (one story has Yadava attempting to have his student murdered).

Rāmānuja married young, but married life interfered with his studies, and he left his wife to become a *sannyāsin*. Eventually, he became head of the temple at Srīrangam, where he spent much of his life teaching and writing. He also traveled extensively in South India, teaching and proselytizing. He died at Srīrangam, having supposedly reached the age of a hundred and twenty.

Rāmānuja belonged to a devotional sect, *Srī Vaiṣṇavas*, which saw *Brahman*—impersonal in Saṁkara's *advaita* approach—as being a personal divinity, Viṣṇu. Though accepting much of Saṁkara's argument against the dualist and pluralist schools of thought, Rāmānuja held the *advaita* position to be too extreme, too academic and cold for his taste. His solution was to divide reality into three: *Brahman* in personal form (as Viṣṇu); material things; and individual souls. The latter two can't exist without the first—but nor can the first exist without the latter.

Though accepting that there is only one reality, Rāmānuja argued that *Brahman* is affected—is qualified—by individuals, hence the label applied to his philosophy: *vi siṣtādvaita*, usually translated as "qualified non-dualism" (or "qualified monism"). It's important to see that Rāmānuja isn't saying that his non-dualism is qualified, but that *Brahman* is. As a personal being, *Brahman* has qualities (such as compassion and love), which are defined in terms of (perhaps consist in) its relationship with individuals.

Rāmānuja rejects Saṁkara's argument that *Brahman* is unknowable unless we lose our individuality. Knowledge of *Brahman*, and *mokśa* comes through *bhakti* (worship, or love), which we practice as individuals. Our beliefs about the world can't be illusory (whose illusions would they be? Not those of *Brahman*, for *Brahman* can't go wrong, and not those of other human beings, for they're part of the illusion).

Though Saṁkara's *advaita vedānta* remained the most influential of the Vedānta schools, the *vi siṣtādvaita vedānta* school developed and consolidated by Rāmānuja attracted many of a more theistic disposition.

In a nutshell:
The world is an interdependent whole, made up of Brahman, *the material, and souls.*

ABŪ HĀMID MUHAMMED IBN MUHAMMED AT-TŪSI AL-GHAZĀLĪ

BORN c.1058, Tūs, Persia	**DIED** 1111, Tūs, Persia

MAIN INTERESTS   Metaphysics

INFLUENCES   al-Fārābi, ibn Sīnā

INFLUENCED   ibn Rushd, Sohravardī, Nicholas of Autrecourt

MAJOR WORKS
The Opinions of the Philosophers,
The Incoherence of the Philosophers,
The Revival of the Religious Sciences

Sūfism, a mystical Islamic movement, began in the early 10th century and grew popular in the 11th and 12th centuries. Its mysticism has some resemblance to both early Christian mystic sects and neo-Platonism.

Though al-Ghazālī had no intention of rejecting philosophical reasoning, his work probably contributed to the stifling of philosophy in the Muslim world more than a century later.

Born in what is now the province of Khorasan in Iran, al-Ghazālī (Algazel) was orphaned early in life, but received an extensive education—in Tūs, Jurjān, and Neyshābūr, where he studied with the leading theologian al-Juwaynī. During this time he wrote respected treatises on law and theology. After his teacher's death in 1085 he was invited to Baghdad by the vizier Niẓām al-Mulk. Here he studied privately, and probably wrote his two most important books, *The Opinions of the Philosophers*, in which he laid out the arguments of Christian and Muslim neo-Platonic Aristotelian philosophers, and *The Incoherence of the Philosophers*, in which he set out arguments against them (*Incoherence of the Incoherence* was **ibn Rushd's** response). In 1091 the vizier appointed him to the Niẓāmiyyāh school, where he spent four years as a popular and respected teacher.

In 1095 al-Ghazālī underwent some sort of nervous breakdown; this, together with what may have been political considerations, caused him to give up his position and wealth to live as a wandering Sūfi. He writes in the autobiographical work *The Deliverance from Error* (often compared with **Augustine's** *Confessions*) that part of the reason for his abandonment of his previous life was religious, and he spent the next ten years or so on pilgrimage and in meditation. Finally, the son of Niẓām al-Mulk persuaded him to teach again, and he returned to Baghdad. He spent the last years of his life in his native Tūs, where he had founded a sort of monastery for the teaching of Sūfism.

Al-Ghazālī accepted the methods of Aristotelian natural science and logic, advocating the use of the latter in philosophy and theology, but he rejected much of the metaphysics developed by Jewish, Christian, and Muslim thinkers as being inconsistent with the teachings of Islam. In *The Incoherence of the Philosophers* he emphasizes the unacceptability of three metaphysical claims: the denial of bodily resurrection; the limitation of divine knowledge to universal, eternal truths; and the doctrine of creation by emanations (together with the related claim that the world is eternal). Claiming that anyone holding these beliefs was an infidel, he set about refuting them. Though his primary motive was religious, he used Aristotelian logic to reject each claim. In doing so, he dealt interestingly with a number of subsidiary questions, including causality. He developed the view that there are no genuine causes within the world, attributing all causal powers to god (compare with **Malebranche's** Occasionalism).

In a nutshell:
Religious faith is essential, but it can and should be supported by reason.

OVERVIEW
PHILOSOPHY AND RELIGION

In all the major intellectual traditions, the relationship between religious thinking—and especially theology—and philosophy has often been a close one. Indian philosophy grew out of the sacred texts, the Veda; Chinese philosophical traditions, however nonreligious to begin with, were generally transformed into religion, their founders treated as objects of worship; and though the beginnings of Western philosophy are to be found in the attempt to move away from religious stories about the world to proper explanations, later developments, and especially the medieval period, saw the two ways of thinking brought back into touch.

Though the differences between philosophy and religion are evident in most areas, the boundaries may seem to become more blurred when we come to the philosophy of religion. How does this differ, not only from theology, but also from the sociology, the psychology, and the history of religion? Differences from the last three are, in fact, fairly easy to establish: philosophy differs from all of them in being concerned with the *truth* of religion. The question of theology is a little more complex, partly because the term "theology" can be used in a number of ways, of which three are prominent.

THE NATURE OF THEOLOGY
Revealed theology is concerned with religious beliefs and doctrines that are gained through revelation (personal or scriptural), not through reason alone. Natural theology is concerned with religious beliefs and doctrines that are gained through the use of reason. Speculative theology is the most influenced by philosophy and metaphysics, and might be described as the philosophy of religion done by believers.

This last definition gives the key to all of them: theology is the study of religion as carried out by religious believers. The philosopher is (or ought to be) prepared to question anything and everything, whereas the believer starts from a core set of beliefs that are beyond question. That isn't to say that the theologian ignores or avoids problems that arise from her faith; she will grapple with

and challenge many issues that ordinary believers would hold to be fixed and beyond question (such as the occurrence of miracles, the efficacy of prayer, even the nature of god). In fact, the religious beliefs of theologians in all religions tend to move further and further away from those of ordinary believers.

One effect of philosophical thought on religion, especially in the West, was to push it toward non-rationalism. As the main rational foundations of belief (such as arguments for the existence of god) were exposed as unsound, and there arose more and more problems with aspects of religious belief (such as the problem of evil), the notion of faith as a sort of belief without rational grounding (or even belief in what could not be understood) became central, and was eventually declared to be a virtue in itself.

As the rational foundations for religious belief crumbled and faith took on a greater importance, Western religious philosophers, became preoccupied with moral concepts such as good and evil. Augustine's neo-Platonic work De Civitate Dei, *for example, defends the City of God against the City of Satan.*

PIERRE ABELARD

BORN 1079, Le Pallet	**DIED** 1142, Chalôn-sur-Saône

MAIN INTERESTS Logic, language, metaphysics

INFLUENCES Aristotle, Porphyry, Boethius

INFLUENCED John of Salisbury

MAJOR WORKS
Sic et Non

The same act may be done by the same man at different times. According to the diversity of his intention, however, this act may be at one time good, at another bad.

Abailard's Ethics, *p.46*

Born in Brittany, Pierre le Pallet was the eldest son of minor nobility, and so was destined for a military career. He rejected this course, however, and left home to study, first at Loches (in Touraine, under Jean Roscelin, a nominalist philosopher), then at the Cathedral School in Paris (under William of Champeaux, a realist). During this time he adopted the surname "Abelard" (or "Abailard," or "Abaelardus"). By about 1105 he'd started his own school at Melun in Seine-et-Marne, later moving along the Seine to Corbeil, and finally returning to Paris in 1108. At some stage, probably between Corbeil and Paris, he temporarily left philosophy to study theology under Anselm of Laon, in part because of health problems. This ended badly; he seems to have quarreled with every teacher he had, and with many others too, but this didn't prevent him from quickly gaining a reputation throughout France and beyond both as a thinker and as a teacher. In 1113 he was appointed to a chair at the Cathedral School, teaching rhetoric and dialectic. He was handsome, charismatic, a very popular teacher, and renowned for his wit and intelligence, but also for his arrogance. As well as many friends and admirers, he gained a number of enemies.

ABELARD AND HÉLOÏSE
In 1117 he became tutor to the niece of one of the canons at Notre-Dame. The sixteen-year-old Héloïse had already achieved some renown herself for her scholarship; she spoke Latin, Greek, and Hebrew, and was well-versed in the classics, philosophy, and theology. They quickly became lovers, and Héloïse became pregnant. The two married secretly; though Abelard wasn't in holy orders, and so was not committed to celibacy, the relationship would have hurt his career, not least because he had been effectively *in loco parentis* to his student. There followed a complicated series of misunderstandings involving Héloïse's uncle, ending in a violent attack on Abelard, and his castration. Héloïse became a nun at Abelard's insistence, and Abelard a Benedictine monk, their son Astrolabe having been sent off to be brought up by Abelard's sister.

After this, one of the most dramatic episodes in the history of philosophy, Abelard went on to court further disasters. He had to flee the monastery of Saint Denis to which he'd retired, having questioned the legend of its patron saint, and his first book to be published, *Treatise on the Divine Unity and Trinity* (c.1120) caused him to be tried before the Council of Soissons in 1121 (possibly as a result of a campaign waged against him by some of the enemies he had made), and though the book seems not to have been condemned directly, he was forced to burn it. What with this, and the continuing enmity of the monks of Saint Denis, he fled to the countryside near Troyes in the Champagne, where he hoped to find peace and solitude.

Romantic love

The correspondence between Abelard and Héloïse after they were separated survives, and has been for centuries an emblem of romantic love—though it is in fact more effective at showing the sharpness of their intellects (and the selfishness of Abelard).

Always surrounded by controversy, Abelard sought to become the teacher of the prodigious young Héloïse. They fell in love and theirs is probably one of the most famous and celebrated of tragic love affairs.

Instead he was sought out by students, and he taught there for some time, in an encampment of tents and huts, and built an Oratory called The Paraclete. He also wrote works of logic and theology, as well as his most famous book, *Sic et Non* (*Yes and No*). Around 1126 he was appointed abbot of the monastery of Saint Gildas de Rhuis in Brittany, and Héloïse became abbess at The Paraclete, becoming famous for her scholarship and ability as an administrator. Abelard wrote an autobiographical work, *Historia calamitatum mearum* (*History of My Misfortunes*) (1132), through which we know many of the details of his life until that time. He also gained the enmity of the monks of Saint Gildas for his strictness, however, and in 1132 they tried to kill him. He returned to Paris, and was teaching there when he made a new and powerful enemy, Bernard of Clairvaux. The result was Abelard's condemnation by the Council of Sens and by the pope. Abelard's appeal against this failed, and after a relatively peaceful time at the monastery of Cluny, and then at a daughter house at Chalôn-sur-Saône, where he had continued to write, he died in 1142. Héloïse died in 1164, and was buried beside him. Their remains were moved to a single tomb in Paris in 1817.

WORDS AND THINGS

Philosophically, Abelard was a prominent nominalist; he argued that only individuals exist in the world, universals such as "hat" or "animal" being simply words. He was careful, however, to make clear that the universal isn't the physical word (the *vox*: the marks on the paper or the uttered sound), but the word as a logico-linguistic item that has meaning (the *nomen* or *sermo*). His positive thesis isn't clear, but he seems at times to think that universals *sermones* gain their meaning from our ability to spot similarities between individuals, so that we form a confused or blurred notion that stands for them all (compare **Berkeley** on abstract ideas). This is one of the things cited against him in the earlier accusations of heresy, for it seems to mean that the three persons of the Christian trinity genuinely exist (as individuals), but that the one god didn't, being only a confused idea.

Aside from his influential work on logic and language, Abelard wrote on more centrally theological issues such as sin and Biblical exegesis, as well as on the problem of free will and divine foreknowledge. It could be said that he was the first important *scholastic*; he lived at a time when the great European universities were beginning to be founded (and, indeed, he has been credited with being an important influence on the creation of the University of Paris).

In a nutshell:
Universals aren't things, though talk about universals isn't merely about words.

IBN RUSHD

IBN RUSHD ABŪ AL-WALĪD MUHAMMAD

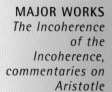

BORN 1126, Córdoba, Spain	**DIED** 1198, Marrakesh, Morocco

MAIN INTERESTS   Epistemology, politics, metaphysics

INFLUENCES   Plato, Aristotle, Porphyry, al-Fārābi, ibn Sīnā, al-Ghazālī

INFLUENCED   ben Maimon, Roger Bacon, Siger of Brabant, Aquinas

MAJOR WORKS
*The Incoherence
of the
Incoherence,
commentaries on
Aristotle*

*Now since [Islam] is true
[...] we the Muslim
community know
definitely that
[philosophy] does not
lead to [conclusions]
conflicting with what
Scripture has given us;
for truth does not oppose
truth, but accords with it
and bears witness to it.*

Faŝl al-Maqāl //

Ibn Rushd (Avén Ruiz, Averroës) was the son and grandson of Córdoban *qādīs* (judges), both important men in the politics of Andalusia, and was himself educated (partly by his father) in jurisprudence, as well as in medicine, philosophy, theology, and mathematics. The caliphs of Córdoba during his lifetime—Abū Ya'qūb Yusūf (1163–1184) and his son Abū Ya'qūb al-Mansūr (1184–1199)—ruled over an enlightened state, in which great freedom was extended to intellectual activity of all kinds—far greater than in the rest of the Islamic and Christian world.

Ibn Rushd flourished in this environment, both intellectually and professionally. He was appointed *qādī* of Sevilla in 1169 and of Córdoba in 1171, before becoming court physician to Abū Ya'qūb Yusūf in 1182. The caliph was interested in philosophy, and under his patronage ibn Rushd began to work on his commentaries on **Aristotle** (this side of his work—the commentaries on Plato, Porphyry, but especially Aristotle—earned him the title "the Commentator").

When the caliph died, his son succeeded him. At first, little changed; ibn Rushd remained court physician and counselor, and became even more prolific in his writing. However, though intellectual circles continued to enjoy controversy and debate, the uneducated masses, influenced by more fundamentalist clerics, were turning against learning, and especially philosophy.

In a nutshell:
Philosophy, theology, and rhetoric are three ways to truth, each appropriate to a different level of society.

There was popular resentment, in particular, of ibn Rushd's defense of reason, and his attempts to show that the findings of philosophy could be reconciled with the teachings of Islam, and he was even physically attacked. In addition to all this, the caliph had political problems, which made it important that he have the support of the clerics. In 1195 ibn Rushd was accordingly accused of heresy, stripped of his posts, and banished from the court in Marrakesh; all his books, apart from the purely scientific works, were burned.

In 1198, the caliph's political and military problems having eased, ibn Rushd was pardoned and brought back to Marrakesh, but he died later that same year. His influence on philosophy in the Christian West was immense (throughout and beyond the medieval period), though he was known almost wholly for his work on Aristotle. His work was taught in the European universities, and in the thirteenth century a group of self-proclaimed Averroists grew up around Siger of Brabant. His influence in the Muslim East was slight, partly because his death came as the forces of Muslim religious

For many years ibn Rushd enjoyed the respect of his fellow intellectuals, while the uneducated masses found it difficult to reconcile his philosophy with the teachings of Islam. He played an important role in the defense of Greek philosophy against Islamic theologians, and is known for his work on Aristotle. However, the rise of Muslim religious orthodoxy led to an accusation of heresy and a burning of his books.

orthodoxy were winning their battle against philosophy, leaving Islam without the rational component that played such a huge role in the development of Christianity in the West. Ibn Rushd, or Averroës as he was known in Christian Europe, was the last of the great Muslim philosophers.

DOUBLE TRUTH

The philosophical position for which he is best known is, in fact, one that he didn't hold: the theory of double truth. This is the thesis that there are two kinds of truth, the philosophical and the religious (and sometimes that only the former is genuine). His actual position differs from this in two respects. First, he in fact drew a distinction between different means to the truth rather than different kinds of truth; secondly (after Aristotle), he distinguished between three means to the truth, each appropriate to a different section of society: philosophical demonstrations, which can be followed by the rulers; dialectical discussion, which can be understood by theologians; and rhetoric, which can be followed by the ordinary mass of people. Ibn Rushd follows his predecessors, such as **al-Fārābi**, in accepting a roughly Platonic notion of the ideal state (replacing the philosopher-kings with philosopher-prophets), with each section of society receiving education appropriate to its level.

His commentaries on Aristotle were themselves divided into three levels, each level being of a different length: the shortest, *jami*, were mainly elucidatory paraphrases, essentially giving Aristotle's conclusions; the *talkhis*, the middle length, added explanations, and contained some of ibn Rushd's own thoughts; the longest, *tafsir*, presented detailed commentary, and presented the thoughts of both Aristotle and ibn Rushd in great depth and detail. His main aims were to cleanse the Aristotelianism of the time of the neo-Platonist influence, and to distinguish between the philosophical and the theological arguments of such writers as **al-Fārābi** and **ibn Sīnā**.

IMMORTALITY OF THE SOUL

One of ibn Rushd's best-known positions comes out of his examination of Aristotle's account, in *De Anima*, of the intellect. In some ways his account follows that of earlier writers, such as al-Fārābi, but his version includes the strikingly original view that Aristotle's "passive intellect," which earlier writers had identified with an aspect of the body, or an individual mentality, is in fact an aspect of a single, unified intellect—immaterial and universal. This implies that, contrary to ibn Sīnā's view, there is no immortality of the soul, except in some general sense very different from the usual Islamic (or Christian) notion.

ZHU XI

BORN 1130, Youxi	DIED 1200

MAIN INTERESTS   Metaphysics, ethics, politics

INFLUENCES   K'ung fu-zi, Meng-zi, Zhou Dunyi, Cheng Yi, Cheng Hao

INFLUENCED   Wang fu-zi, Kang Youwei, Feng Youlan

MAJOR WORKS
*Reflections on Things at Hand,
Analects*

Everything has an ultimate qi, which is the ultimate li.

Recorded Sayings *94*

Zhu Xi (Chu-shi, Chu Yülan-Hui, Chu Wen-kung) was born toward the end of the Song dynasty in what is now Fujian Province in China; he was the son of a minor local official who had left the capital in protest against government actions. After a precocious performance in the Imperial examinations in 1148, Zhu Xi spent the next nine years in the civil service. He wasn't an ideal civil servant, being honest and straightforward, and was eventually fired. He lived for the next twenty-one years in relative poverty, studying, writing, and teaching, before rejoining the civil service in 1179. Like his father, however, he remained in the lower echelons as a result of his openly critical attitude toward the government, and was eventually fired again.

He'd made a number of enemies, and in 1196 they managed to get his works banned, an Imperial censor having accused him of a list of ten crimes, which included refusing to serve the state and spreading false ideas. Though there were moves to have him executed, these came to nothing, and he died in official disgrace, though his funeral is said to have attracted a large crowd of mourners.

Zhu Xi wasn't, as is sometimes claimed, the founder of neo-Confucianism, but he was certainly one of the most important of the philosophers for its development; it would be fair, in fact, to say that he provided the synthesis that gave neo-Confucianism its

In a nutshell:
Daiji, the Great Ultimate, is the formal essence of the universe, and each of us is a reflection of the whole.

strength and made it as influential as it was, not only in China, but also in Japan and Korea. He was certainly responsible for its place in the educational system of Song dynasty China. It was Zhu Xi who chose and annotated the four classics—*Lun-Yu* (*Analects*), *Meng-zi*, the *Great Learning*, and the *Doctrine of the Mean*—that were eventually (two centuries after his death) prescribed for the Imperial examinations. Zhu Xi's version of Confucianism was known as *Lixue*, or the School of Principle.

He'd been attracted in early life by both Buddhism and Daoism, but during his thirties he settled on Confucianism, and his great achievement was the Great Synthesis of all the major neo-Confucian philosophers. Whereas Confucianism had concentrated almost wholly on ethics and political theory, the neo-Confucians introduced an interest in metaphysics and epistemology, which arose in large part from their engagement with Buddhist and Daoist thought. Zhu Xi took major elements from each of the neo-Confucians and built a rational, coherent system out of them.

Confucianism in the Song dynasty

At the beginning of the Song dynasty (960–1279), Confucianism had sunk to a stagnant, superstition-ridden state of neglect; the work of the neo-Confucian philosophers, and especially of Zhu Xi, revitalized it, and it gained influence not only in China, but also in Korea and Japan, in both countries becoming the state philosophy.

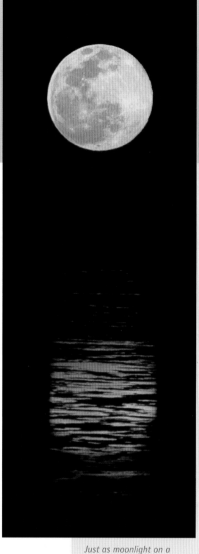

LI AND QI

His position centered on the notions of *li* (principle, form, idea) and *qi* (or *ch'i*; energy, or material force). *Li* was, of course, at the heart of ancient Confucianism, but there it meant something like propriety, the rules of right conduct; in the work of Cheng Yi, from which Zhu Xi took it, it's closer to the Platonic notion of a Form, or even the Daoist *dao*. If we think of *li* as the formal essence of a thing, then *qi* is its material essence. This is what **Descartes** called a Real Distinction: the claim isn't that *li* and *qi* are separate, but that they are distinct sorts of things. In fact, *li* and *qi* are never found separately, for *qi* is what *li* inheres in, and *li* is what gives *qi* its form. As Cheng Yo wrote: "Everything in the world is controlled by *li*. A thing must have its *qi*. A thing must have its *li*" (*Posthumous Papers*, V: 18). *Li* is unchanging and eternal, whereas *qi* is temporal and mutable.

THE GREAT ULTIMATE

Zhu Xi held that *li* is single and unified—and as a unified whole it is *daiji* (or *tai ch'i*; Great or Supreme Ultimate. This part of the synthesis comes from the work of Zhou Dunyi). *Daiji* is everything, and is in everything; it's the *li* of the universe. That isn't to say, though, that things in the world are part of the *daiji*, that the *daiji* is divided:

This *daiji* is received by each individual in its entirety and undivided. It's like the moon shining in the sky; although it's reflected in rivers and lakes, we shouldn't say that it was divided (*Recorded Sayings* 94).

So just as moonlight on a puddle isn't a certain fraction of moonlight, but the moon shining on the puddle, so the *li* in an individual isn't a certain fraction of *li*, but *daiji* informing the individual.

THE SCHOOL OF PRINCIPLE

Upon this metaphysical system is founded the ethical and political views of the School of Principle. Every human being, as informed by *daiji*, has within him- or herself the Four Virtues: benevolence, righteousness, propriety, and wisdom. Wrongness comes only when we're controlled by *daiji* rather than by our own mixture of *li* and *qi*. In practice, this means restricting ourself to natural needs, and avoiding artificial human desires. A well-balanced, virtuous society would result from everybody achieving this avoidance of desires, so that they lived in accordance with natural principles.

Just as moonlight on a puddle isn't a fraction of moonlight, but the moon shining on the puddle, so the li in an individual isn't a fraction of li, but the unified whole li—daiji.

MOSES BEN MAIMON

BORN	1135, Córdoba, Spain	DIED	1204, Fostat, Egypt

MAIN INTERESTS Law, ethics, metaphysics

INFLUENCES Aristotle, al-Fārābi, ibn Sīnā

INFLUENCED Aquinas, Albertus Magnus, Spinoza

MAJOR WORKS
Guide for the Perplexed, *Mishnah Torah*

Ben Maimon famously redrew the Jewish Menorah, claiming that it was not a common candelabra. The Menorah's structure, like a tree growing upward, served more for spiritual than for physical light.

Ben Maimon (Maimonides, Rambam) was born of Spanish-Jewish parents in Córdoba, southern Spain; he was educated by his father and other teachers in rabbinic studies, science, and philosophy. When he was thirteen, his family left Córdoba after it was attacked and taken by the Almohads (North-African Muslim reformers, who forced Islam on non-Muslims). After wandering from place to place in Christian Spain, the family moved to Fez in northern Morocco, where they stayed for some time, allowing ben Maimon to continue with his studies, which now included medicine, and to continue writing his first major work, the *Book of Illumination*, a commentary on the Mishnah.

Fez, however, was also under the rule of the Almohads, and though they managed to avoid the attention of the authorities for a time, ben Maimon's growing reputation as a scholar made it difficult for them to remain unnoticed, especially as both ben Maimon and his father became active trying to help the Jewish community, who had been forced to convert to Islam but still practiced Judaism. Eventually, after a near disaster, which they escaped only with the help of a Muslim friend, in 1165 the family moved on.

They traveled first to Palestine, and finally to Egypt, where they settled in Fostat, the Old City of Cairo. When their father, Rabbi Maimon, died, his elder son David supported the family by trading in gems, but in 1169 David died at sea, and the family's finances

(together with the large sums he was carrying for other merchants) were lost with him. It was now the younger brother's task to support the family, and he started practicing medicine. He had great success in this profession, eventually becoming court physician to the vizier of Salah ad-Din Yusuf (Saladin). He also began to gain great fame throughout Judaism for his learning as a rabbi, and he engaged in correspondence with many Jewish communities, responding to appeals for advice and using his political influence to help people. He became head of the Egyptian Jews in 1177, and spent much time studying and writing on the Talmud, producing his greatest non-philosophical work, the *Mishnah Torah* (a codification of all Jewish law). When he died, his body was taken to Palestine, where he was buried at Tiberias.

ARISTOTLE AND JUDAISM

Like his Muslim and Christian peers, ben Maimon's philosophy was grounded in Aristotelianism, but like them he departed from Aristotle's views where they conflicted with his own philosophical and theological position. Indeed, one of his main aims was the reconciling of Aristotelian, rational thought with the tenets of traditional Judaism. Perhaps his most significant departure from Aristotelian orthodoxy was his argument for the creation of the world out of nothing at a particular time. His most significant departure from the methods of other philosophers at the time, however, was

Rabbinic literature

Torah ("teaching")—variously used to refer to the first five books of the Hebrew Bible (the Pentateuch), the whole of the Hebrew Bible, the oral Jewish teachings, or even the whole Jewish law.

Midrash—tradition of Biblical exegesis found in rabbinic literature.

Mishnah—2nd century C.E. rabbinical text, edited from earlier collections, primarily concerned with the legal side of Biblical exegesis.

Talmud—main rabbinical text, commentary on the Mishnah: Palestinian Talmud, 4th century C.E.; Babylonian Talmud, 5th century C.E.

in not producing any work of academic philosophy—either commentaries on Aristotle or (aside from a very early work of logic) expositions of or arguments for his own views. His writings were either theological, legal, or practical, and their philosophical component lies in the way in which ben Maimon applies his philosophical thinking to those issues.

DISPELLING PERPLEXITY

The most philosophical, and the most important, of his works outside the strictly religious context was the *Dalālat al-Ha'irīn*, or *Guide for the Perplexed*, known by Christian philosophers of the next two centuries as Rabbi Moses' *Doctor Perplexorum*. This had a tremendous influence on European philosophy from the beginning of the thirteenth century onward. Yet it's an odd book. It's presented as though written to one of ben Maimon's former students, Joseph ben Judah, and is definitely not intended for the interested non-philosopher; it's often obscure and oddly organized. In common with rabbinic custom and with the views of many of his Muslim predecessors (especially of his contemporary **ibn Rushd**), ben Maimon considered philosophical (and theological) discourse to be appropriate only for a small minority of people; he therefore designed his book to be intelligible only to the properly educated. Moreover, it's aimed at the religious believer with philosophical interests, for it assumes the truth of Judaism, and largely concerns

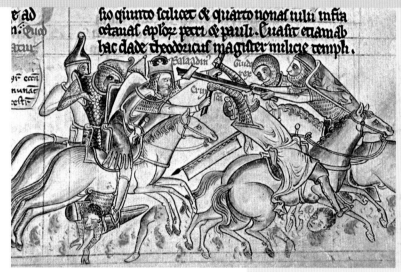

Ben Maimon lived his life in Islamic society. In Egypt he was court physician to the vizier of Muslim warrior Salah ad-Din Yusuf, who defended the Holy Lands against the invasion of the Christian Crusaders. Some say his fame as a physician was so widespread that even the Crusaders sought him out.

problems that arise out of certain biblical passages. Ben Maimon is very much concerned with anthropomorphic interpretations of the Bible, against which he argues.

He spends time on discussion (and, generally, refutation) of the work of previous philosophers, offers a number of arguments for the existence of god, and discusses the divine attributes, about which he adopts the doctrine of negative attributes (that is, god's essential nature can be understood only by saying what he is not—he's not limited in power or knowledge, and so on; any positive attribution will inevitably be inadequate).

In a nutshell:

Philosophy is the highest form of thought, though where it provides no answer, revelation can fill the gap.

ROGER BACON

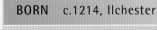

BORN　c.1214, Ilchester	**DIED**　1292, Oxford

MAIN INTERESTS　Science, epistemology

INFLUENCES　Aristotle, Augustine, al-Kindī, ibn Sīnā, ibn Rushd, Grosseteste

INFLUENCED　Experimental science

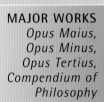

MAJOR WORKS
Opus Maius,
Opus Minus,
Opus Tertius,
Compendium of
Philosophy

[...] experimental science
is the mistress of the
speculative sciences, it
alone is able to give us
important truths within
the confines of the other
sciences, which those
sciences can learn in no
other way [...]

Opus Maius, *p.616*

Little is known about the early life of Bacon, who was born in or near Ilchester in Somerset. His family had been wealthy, but chose the wrong side in the war between Henry III and the barons under Simon de Montfort, losing their property. He was educated at Oxford, and then traveled to Paris, where he took a degree when he was about thirty-three, and taught there for a time. This was the time when it was forbidden to teach many of **Aristotle's** works at the University of Paris (indeed, in 1245 the pope had extended the prohibition to the University of Toulouse). The prohibition covered the works of natural philosophy, which would have included the *Metaphysics*. Bacon wasn't alone in ignoring the ban, but the flouting of rules was to be typical of much of his career.

His interest in the sciences had been instilled by Franciscans teaching at Oxford and Paris, possibly including Robert Grosseteste (c.1168–1253), and at some time, probably a few years after his return to Oxford in 1248, he joined the Franciscan order himself. This would have made considerable sense at the time, for the Franciscans were, along with the Dominicans, the foremost intellectual Christian order. Nevertheless, it proved to have been a mistake, for after a long period at Oxford spent teaching, writing, and performing scientific experiments, in 1260 the Franciscan order imposed on him a rule of internal censorship; that is, he was forbidden to publish any work outside the

In a nutshell:
Science demands careful observation,
and is grounded in mathematics.

order unless he gained the permission of his superiors. The reason for this isn't entirely clear, though it was probably a mixture of his outspoken disdain for theologians and the fact that his interest in the natural sciences was somewhat undiscriminating, including as it did a belief in astrology and the alchemists' Philosopher's Stone.

At some point Bacon found himself under what was effectively house arrest in Paris, though at the request of Pope Clement IV (who seems to have cared little for the Franciscans' refusal to allow Bacon to publish), he wrote *Opus Maius* (the Greater Work), the *Opus Minus* (the Lesser Work), and the *Opus Tertius* (the Third Work), which together form his most important writings. Perhaps as a result of the pope's intervention, perhaps because of his ill health, Bacon was allowed to return to Oxford in about 1289, where he wrote one more work (the *Compendium of Theology*) before he died.

MYTH AND MAGIC
Bacon was a strange character—on the one hand a hard-headed empirical scientist and rigorous philosopher, and on the other hand

Philosopher's Stone

The Philosopher's Stone was one of the goals of medieval alchemists. It was supposed to be a substance of such perfection that it could be used to increase the quality of base metals until they transformed into gold.

The north view of Friar Bacon's study in Oxford. His house on Folly Bridge was said to be the site of many alchemical and occult experiments.

a gullible believer in various myths, legends, and fabrications. Both aspects were the subject of later invention and fantasy. He was credited with the invention of spectacles and gunpowder, but there's no evidence for the former (though he certainly did important work in optics), and the Arabs, with whose work he was familiar, had already used gunpowder. Tales were also told of his occult powers, and a house on Folly Bridge, Oxford, is still pointed out as the site of his magical exploits; this side of his life, much exaggerated, was further emphasized by writers in the sixteenth century, who collected, passed on, and embellished popular tales of his magical researches.

EPISTEMOLOGY

Of much more importance are Bacon's discussion of perception (primarily vision), his insistence on a central role for observation in the gaining of knowledge, and especially his arguments for the usefulness of mathematics in the sciences and in practical affairs. On this last point, which is crucial for the development of science, he mixes together two claims: that mathematics should be the ground and support of experimental science, and that it should be the first part of the sciences to be studied. He offered eight arguments for these positions, of which the most important are, first, that science needs the clarity and certainty of mathematics, and second, that mathematical knowledge is "almost innate" (we would say that it's a priori knowledge),

needing no justification by experience or learning, so properly acts as a foundation for knowledge that is in need of such justification.

Even on such matters as the value of experience his double nature showed itself, for he included in this category not only perceptual experience gained through observation and experiment, but the divine illumination of the mind. Similarly, though he was very well read in ancient and Muslim philosophy, he accepted as genuine various fake works attributed to Aristotle, such as the *Book of Causes* and the *Secret of Secrets* (the latter was supposed to be a letter from Aristotle to Alexander the Great, containing [in addition to genuine political advice] material on astrology, magical herbalism, and numerology).

Bacon, then, could have been a tremendously influential figure in the development of philosophy, but his intellectual immaturity tended to push him to the sidelines. Nevertheless, his ability was such that he still made a mark on the intellectual life of the period, especially after his death.

THOMAS AQUINAS

| **BORN**   c.1225, Roccasecca, Italy | **DIED**   1274, Fossanuova, Italy |

MAIN INTERESTS   Metaphysics, epistemology, ethics, politics

INFLUENCES   Aristotle, Boethius, Eriguena, Anselm, ibn Rushd, ben Maimon

INFLUENCED   Everyone who came after him

MAJOR WORKS
Summa contra Gentiles, Summa Theologiæ

Like all the medieval Aristotelians, Aquinas' understanding of Aristotle was filtered through several layers of his predecessors (in his case, neo-Platonism, the Muslim philosophers, ben Maimon, and pseudo-Dionysius), as well as through his own Christian world view. He had something of an advantage over earlier philosophers though, for he had access to new, more accurate translations of Aristotle into Latin.

Born of an aristocratic family (his father was the count of Aquino, and his mother was the countess of Teano), Aquinas' early education was at the nearby Benedictine abbey of Monte Cassino. He went on to study at the University of Naples from 1239 until 1243, where he was taught by Pietro Martini and Peter of Ireland, and joined the Dominican order the following year. His family had been opposed to his interest in the Dominicans, and now, his father having died, his brothers had him kidnapped, keeping him captive for about a year and attempting what we'd now call "deprogramming." They failed, and eventually he was released.

He went first to Rome, then to Paris, and eventually to Köln, where he undertook further study under Albertus Magnus (c.1200–1280). After a brief period in which Aquinas' heavy build and quiet manner led his fellow students to nickname him "the Dumb Ox," Albertus recognized and proclaimed his ability with the famous and prophetic comment: "We call this boy a dumb ox, but one day his bellowing will resound throughout the world."

After some to-ing and fro-ing between Paris and Köln, during which time he was ordained as a priest, Aquinas settled in Paris in 1252 for further study, and in 1256 received his master's degree (the license to teach, for which he needed a papal dispensation, as he was under age). That year also saw his first publication (on the work of

In a nutshell:
There aren't two truths, so if philosophy and religion disagree, one of them must be wrong, and reason is the only tool we have to tell us which it is.

Italian theologian Peter Lombard), and he continued to write and publish throughout his career. In 1259 he was summoned to act as adviser to the papal court, and he spent a nine-year stint traveling with the court, returning to Paris in 1268.

His main concerns for the next three or four years were theologico-philosophical battles with the followers of **ibn Rushd**, the self-named Averroists, led by the French philosopher Siger of Brabant (c.1240–c.1284), and with the Franciscan Augustinians, led by the Englishman John Peckham of Brighton (c.1225–1292). He was sent to Naples in 1272, where, a year later, he suddenly stopped writing, saying: "I can do no more. Such things have been revealed to me that all I have written now appears to be as straw." He fell ill while traveling from Naples to Lyons, and died at the abbey of Fossanuova in 1274.

RECONCILING RELIGION WITH PHILOSOPHY
Aquinas' philosophical work was rooted in the belief that we've already seen expressed

by ibn Rushd: given that philosophy and science lead to the truth, and if one believes in the truth of religion, then they can't be in disagreement. Moreover, he tended to equate the truths of philosophy and science with the work of "The Philosopher," **Aristotle**. That is, he believed strongly that, for the most part, Aristotle's philosophical and scientific conclusions were true, and so must be in agreement with the revealed truths of religion—in particular, the contents of the Bible. Where there was apparent disagreement, it had to be the result of a misinterpretation, and on the whole that meant a misinterpretation of the Bible rather than of Aristotle. After all, Aristotle's work was straightforward, plain, and clear, whereas the Bible was written in the form of stories, histories, poetry, parables, and the like.

This isn't to say that Aquinas stuck slavishly to Aristotle's philosophy. He often extended, deepened, or simply reworked what Aristotle had written, either from religious motives, or simply because as a philosopher he saw problems and arguments that Aristotle had missed. Nevertheless, where Augustine had accepted **Plato's** thought where it agreed with Christian teaching, and amended it where it disagreed, Aquinas was much more ready, not to amend, but to reinterpret Christian teaching where it conflicted with Aristotle.

REASON AND REVELATION

Aquinas did in fact disagree with ibn Rushd with regard to the relationship between religion and philosophy, which was the main reason for the strength of his opposition to the Averroists. Where the Muslim philosopher and his Christian followers held that philosophy and revealed religion were completely independent of each other, Aquinas held that the relationship was more complex. Philosophical and religious knowledge must coincide, for the notion that there could be contradictory truths is absurd and self-defeating; thus there's a realm of knowledge that can be attained either philosophically or through revelation (such as the existence of god). However, there's a larger realm of knowledge attainable only through philosophy (such as knowledge of the structure of the natural world), and a realm of knowledge attainable only through revelation (for example, Anselm and the incarnation and the trinity).

On the one hand, Aquinas saw himself as protecting Christian theology from the views of philosophers such as the Averroists; on the other, he was protecting philosophy and the sciences from an anti-rationalist tendency in the church. His followers, known as Thomists, were to be extremely influential in the development of Christian, and especially Catholic, theology. Aquinas' rigor and clarity of thought were equally influential in the development of philosophy.

Aquinas' great achievement was to absorb the teachings of Aristotle into Platonized Christian philosophy.

[...] man wills Happiness of necessity, nor can he will not to be happy, or to be unhappy.

Summa Theologiæ
Pt. I, qu. 13, a. 6

WILLIAM OF OCKHAM

BORN	c.1285, Ockham, Surrey	DIED	1349, München

MAIN INTERESTS   Epistemology, logic

INFLUENCES   Aristotle, Porphyry, Duns Scotus

INFLUENCED   Buridan, Suárez, Descartes, Locke, Leibniz, Berkeley, Hume

MAJOR WORKS
*Summa Logicæ,
Ordinatio,
Dialogus*

The name "Ockham's Razor" is given to the principle that we shouldn't include in our theories more kinds of thing than are strictly needed: "entities should not be multiplied beyond necessity." It can be found in Aristotle, in fact, and in many of Ockham's medieval predecessors—though neither there nor in Ockham's work does it appear in that wording. It has been given Ockham's name because he makes central use of the principle in a particularly rigorous way.

Born in the village of Ockham (Occam) in about 1285 (dates offered by different writers range between 1280 and 1289), William entered the Franciscan order (probably in London) before going on to study at Oxford and then Paris. There's reason to believe that he was a student of **Duns Scotus** in Paris, and he was certainly much influenced by his fellow Franciscan. On his return to Oxford he set out to complete his studies, but failed to receive his mastership (the doctorate, or license to teach) because in 1323 the chancellor of the university, an overzealous Thomist John Lutterell, charged him with "erroneous teaching," and he was summoned to the papal court at Avignon for an inquiry into his writings.

Ockham wasn't ever convicted, in fact, because the inquiry went unfinished. While he was waiting at Avignon, the Franciscan minister general Michael of Cesena arrived for an inquiry into his (Ockham's) attacks on the papacy over a dispute concerning the poverty of Jesus and the apostles. He made an ally of Ockham, and in 1328 they fled Avignon together (and were both excommunicated). They went to Pisa, where they accepted the protection of Ludwig of Bavaria (the Holy Roman Emperor, and an opponent of the pope). From Pisa they traveled with Ludwig to München, where Ockham lived for the next thirty years, writing political tracts against the papacy and in favor of the separation of church and

In a nutshell:
Only individuals exist.

state, as well as philosophical and theological works. Ludwig's death in 1347 left Ockham in a vulnerable position, and he began to prepare for a reconciliation with the papacy. He died (probably of the Black Death) in 1349, possibly before the reconciliation was complete.

Like Duns Scotus, Ockham's main work is his commentary on Lombard's *Sentences*. This comes in various versions, including the author's own edition (the *Ordinatio*) and various *Reportata* produced by his students. He also wrote on **Aristotle** and Porphyry, on physics, and on logic (especially his *Summa Logicæ* (Summary of the Whole of Logic).

WIELDING THE RAZOR
Ockham was one of the main opponents of **Aquinas'** approach to philosophy and religion, arguing that it is not possible to demonstrate by reason such religious doctrines as the nature of the divine attributes, creation, and especially the immortality of the soul. Such beliefs depended solely upon revelation. He was also one of the chief, and perhaps the greatest, defenders of nominalism, denying the existence of universals—that is, properties independent of the things that have them.

The Papacy in Avignon

Between 1309 and 1377 the papacy was based at the Pope's Palace in Avignon instead of the Vatican, as the popes felt unsafe in Rome (Boniface III having been arrested in his palace by French-employed mercenaries). This period was known as the Babylonian Captivity.

The Pope's Palace, Avignon.

We don't need to invoke such things in order to explain the world and our experience of it, therefore (by Ockham's Razor) we shouldn't include them in our theories. (Of course, as with most controversies of this sort, Ockham's opponents, the Realists, didn't deny Ockham's Razor; rather, they argued that such things as universals *are* necessary to understand the world.)

Ockham's nominalism wasn't confined to universals. He applied the Razor to such metaphysical concepts as time, arguing that, just as people wrongly assumed that the use of words such as "redness" meant that there was a sort of abstract color floating around independently of red things, so they wrongly assumed that talk about events occurring in time means there's something called "time" that is a sort of container for these events. He didn't offer only a negative thesis, though. One of Ockham's main interests was logic, and he used it to show how the role of universals in language and understanding could be filled without our having to accept their existence. As well as logic, Ockham appealed to religion, and especially to god's omnipotence, though he was careful not to take his thesis too far; the idea that god has created things completely differently from the way in which we perceive them, together with Ockham's logical principles, could lead to extreme skepticism about experience, but though Ockham is a skeptic about some things, he never slides into a general skeptical position.

MODALITY

Though he was interesting in some areas of the philosophy of religion (for example, the Divine Command theory of morality), and his nominalism had a great effect on future philosophy of language and metaphysics, Ockham's main influence was in the field of logic, particularly his development of the logic of possibility and necessity. However, the medieval rise of logic (and of scientific method) during the fourteenth century was swept away by the Renaissance; science returned to the forefront in the sixteenth century, but logic had to wait another three hundred years for any real development.

Nevertheless, it wouldn't be too much of an exaggeration to say that, together with his fellow Franciscan Duns Scotus, Ockham set British philosophy on a course that led more or less directly to the empiricists of the seventeenth and eighteenth centuries, a period considered by many to have been the golden age of British philosophy.

That no universal is a substance existing outside the mind can be evidently proved.

Summa Logicaæ, Opera Philosophica I, p.50

JOHN DUNS SCOTUS

BORN	c.1266, Duns	DIED	1308, Köln

MAIN INTERESTS   Logic, metaphysics

INFLUENCES   Aristotle, ibn Sīnā, Aquinas

INFLUENCED   Ockham, Peirce, Heidegger

MAJOR WORKS
*Quodlibetal
Disputations,
Treatise on the
First Principle,*
commentaries on
Lombard's
Sentences

*The doctrine of the
Immaculate Conception
was that Mary, mother of
Jesus, was born sinless,
free from the taint of
Original Sin. It's distinct
from the doctrine of the
Virgin Birth (which arose
out of a mistranslation of
the Greek).*

*In the continuing battles
between the medieval
followers of Duns Scotus
and Aquinas, the
Scotists lost to the
Thomists, and the term
"dunce" (for "Dunsman")
was one result.*

Duns Scotus was born in Duns, Berwickshire (now the Scottish Borders), and received his early education at the Franciscan friary at Dumfries. He became a Franciscan friar in about 1281, and was ordained a priest at Northampton ten years later. In the interval he probably went on to further study in Oxford. By 1300 he was lecturing at Oxford, and in 1302 he moved to Paris, but was exiled from France in 1303 as part of a dispute between the king and the pope. Returning to Paris the following year, he completed his advanced studies, and developed his defense of the doctrine of the Immaculate Conception (which became Catholic dogma in 1854). This side of his thought earned him the nickname "the Marian Doctor." He was sent by his order to Köln in 1307, where he taught until his death a year later. He was extremely influential for two centuries after his death, and his influence extended into the nineteenth and twentieth centuries.

Duns Scotus wrote relatively little, and much of what has been ascribed to him in the past has turned out to be by other writers; some of the remainder are in the form of his students' lecture notes, or are works written for his own use rather than for publication. His philosophical arguments and positions are found most fully in the lectures that he gave on the *Four Books of Sentences* by theologian Peter Lombard (c.1100–1160); various versions of these have been collected, edited, and annotated, the most

In a nutshell:

Every individual or thing has a unique haecceity *or "thisness"—an essence that makes it just that individual or thing.*

important versions being the *Opus Oxoniensis* (Oxford Commentary), edited and revised by Duns Scotus, and the shorter *Reportata Parisiensa* (Paris Commentary).

Though he was a realist, he was in other respects opposed to views of **Aquinas**, not least in holding that theology and philosophy are distinct disciplines (philosophy being completely independent of theology, though theology needs to use philosophical tools). He also rejected the claim that divine revelation (or "illumination") is required for any of our knowledge, and argued that perception gives us direct knowledge of individuals rather than, as Aquinas held, the need for mediation by universals.

Among Duns Scotus' more important and well-known discussions are his account of the will and his discussion of possibility and necessity. However, what make him important and interesting are the rigor and thoroughness of his arguments, which mark him as one of the most typical of the scholastic philosophers.

NICHOLAS KRYFTS

| BORN | 1401, Kues, Rhineland | DIED | 1464, Todi, Tuscany |

MAIN INTERESTS   Politics, metaphysics

INFLUENCES   Augustine, Proclus, Boethius, Erigena, Anselm

INFLUENCED   Copernicus, Bruno, Leibniz, Spinoza

MAJOR WORKS
On Learned Ignorance, The Books of the Idiot, On the Pursuit of Wisdom

It's not only the universe as a whole that mirrors god, but every part of the universe, especially human beings; each thing and each person is a microcosm, a tiny version of the universe. This view was later taken and extended by **Leibniz**.

Nicolas Kryfts or Krebs (Nicholas of Cusa, Nicholas Cusanus) was born in Kues (Cusa) on the River Mosel, between Trier and Koblenz. He was educated first in Deventer, the Netherlands, at a school run by the Brothers of the Common Life, a monastic order founded by the Dutch mystic Gerhard Groote (1340–1384). From there he went on in 1416 to study philosophy at the University of Heidelberg, traveling in 1417 to Padua, where he studied canon law, receiving his doctorate in 1423. He then studied theology at Köln, and worked as a legal assistant for the papal legate to Germany.

He was a proponent of political reform, and in about 1433 wrote *On Catholic Unity*, advocating the supremacy of church councils over the pope. He was actively involved with the Council of Basel as a lawyer and delegate, but when the Council failed to deliver any reform, he changed his views, becoming a supporter of the papacy. This led to a successful career, in which he carried out a number of papal missions. In 1448 he was made a cardinal, and in 1450 became Bishop of Brixen (now Bressanone in Italy), an ecclesiastical principality. This led to conflict with the Archduke Sigismund, who objected to Kryfts' reforming intentions, and even imprisoned him for a time (for which the archduke was excommunicated). Kryfts died at Todi, Tuscany, at age sixty-three.

Kryfts stands at the transition between the medieval age and the Renaissance. His medieval credentials include the Christian assumptions that underlay his philosophizing, but he rejects Aristotelianism in favor of neo-Platonism, a move that was to typify the Renaissance. His main importance lay in his *theologia negativa*, according to which the nature of the universe mirrors the nature of god; god is unknowable by human beings, all that we can really know is that we're ignorant, so our only knowledge of god (and hence of the universe) is what he is not. For example, he's not limited—he's infinite; insofar as the universe mirrors god, it too must be unbounded (though not genuinely infinite). Therefore, the Earth can't be at the center of the universe, for there is no center of an unbounded space; nor can it be said to be at rest, for motion or rest must be relative, dependent on the observer. (Note that, however modern this may sound, it is based not on science, but on a mystical theology.)

Politically, Kryfts rejected the notion that the monarch's authority came from god, arguing that monarchs received their authority from their subjects—a position also held by **Suárez**, and developed by early-modern philosophers such as **Locke**.

In a nutshell:
As above, so below; the nature of the creator mirrors the nature of the created world.

NICCOLÒ DI BERNARDO DEI MACHIAVELLI

BORN 1469, Florence		**DIED** 1527, Florence	

MAIN INTERESTS   Politics, ethics

INFLUENCES   Aristotle, Cicero

INFLUENCED   Hobbes, Montesquieu, Rousseau, Nietzsche

MAJOR WORKS
The Prince,
The Discourses,
The Art of War

Political philosophy had been around ever since **Plato's** *Republic, but with Machiavelli, political science was born. Political science isn't really concerned with what ought to be the case, with the best form of government—it's concerned with what in fact is the case, with the most efficient form of government.*

Machiavelli was born into a Florence unofficially ruled by the Medici family—a city-state that was wealthy yet vulnerable to foreign powers, culturally rich but politically unstable. We know little of his early life; the first real evidence we have is a business letter written toward the end of 1497.

Machiavelli's life was spent in pursuit of the dream of a unified Italy that would be strong enough to be secure from foreign invasion and internal wars. His early political career, until the return of the Medici in 1512, was spent as secretary to the Ten—the council in charge of the Florentine Republic's military and diplomatic activity. This involved missions to France and Germany, where he came across the papal prince Cesare Borgia. Borgia was cruel and wily, and Machiavelli had no love for him or his policies, but he believed that a ruler of such strength and cunning was the only way that Florence could unite Italy.

When the Medici returned to power in Florence, they dissolved the Republic, and Machiavelli was linked (apparently wrongly) to an anti-Medici plot. He was arrested and tortured, but was eventually let off with a fine. That was enough to keep him out of government, however, and he spent the next fifteen years on his estate near Florence, writing his best-known works, *Il principe* (The Prince) (1513) and *Discorsi sopra la prima deca di Tito Livio* (Discourses on the first Ten Books of Titus Livius) (1517). The

In his own words:

[...] a prince, and especially a new prince, cannot observe all those things which are considered good in men, being obliged, in order to maintain the state, to act against faith, against charity, against humanity, and against religion.

The Prince 18

first of these was a pamphlet dedicated to Lorenzo de' Medici, the de facto ruler of Florence. Machiavelli's attempts to gain favor with the Medici were unsuccessful, but they ensured that when the Republic was restored in 1527 (only to fall again in 1531), he was kept out of government by the Florentines too. He died the same year.

In *The Prince*, Machiavelli argues that the medieval notion of the ruler as being the embodiment of the virtues is unrealistic and dangerous; the ideal ruler is the one who does what's necessary, who does what's successful rather than what's morally praiseworthy. He makes clear, though, that he's concerned to discuss the nature of monarchies. In *The Discourses*, on the other hand, Machiavelli writes from an openly republican viewpoint; many of the same points are made, though more elaborately, yet the feeling of the book is wholly different from the radicalism of *The Prince*.

FRANCISCO SUÁREZ

BORN	1548, Granada, Spain	DIED	1617, Lisbon or Coimbra

MAIN INTERESTS   Metaphysics, law, politics

INFLUENCES   Aristotle, Aquinas, William of Ockham

INFLUENCED   Grotius, Descartes, Leibniz, Wolff, Schopenhauer

MAJOR WORKS
*Metaphysical
Disputations*

Scholasticism is generally regarded as dying out in the mid-fifteenth century, slowly to be replaced by Renaissance humanism, before the advent of early modern philosophy. There was, however, a scholastic revival in sixteenth-century Spain, led by Dominican and Jesuit philosophers and theologians. Suárez was the greatest of these, though Francisco de Vitoria (1480–1546) was also important, albeit less for his philosophical than for his legal writings.

Born in Granada, the son of a lawyer, at the age of sixteen Suárez became a Jesuit in Salamanca, where he studied for five years. He failed his entrance examination twice, but went on to complete his philosophy course with distinction, before studying theology. He then taught philosophy at Avila and Segovia, becoming a priest in 1572, and going on to teach theology. He even taught in Rome (where the pope attended his first lecture). Despite his teaching, and traveling, he was a prolific writer, producing works on law, the relationship between church and state, metaphysics, and theology. During his lifetime he was regarded as the greatest living philosopher and theologian, and his reputation increased after his death. He is generally regarded as being the greatest scholastic philosopher after **Aquinas**. His main philosophical achievements lie in metaphysics and the philosophy of law.

Metaphysics, he said, was the science of being—that is, of real essences and existence. Real being (as opposed to conceptual being) can be either immaterial or material, but metaphysics is mostly concerned with the former. Though Suárez agrees with earlier scholastics that essence and existence are the same in the case of god, he disagrees with the view that, in the case of created, finite beings, essence and existence are really distinct (that is, they can exist separately); rather, he argues, they are merely conceptually distinct (that is, can conceive them separately). He was a nominalist with regard to universals, and held that we have direct knowledge of individuals.

With regard to law, his main importance lies in his treatment of natural law, as well as in his arguments about human law and the status of a monarch. Suárez argues against the social contract theory that was to become dominant in early modern political philosophy—namely, that human beings have a (god-given) social nature, accompanied by the potential to legislate. Rather, when a political society is formed, its nature is chosen by the people, they bestow the legislative power on the government. If a government is imposed on people, they have the right to revolt against it in self-defense (up to and including killing the tyrant); if their *chosen* ruler behaves badly, they also have the right to revolt—they gave the power, so can take it away (but they have to behave justly, killing the tyrant is ruled out).

In his own words:
[...] all the other sciences often use metaphysical principles, or presuppose them in order to move forward in their demonstrations or arguments; and hence it often happens that errors in the other sciences come about through ignorance of metaphysics.

Metaphysical Disputations *I, iv,5*

The early modern period in European philosophy stretched from the beginning of the seventeenth century, with Descartes as its main progenitor, to the beginning of the nineteenth century, with Kant as the philosopher who ushered in a new era. This is an arbitrarily defined period, chosen with regard to a certain sort of philosophical concern.

The beginning is reasonably uncontroversial, for Descartes not only marks a new approach to philosophy but influenced everyone who came after him, in all areas of philosophy. Slightly

1588

1588

1596

1619

more controversially, Francis Bacon's work marks a change in the nature of the physical sciences and in the attitude of philosophy to science. The end of the period is less clear-cut; with regard to metaphysics and epistemology, and to a certain extent ethics, Kant's work certainly sent philosophy in new directions, but did not really influence other fields, such as politics. There, however, two major influences ushered in a completely new era: the Utilitarianism of Bentham, and the political and

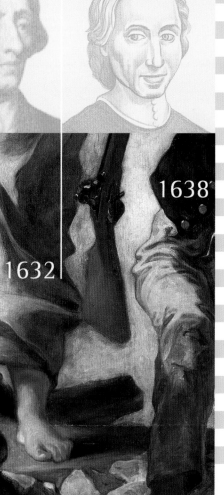

1588 Defeat of Spanish Armada

1591 Defeat of Songhai Empire by Moroccan troops

1593 Edict of Nantes

1603 Union of English and Scottish crowns

EARLY MODERN
1600–1800

1605 Gunpowder Plot

1609 Dutch independence from Spain. Expulsion from Spain of 250,000 Moriscos

1616 Shakespeare and Cervantes die. Edict of Inquisition against Galileo's astronomy

1618 Thirty Years War begins

1620 Pilgrim fathers settle in New England

1640 Long Parliament begins in England

1642 Outbreak of English Civil War

1644 Qing dynasty instituted by Manchus

1648 End of Thirty Years War

1649 End of English Civil War; execution of Charles I

1653 Cromwell becomes Protector

1658 Cromwell dies

1660 Restoration of English monarchy under Charles II

1665 Great Plague of London

1666 Great Fire of London

1672 The de Witt brothers murdered in Amsterdam

1673	Test Act deprives English Catholics and Non-Conformists of public office
1683	Siege of Vienna by Turks
1685	Revocation of the Edict of Nantes
1688	"Glorious Revolution." William and Mary accede to English throne
1692	Massacre of Glencoe
1707	Act of Union uniting English and Scottish Parliaments
1715	Defeat of Jacobites at Preston and Sherrifmuir
1723	Christopher Wren dies
1746	Battle of Culloden
1750	J. S. Bach dies
1751	Chinese conquest of Tibet
1755	Lisbon earthquake
1756	Outbreak of Seven Years War. Black Hole of Calcutta
1759	Handel dies. Voltaire publishes *Candide*
1773	Jesuits suppressed by the pope. Boston Tea Party
1774	Warren Hastings appointed first governor general of India. Joseph Priestley discovers oxygen
1776	American Declaration of Independence
1784	Samuel Johnson dies
1787	Drafting of American Constitution
1789	Storming of the Bastille. Washington becomes first president of the U.S.
1792	Denmark first country to ban slave trade. French republic founded
1793	Louis XVI beheaded
1794	Revolt of slaves in Haüti, led by Toussaint l'Ouverture
1798	Battle of the Nile

religious Radicalism of the latter part of the eighteenth century. Between them these helped lay the foundations for philosophers such as John Stuart Mill, as well as helping to give birth to revolutions in France and North America.

THE INFLUENCE OF THE RENAISSANCE

One of the important influences on the new philosophy was a move away from the Aristotelianism of the medieval period, and especially of the schools, a move that began as what is generally known as the Renaissance. This was partly the result of the fall of

1646　1685

Constantinople, and the consequent flood of refugees, which led to the reintroduction to fifteenth-century Western Europe of many ancient works, including some of those of Plato, and the translations of Plato's dialogues by Marsilius Ficino (1433–1499). A new understanding of Plato resulted from reading his own works rather than those of his various commentators and critics, and this had a tremendous influence on philosophy and the sciences.

RATIONALISM AND EMPIRICISM

At the heart of this period of philosophy is the distinction between the Rationalists and the Empiricists—it's used to organize university courses and introductory books, so few students of philosophy can have escaped its influence. Yet at best it's arbitrary, and at worst it can be extremely misleading. The distinction is roughly between the philosophers of mainland Europe, primarily Descartes, Leibniz, and Spinoza, who held that knowledge can be gained through the use of reason alone, and the British philosophers, primarily Locke, Berkeley, and Hume, who held that knowledge can come only through sense

as providing a third way of doing philosophy, reconciling and transcending the two methods of intellect and sense, Rationalism and Empiricism. As these brief sketches of the relevant philosophers show, the methods of and relationships between the various philosophers are much more complex.

One reason for all this is that Kant divided the two traditions in terms of epistemology; if he'd looked at the various philosophers' metaphysical positions, or at their attitudes to ethics, or to language, he'd undoubtedly have drawn the distinction very differently. In fact, though, with regard to epistemology, the distinction runs into problems.

1689   1710   **z**   1711   1748

experience. The Rationalists, then, take mathematics and the Empiricists take the physical sciences as their models for knowledge.

Even those who consider this distinction to be harmless and even useful don't claim that it represents an historical fact about the philosophers concerned. No one in the seventeenth and eighteenth centuries thought of themselves in these terms, nor even as working in separate traditions. The one exception, and a major (if not *the*) source of the mistake is Kant, who saw himself

For example, even restricting ourselves to the traditional big three Rationalists—Descartes, Leibniz, and Spinoza—we find them enthusiastic and knowledgeable about the physical sciences, whereas of the traditional big three Empiricists—Locke, Berkeley, and Hume—only Locke had any real scientific training and expertise.

x

y

SIR FRANCIS BACON

BORN 1561, London	DIED 1626, London

MAIN INTERESTS Science

INFLUENCES Democritus, Plato

INFLUENCED Diderot, Hobbes, Hume, Haack

MAJOR WORKS
Essays, The Advancement of Learning, New Organon

Bacon was imprisoned in the Tower of London, in 1621, after admitting to charges of bribery while serving as a judge. It was probably a political, rather than a moral, issue. Many in Parliament disapproved of the King's friendship with Bacon, and used the opportunity to oust Bacon from public life. King James instigated his release from the Tower after four days.

Francis Bacon (Baron Verulam, Viscount St. Albans) was the youngest son of a highly placed, powerful, and learned family (his father was Lord Keeper of the Great Seal under Elizabeth I, and his mother—the daughter of a royal tutor—was well educated, reading Greek and Latin, and speaking French and Italian). He was first tutored at home, then in 1573 went up to Trinity College, Cambridge (entering university at age twelve was less uncommon then than now, though Bacon was in fact considered precocious), where he learned to dislike the late-Scholastic, hidebound approach to philosophy, with its virtual worship of Aristotle. In 1576 he began the study of law at Gray's Inn, though the next year he accepted a diplomatic post in France.

Bacon is yet another philosopher whose father died when he was young—he was eighteen—but the event was all the more traumatic because it left him virtually penniless. He was forced to go back to his legal studies, graduating in 1582, and two years later was elected a Member of Parliament. His career was initially hampered by two things: the failure of his rich and influential relatives to do much to help him, and his naïveté in arguing against the queen's taxation policy just as he was about to be appointed attorney general.

Fortunately for Bacon he had a powerful friend in the earl of Essex, a favorite of the queen. Essex did his best to persuade her to appoint his friend to high office, and (when, out of distrust of Bacon, she proved reluctant) he himself gave Bacon one of his estates. It wasn't long, though, before Essex was in trouble with the queen, and though Bacon managed to intercede successfully for his patron once, he was unable to do so again when Essex foolishly tried to start a rebellion in London. Bacon did try to gain clemency for Essex, but Elizabeth instructed him to prepare the prosecution case, which he did; Essex was executed in 1601.

It wasn't until Elizabeth's death and the accession of James I that Bacon's fortunes rose. He was appointed solicitor general in 1607, attorney general in 1613, Lord Keeper of the Great Seal—like his father—in 1617, and finally, in 1618, Lord Chancellor. And then in 1621, at age sixty, he was arrested and charged with accepting bribes. He admitted the charge and stoically accepted his punishment, which was to be stripped of all his offices, fined heavily, and imprisoned in the Tower of London. In fact he served only a few days of his imprisonment and the fine was waived, but he was banned from public office.

Bacon's use of "empiric"

Bacon uses "empiric" in the sense that went back to the ancient Greek physicians (see **Sextus Empiricus***). Empirics were those who held that it was impossible to learn about what isn't visible, whether by speculation or by inference from what is visible.*

King James, under whose monarchy Bacon enjoyed a rapid rise in rank, wrote several works on theology and the justification of Divine Right. His version of the Bible is one of the most famous works written in the English language.

Bacon spent his final years on his writing, and especially on his scientific interests. His death was bizarre yet typical of him; in the course of his investigations into the preservation of food, he went out and collected snow to stuff a chicken, which led to his death from bronchitis.

THE GREAT INSTAURATION

Though Bacon's early work, the *Essays*, covered a wide variety of topics, and he later produced historical and legal works, his main interest for philosophers lies in his philosophy of science. This is in two parts: a criticism of scholastic and the contemporary Renaissance approach to science, and a carefully worked out methodology with which to replace it. He called his project to reform the sciences "the Great Instauration" ("instauration" = "restoration," "renewal"), and this was the title of what was to have been his master work, of which he completed only the first of three parts, the *New Organon* (a reference to **Aristotle's** logical works, known collectively as the Organon ["tool" or "instrument"]).

Bacon's attitude to what had gone before is summed up in a set of similes, with which he characterized the traditional metaphysicians, the Empirics such as alchemists, and the ideal scientist: the metaphysicians were like spiders, spinning beautiful and ingenious webs that floated in the air, produced purely from within their own bodies; the Empirics were like ants, scurrying around collecting quantities of material and piling them up, without making anything new from them. We should be like the bees—working together to collect and *transform* what we've collected. Scientists should interpret the data that comes from experience, should carry out experiments to collect new data, and so slowly build up our knowledge of the world.

THE IDOLS

We're handicapped by our human tendency to prejudice and preconception, which Bacon characterized as *Idols of the Mind*: the *Idols of the Tribe* are common to all human beings, who uncritically take what their senses tell them as representing the nature of the world accurately; the *Idols of the Cave* are peculiar to each individual, formed by education, upbringing, reading, and so on; the *Idols of the Market Place* arise out of social interaction, primarily language, which serves to obstruct rather than assist understanding; finally, the *Idols of the Theatre* are the results of philosophical systems, which he characterizes as "so many stage-plays" (he could, following his other simile, have called them the "Idols of the Web").

What is Truth; said jesting Pilate; And would not stay for an Answer.

Essays, p.7

In a nutshell:
Science is for teams in laboratories, not individuals in armchairs.

THOMAS HOBBES

BORN 1588, Malmesbury	DIED 1679, Hardwick

MAIN INTERESTS   Politics, metaphysics, language

INFLUENCES   Aristotle, Machiavelli, Francis Bacon, Galileo, Gassendi

INFLUENCED   Spinoza, Leibniz, Locke, Rousseau, Bentham, Mill, Marx, Rawls

MAJOR WORKS
Leviathan, The Elements of Law, Natural and Political

And the life of man, solitary, poore, nasty, brutish, and short.

Leviathan 1:13

The younger son of a country vicar, Hobbes was educated at Oxford. He began his career as a tutor, traveling around Europe with his pupil (William Cavendish) which gave him the opportunity to meet such luminaries as Galileo and Descartes. His first philosophical work was *The Elements of Law, Natural and Political*, which placed him firmly on the Royalist side in the growing conflict between king and parliament. Though the book wasn't published for more than ten years (in 1650), it circulated privately in 1640, at a time when matters between the two sides were beginning to come to a head. Hobbes decided that he was potentially at risk, and went to live in France for eleven years. This caution (which some might have considered excessive) was a recurrent theme throughout his life, and goes some way to explaining the great age to which he lived.

During his time in France Hobbes became part of **Mersenne's** circle, and wrote the Third Set of Objections to **Descartes'** *Meditations* (to which Descartes' Replies were dismissive and hostile), and a number of books: *Elements of Law* and *De Cive* (The Citizen) in 1642, the latter containing his first real attempt to produce a political science (or "civil philosophy" as he called it); *Human Nature* in 1650; and *Leviathan*, his master work, in 1651. The anti-Catholic sentiment of parts of this last book got him into trouble with the French authorities, however, and he fled back to England, where Cromwell's Commonwealth came to an end

and Hobbes found himself back in favor. However, his troubles were not yet over; Parliament included him in an investigation it had launched into atheist writings, and Hobbes burned some of his papers and delayed publication of a number of works. His caution paid off, and he survived—and in his eighties produced verse translations of both the *Iliad* and the *Odyssey*.

THE SOCIAL CONTRACT

The foundation of Hobbes' political philosophy was a mechanistic naturalism: the universe, including human beings, is a vast machine, running according to natural laws. Society is to be explained in the same way that physics explains the rest of the world, in terms of the regular interaction of its constituent parts; human beings take the place of particles, which in their natural state would simply bounce around and off each other, with no thought of cooperation. In this nasty and brutish state, each particular person goes in fear of their fellows; the order brought by society means that, in return for the complete freedom they surrender, individuals gain security against each other. This order is possible only if imposed by a small group, or preferably by a single person; this is the absolute power that Hobbes compares to Leviathan, the great sea monster of the book of Job. In other words, society functions to free us from mutual fear, and it does so by means of a contract between its members in which we submit to a sovereign in return for

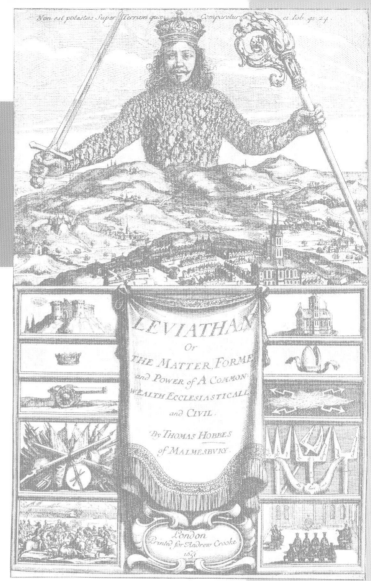

protection against chaos. This chaos is the *state of nature*, and is less an historical state than a constant threat. Most other contract theorists, such as **Locke** and **Rousseau**, were moved to argue against absolute monarchy; Hobbes is unusual in using the theory to argue for it.

Though best known for his political writing, Hobbes' philosophical interests spread much further, as his Objections to Descartes' *Meditations* indicate. His metaphysical and epistemological positions were similar to those of **Gassendi**, being materialist and empiricist, though he went further than Gassendi in including the nature of god in his materialism; god was merely a more refined material being. His religious views were in other ways also considerably less conventional than Gassendi's, and his arguments for religious toleration (except for Catholics) and disestablishmentarianism led to his being dubbed an atheist and nicknamed "the beast of Malmesbury."

LANGUAGE AND THE WORLD
Hobbes also developed an antirealist position, according to which the nature of the world is independent of our understanding of words and ideas; truth and falsity concern the ordering of our statements, not the relationship between what we say and the way the world is. This derives from his materialism, for he explained thought in terms of physical movements in the brain—though he accepted that such movements have their origins in movements in the external world. A version of the social contract came in here too, for the starting definition of words have to be fixed by common consent.

Hobbes took language very seriously, and the misuse of language was one of his central concerns. He held that many significant errors arise because we fail to distinguish between linguistic structure and logical structure (and so what seem to be philosophical problems in one language group wouldn't arise at all in another).

MARIN MERSENNE

BORN	1588, Oizé, Maine	**DIED**	1648, Paris

MAIN INTERESTS Mathematics, science

INFLUENCES Augustine

INFLUENCED Descartes

MAJOR WORKS
Second & Sixth
Sets of Objections
to Descartes'
Meditations,
*The Truth of the
Sciences against
the Sceptics or
Pyrrhonists*,
*The Impiety of
the Deists*

*Do we know whether the
braying of a donkey is
not more pleasant than
our music according to
nature, given that it is
more pleasant to that
animal?*

The Truth of the Sciences against
the Sceptics or Pyrrhonists 2

In a nutshell:

*Mersenne was a seventeenth-century
communications hub, linking
philosophers and scientists.*

Mersenne was born into a poor family, his father a laborer. Having been educated by the Jesuits at La Fléche, followed by study in philosophy at the Sorbonne, in 1611 Mersenne joined the Minims—a religious order who regarded themselves as the least of the religious, hence their name. His education continued within the order, and after ordination as a priest he taught philosophy at a convent at Nevers from 1614 to 1618. He then returned to Paris, where he became a central figure in the intellectual world, both locally (eminent scholars such as Pierre de Fermat, **Pierre Gassendi**, and Blaise Pascal met at his cell) and more widely through extensive correspondence.

Mersenne was important as a mathematician, musicologist, scientist, theologian, and philosopher. He suggested to Christiaan Huygens the use of a pendulum as a timing device, measured the speed of sound to within 10 percent of the modern figure, calculated the frequency of vibration of musical notes, introduced much of Galileo's work outside Italy through his translations and commentaries, as well as through his own scientific work, and was a key friend and mentor of **René Descartes**. He not only defended Descartes against attack, but encouraged him to return to philosophy and science when he seemed likely to drift away, and helped him to get his work published. When Descartes replied to the various sets of Objections to his *Meditations*, he was respectful toward those

contributed by Mersenne (in fact Mersenne was responsible, not only for writing the Second and Sixth Sets of Objections, but for prompting and gathering together all the other sets apart from the first).

Mersenne's early work was mainly concerned with criticisms of atheists and skeptics, but he later turned to philosophy, and especially to the sciences and mathematics (in which he's best known for his work on prime numbers; when $2n$-1 is prime [where n is a prime] it's still called a *Mersenne prime*). His work in these fields is interesting, and often had great influence on his contemporaries and successors, but Mersenne's greatest achievement without doubt lay in his role as facilitator and networker. When he died (in the arms of his friend Gassendi), his cell was found to contain letters from seventy-eight correspondents, including Fermat, Huygens, Galileo Galilei, Evangelista Torricelli, and John Pell. Through this huge network he helped to establish the new science, to combat superstitions such as astrology, and to stimulate by his insightful questions and criticisms the scientists, mathematicians, and philosophers who gathered around him.

PIERRE GASSENDI

| **BORN** 1592, Champtercier | **DIED** 1655, Paris |

MAIN INTERESTS   Metaphysics, science, epistemology

INFLUENCES   Democritus, Epicurus

INFLUENCED   Locke

MAJOR WORKS
Fifth Set of
Objections to
Descartes'
Meditations,
Unorthodox
*Essays against
the Aristotelians*,
*Disquisitio
Metaphysica*,
*Syntagma
Philosophicum*

*In 1631 Gassendi became
the first astronomer to
observe the transit of
Mercury across the Sun
(as predicted by Kepler).*

Gassendi was educated at Digne, then at home, and finally at the universities of Aix-en-Provence and Avignon, where he studied philosophy and theology. He received his doctorate in philosophy from Avignon in 1614, and was ordained a priest in 1615. His intellectual promise was recognized early, for at sixteen he taught rhetoric at Digne, and at nineteen he was appointed to teach philosophy at Aix. Somewhat unwillingly he accepted a professorship in mathematics at the Collége Royale, and in Paris he met and befriended **Marin Mersenne**, and became part of his extensive network, corresponding with Galileo and Kepler, among many prominent scientists. This helped him to develop his interest in astronomy; he was an excellent observer and an acute defender of the Copernican system against its critics (though he seems not to have fully accepted the system himself).

Mersenne encouraged him to abandon mathematics and science in favor of philosophy, and Gassendi became the author of one of the sets of Objections to **Descartes'** *Meditations*; he later expanded these, first in his *Instances*, and then into a book, *Disquisitio Metaphysica* (1644).

His disagreements with Descartes were wide ranging; aside from a number of important issues in their scientific theories about the nature of the world, they differed deeply about the nature of philosophical and scientific method. Though Gassendi shared Descartes' opposition to the Aristotelianism of the time, he was a champion of **Epicurus**, whose philosophy he tried to bring into line with Christian thought. At the center of this position is a mechanistic, atomistic view of the world, though Gassendi added a belief in the immortality of a soul that lay outside the physical. Nevertheless, he rejected both Descartes' argument for dualism and his account of the relationship between mind and body.

The chief disagreement between the two philosophers, though, was epistemological. Gassendi especially rejected Descartes' use of universal doubt, and his appeal to knowledge gained through reason alone. Systematic doubt was acceptable, but to doubt *everything* was unreasonable—indeed, not clearly possible. He held both the Aristotelians and Descartes guilty of rejecting the help of as wide a range of writers as possible: Epicurus of course, but also Plato, Democritus, and other ancient writers. In rejecting the appeals to authority of the Aristotelians, Descartes had gone too far the other way, and tried to do everything unaided. Gassendi's mature view was that, though reason must play its part, all knowledge must *start* with the senses.

In a nutshell:
*The world's a machine, and we have to
learn about it by looking at it.*

RENÉ DESCARTES

BORN 1596, La Haye	DIED 1650, Stockholm

MAIN INTERESTS   Metaphysics, epistemology, science, mathematics

INFLUENCES   Plato, Aristotle, Anselm, Aquinas, Ockham, Suárez, Mersenne

INFLUENCED   Everyone who came after him

MAJOR WORKS
Discourse on the Method, Meditations on First Philosophy, The Principles of Philosophy

Descartes anticipated reflex theory. He suggested that the human body had a mechanism for automatic response. Here, the heat from the flame, starts a process at the heat-affected spot, which travels to the muscles that will pull the hand away from the flame.

Educated, like **Marin Mersenne**, at the Jesuit College of La Fléche, Descartes went on to study law, which he never in fact practiced; instead he opted for a military career. This took him to the Netherlands and Bavaria, and it was in Bavaria that he conceived his philosophical task: not merely to add to philosophy, but to rebuild it from first principles. He spent much of the rest of his life in the Netherlands, at least in part out of fear of persecution by the Catholic authorities in France (a fear that was probably not very well founded). It was there that he wrote most of the works for which he became famous. At the age of fifty-three he was invited to Stockholm by Queen Christina of Sweden, with whom he had been corresponding; the rigors of the climate, together with the early hour at which he was expected to attend the queen, led to his death a year later.

Descartes was not only a philosopher, but a mathematician and scientist; he published significant contributions to optics, geometry, physiology, and cosmology (though the treatment meted out to Galileo caused him to withhold from publication his book *The World*, in which he laid out his account of the origins and workings of the solar system). Of these, mathematics is the field in which he made the greatest contribution; he introduced many of the conventions still in use today (for example, the use of indices to indicate powers, such as 2^3), and gave us the system of Cartesian coordinates, allowing plane lines and curves to be represented numerically.

In a nutshell:
Descartes was the father of modern philosophy.

CERTAINTY
By far the most important of his writings, however, were in the field of philosophy. His great project, to rebuild philosophy from scratch, is unveiled in part in his first book (which he never finished, and which was published posthumously), *Rules for the Direction of the Understanding*. Here he sets out the fundamental principle: the standard for philosophy must be the same as that for mathematics—certainty. The way in which this is to be achieved is worked out in his later books, in particular the 1637 *Discourse on the Method* (which started life as an introduction to a collection of his scientific works) and *Meditations on First Philosophy* (1641). He sent this latter book out to a variety of philosophers before publication, including **Mersenne**, **Gassendi**, **Arnauld**, and **Hobbes**, and their Objections, together with his Replies, were included in the first edition.

DOUBT
The foundation of Descartes' project is the Method of Doubt: he carefully examines each of the sorts of belief he holds,

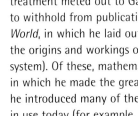

Cogito ergo sum

The famous slogan: "cogito ergo sum," or "I'm thinking, therefore I exist," ("I think, therefore I am") is a misleading expression of what Descartes actually wanted to say. He corrected it in the Meditations to "I am, I exist, is necessarily true whenever it is put forward by me or conceived in my mind."

Descartes sought to rebuild philosophy, and by concentrating on the issue of true and certain knowledge, he made epistemology the starting point.

categorized according to the ways that he acquired them, and tries his hardest to find reasons to doubt them. Once he's gone as far as is possible to go with this procedure, any belief he has left will have been shown to be immune to doubt. In fact the only one that does survive the test is his belief in his own existence, and this forms, not the foundation of his certain and well-structured framework of knowledge, but the firm ground upon which he stands to build that framework.

GOD

In order to proceed, though, Descartes needs to establish the existence of something objective and independent of himself, for which he needs god; this, unfortunately, is where his project fails. He offers two arguments for god's existence, one a version of the cosmological argument, the other a version of the ontological argument; neither is sound, and interest in his project for its own sake ceases at that point. However, Descartes offers much that has value independently of the success or failure of the project as a whole, including an argument for and discussion of mind–body dualism.

DUALISM

Descartes' dualism is one of the areas of his thought that is often misunderstood and misrepresented. Notwithstanding careless or unscrupulous critics, he did not in fact say that the person is just a mind, using the body as some sort of temporary vehicle (a ghost in a machine); indeed, he specifically denied this. Rather, each person is a complex combination of mind and body, both being needed for such crucial matters as perception, memory, imagination, and emotions. Briefly, he argues that it's logically possible for the mind and body to exist separately; nothing can be separate from itself, therefore the mind and body can't be the same thing. It's a subtle and powerful argument, which his detractors tend to ignore or caricature rather than address.

ANIMALS

One final canard should be laid to rest (and of all philosophers Descartes must surely be the most frequent victim of unfounded criticism): he did not argue that nonhuman animals are merely unfeeling automata. His views, as usual, are complex, but as he said clearly in a letter to Henry More in 1649: "Though I regard it as established that we cannot prove there is any thought in animals, I do not think it can be proved that there is none, since the human mind does not reach into their hearts."

Good sense is the best distributed thing in the world: for everyone thinks himself so well endowed with it that even those who are the hardest to please in everything else do not usually desire more of it than they possess.

Discourse on the Method of Rightly Conducting the Understanding *AT VI 1–2*

ANTOINE ARNAULD

BORN	1612, Paris	DIED	1694, Brussels

MAIN INTERESTS   Logic, language, metaphysics

INFLUENCES   Augustine, Descartes, Pascal, Malebranche

INFLUENCED   Leibniz, Reid, Chomsky

MAJOR WORKS
Fourth Set of
Objections to
Descartes'
*Meditations,
Logic, or the Art
of Thinking* (with
Pierre Nicole),
*On True and
False Ideas,*
correspondence
with Leibniz

*I am from such and
such a country, hence I
ought to believe that a
certain Saint preached
the Gospel [...] Whatever
order or country you
come from, you ought
to believe only what is
true and what you
would be disposed to
believe if you were from
another country.*

Logic, or the Art of
Thinking III, 20, i

Born into a prominent family, Arnauld was educated at the Sorbonne, where he received his doctorate and was ordained in 1641. His family were Jansenist anti-Jesuits, and Arnauld adopted their position, defending Jansenism in his book *On Frequent Communion* (1643). This eventually led to his being stripped of his doctorate and expelled from the Sorbonne in 1656. He sought refuge in the Jansenist monastery at Port-Royal des Champs, where his sister had been abbess until her community moved to Paris.

At Port-Royal Arnauld wrote, with Pierre Nicole (1625–1695), his most famous work: *Logic, or the Art of Thinking* (1662), commonly known as the *Port-Royal Logic*. It had four main purposes: to present **Descartes'** epistemology, metaphysics, and physics; to attack the position of empiricists such as **Hobbes** and **Gassendi**; to attack Montaigne's skepticism; and to present a Jansenist response to orthodox Catholic (and Protestant) teachings on a variety of issues, including grace and freedom of the will. The book deals with a range of topics from logic, language, epistemology, physics, to metaphysics, and though for the most part it wasn't terribly original, it was hugely influential, remaining a standard university text until the end of the nineteenth century, and regarded by some modern scholars as the first truly modern work in linguistics.

In 1669 Pope Clement IX tried to end the war between the Jansenists and the Jesuits,

In a nutshell:
Arnauld was mainly a catalyst for other people's philosophy.

issuing an agreement to end the persecution of the Jansenists in exchange for their submission to the authority of the church. Arnauld returned to Paris, and seemed for a time to face a peaceful life, with renewed respect from church and state. However, after a period in which he confined himself to writing against Protestantism, he was eventually unable to resist attacking the Jesuits in print, and in 1679 he was forced to flee to Belgium.

There he engaged in a correspondence with **Leibniz** about some of the key metaphysical notions from what became the *Discourse on Metaphysics*; this marked a significant stage in Leibniz's philosophical career. Arnauld, in fact, participated with some reluctance, being more concerned with his religious preoccupations at this stage. These included an acrimonious debate that he'd started with **Malebranche** (once a friend). In *On True and False Ideas* (1683) he attacked Malebranche's account of grace, and the claim that we see everything in god. The disagreement was not only bitter, but marked by extra-philosophical, political maneuvering, and was ended only by Arnauld's death.

OVERVIEW
MIND AND BODY

Is it our intellect that distinguishes us from animals?

The central concern of the philosophy of mind is our understanding of mind and its place in the physical world. More specifically, in Western philosophy the emphasis is on what is known as the *mind–body problem*—that is, the relationship between the mind and the physical world. The two main kinds of approach are *dualism*, which argues that mind and body are different sorts of things, with different sorts of property, and *monism*, which argues that there is only one kind of thing and property. Though there have been monists (notably **Berkeley**) who have taken that one kind of thing to be mental, the usual position is *materialism or physicalism*.

DUALISMS

For **Plato**, the mind was that part of us that was immortal; in contrast with the body, it had affinities with the eternal and immutable, and was the carrier of the eternal truths. **Aristotle** tried to give what might be called a naturalistic account of the *psyche*, or soul, in terms of its different faculties, such as nutrition and reproduction found in plants, locomotion, sensation, and perception found in animals, and imagination found in man. However, what distinguished man from the rest of the animal kingdom was *noūs* or intellect, which was the immortal part in us. In **Descartes** we find a distinction between mind and body in terms of their essential natures: the essence of mind is thinking, the essence of body is extension. This is closer to Plato's account than to **Aristotle's**, making mind and body different substances, with no properties in common.

Spinoza's thesis of the mind is usually referred to as monism in contrast with Descartes' dualism. However, this is misleading because Spinoza upholds a fundamental duality in his metaphysics. For Spinoza the mind and body were not individual substances but modifications of the one substance (which he referred to as god or nature), under the attributes of thought and extension. Each attribute is not a way of talking about the one substance, but is in itself absolutely irreducible and really distinct from any other attribute. The relation of mind and body to the one substance is one of dependence, both causally and explanatorily.

PHYSICALISMS

Set against all forms of dualism are various materialist/physicalist doctrines of the mind. At the turn of the twentieth century we find the thesis of behaviorism, which claimed that to have a mind is nothing more than to be disposed to behave in a certain way; or in its philosophical or analytical version it claims that any talk about the mind can be translated into talk about behavior. Such a thesis tries to give an account of the mind purely from the external perspective of the theorist, the result of which leads to the absurdity that one cannot suffer in silence. Behaviorism was to a certain extent superseded by physicalism, the thesis that conscious or mental phenomena *are* physical phenomena of some physical or biological system such as a brain. It was put forward as a contingently true doctrine: there might have been minds (that is, Descartes' dualistic hypothesis is intelligible), but as a matter of fact it has turned out that there aren't any minds.

Physicalism is the currently dominant theory of the mind, and it comes in various forms: non-reductive physicalism, for example, claims that though there is only one kind of thing, say the brain, the terms we use to describe it are not reducible to each other. So, though the term "pain" and the phrase "brain processes" refer to the same thing, the mental and the physical descriptions are governed by different rules. Another way of characterizing non-reductionism, and one defended by functionalism, is that the mental is individuated by the functional role it plays in the causal network of inputs and outputs and its multiple realization, be it in a biological system or in a very complex system of silicon chips.

WANG FU-ZI

BORN	1619, Hengyang	DIED	1693, unknown

MAIN INTERESTS	Ethics, politics, metaphysics, epistemology

INFLUENCES	K'ung fu-zi, Zhang-zai, Zhu Xi

INFLUENCED	Yen Yüan, Tai Chen, T'an Ssut'ung, Tang Chuni

MAJOR WORKS
*Ch'uan-shan
i-shu ch'uan-chi*
(complete extant
works)

*What is meant by the
Way [Dao] is the
management of concrete
things. [...] Lao-zi was
blind to this and said
that the Way existed in
emptiness [...] Buddha
was blind to this and
said that the Way existed
in silence [...] One may
keep on uttering such
extravagant words
endlessly, but no one can
ever escape from
concrete things.*

Ch'uan-shan i-shu ch'uan-chi

Wang fu-zi (Wang Ch'uan-shan) was the son of a scholar in the Hunan province in Ming dynasty China. When he was twenty-four, and had just passed his civil service exam, China was invaded by the Manchus, who went on to establish the Qing (Ch'ing) dynasty. Being loyal to the Ming emperors, he spent his life fighting the Manchus, and then hiding from them. He wrote more than 100 books, of which many have been lost.

Wang was a Confucian, but considered that the neo-Confucianism then dominant was a distortion of genuine Confucian teaching; this led him to produce many commentaries on the Confucian classics, five on the *Yi Jing* (*I Ching*—Book of Changes) alone, and to develop his own philosophical system.

Wang's metaphysical position is a sort of materialism: only *qi* (*ch'i*; energy, or material force) exists, and the fundamental Confucian category of *li* (principle, form, or idea) is merely the principle of the *qi*, so does not exist in its own right. As *qi* has always existed, so has the universe. This leads to a view of ethics according to which virtues and values are assigned by human beings, nature itself being value-free. Human nature is a function of the material nature of the person at birth, and of the changes she undergoes through life—changes arising from her relationship as a moral being with other material objects. This relationship is largely a matter of desires, which are not evil, but unavoidable and even beneficial; evil arises

In a nutshell:
We live in a material world, and should respond to the present, not to the past.

out of lack of moderation, not out of the material nature of the world. Our morality is rooted in our human nature, in our feelings.

Wang stressed the need for both knowledge gained from the senses through study, and knowledge gained through reason; both are gained gradually (there's no sudden enlightenment), for knowing and acting are bound together, action being the foundation of knowledge.

Wang's political and historical writings are largely responsible for his popularity in modern China. He argued for an increase in taxation as a means to reduce the power of the landlords, and to encourage landowning peasants. Government is for the benefit of the governed, not of the governors. History continually renews itself; human civilization gradually progresses, against the background of cycles of prosperity and chaos, as a result of the virtues of the emperor and the people. Neither the cycles nor the improvement is a matter of fate, but of the working through of the natural laws of individuals and society. There was no golden age that we must try to emulate (or even imitate).

LADY ANNE FINCH CONWAY

| BORN 1631 | DIED 1679 |

MAIN INTERESTS Metaphysics

INFLUENCES Plato, Plotinus, Hobbes, More, Hobbes, Descartes, Spinoza

INFLUENCED Leibniz

MAJOR WORKS
The Principles of the Most Ancient and Modern Philosophy

[...] when concrete matter is so divided that it disperses into physical monads, such as it was in the first state of its formation, then it is ready to resume its activity and become spirit just as happens with our food.

The Principles of the Most Ancient and Modern Philosophy, chap. III, S.9

Born in 1631, a week after the death of her father (Sir Heneage Finch, Speaker of the House of Commons), she was tutored at home, where she learned Latin (later adding Greek and Hebrew), and showed considerable intellectual curiosity and ability. The Platonist Henry More had tutored one of her brothers at Cambridge, and this led to her correspondence with him on the philosophy of Descartes, which continued after her marriage to Edward Conway in 1651, though their relationship changed from one between tutor and pupil to one between equals.

Conway followed a particularly unusual intellectual course—not only for a woman, but for anyone in seventeenth-century England. Aside from Cartesian philosophy she was influenced by the school of kabbalistic thought founded by Isaac Luria (1534–1572), and by Quakerism (generally loathed and feared at that time), to which she converted. Her philosophical work had another important source: her own physical pain. From youth she suffered from headaches so appalling that she was prepared to try extreme (including trepanning—though no one dared perform this operation, so instead she had her jugular arteries opened), though nothing worked. This affected her philosophical thought in that she was very much concerned to provide a theodicy—an attempt to reconcile the existence of a benevolent god with the existence of suffering and other evils in the world.

Her only work was published posthumously, and itself had a difficult history. She probably wrote it—in English—between 1671 and 1675, and it was first published in a Latin translation in 1690. When an English edition was prepared in 1692, with the title *The Principles of the Most Ancient and Modern Philosophy*, it had to be translated from the Latin translation, the original manuscript having been lost. Her central metaphysical position was a spiritual monism, modified by Christian Platonism: the world began as a spiritual emanation, but degenerated, taking on material characteristics. Thus the spiritual and the material are two forms or states of the same substance, which will one day return to its purely spiritual state. This forms the basis of her theodicy; she argues that everything in the world is capable of improvement, from the most material (such as stones) to the most spiritual (human beings); god's goodness is demonstrated in this creation of a world able to raise itself eventually, not to the level of god, but that of angels.

In a nutshell:
There's only one kind of stuff—spiritual—which coarsened to materiality at the Fall, and which will eventually regain its pure state.

BARUCH SPINOZA

BORN 1632, Amsterdam	**DIED** 1677, The Hague

MAIN INTERESTS   Ethics, epistemology, metaphysics

INFLUENCES   ibn Sīna, ben Maimon, Nicholas Kryfts, Hobbes, Descartes

INFLUENCED   Conway, Kant, Hegel, Davidson

MAJOR WORKS
Tractatus Theologico-Politicus, Ethics

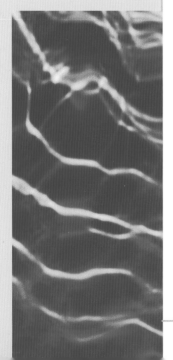

In Spinoza's argument for monism, ripples on a lake illustrate the point that our world is comprised of temporary modifications to the one substance that makes up the world.

Baruch, or Benedict de, Spinoza was born in Amsterdam, a Jew whose family had fled Spain for the religious tolerance of the Netherlands. Educated in the Jewish tradition, he was well versed in Jewish and Arabic philosophy and theology, but became increasingly influenced by modern rationalist philosophy and science, particularly the writings of **Hobbes** and **Descartes**. His thinking moved further and further away from traditional Jewish thought, until in 1656 he was excommunicated from his synagogue. Though he engaged in some teaching, his living came primarily from lens grinding. His friendship with Jan de Witt, a politician opposed to the House of Orange, led to his involvement in public affairs; though this was never great, it nevertheless put him in danger—once when he tried to go to protest the death of de Witt at the hands of a mob, and once when he consented to undertake a minor diplomatic mission to an invading French army.

His life was characterized by personal integrity; he lived frugally, and turned down both a professorship at the University of Heidelberg and a pension from the French king, in both cases because he wanted to avoid any risk of losing his intellectual independence. All accounts testify not only to his rectitude, but to his simplicity, courage, and personal charm. He died at the age of forty-five, the victim of a pulmonary condition, probably the result of his years as a lens grinder.

In a nutshell:
We have a fundamental moral duty to increase our understanding and knowledge of everything that we can.

Spinoza's early works were greeted with considerable hostility, especially the *Tractatus Theologico-Politicus* (1670), whose arguments for toleration, nonstandard approach to the Bible, and defense of secular government displeased the political and religious authorities alike, and provoked attacks from Cartesian philosophers in their attempts to distance themselves from him. Typically, his response to this was neither fear nor outrage, but concern that he should avoid provoking further hostility and unrest; for this reason his master work, the *Ethics*, had to wait for publication until after his death. The *Ethics* is presented in the form of Euclid's *Elements*, with numbered definitions, axioms, and propositions, each with a demonstration. This is slightly misleading; much as Spinoza might have wanted philosophy to be as clear and ordered as mathematics, it isn't. The *Ethics*, therefore, has to be read carefully and critically.

SUBSTANCE MONISM, ATTRIBUTE DUALISM
Spinoza's system starts from an argument for monism—the existence of a single substance,

What is Pantheism?

Pantheism is the belief that god is everything and everything is god. This has been dismissed by writers such as Schopenhauer, who argue that it makes "god" just a superfluous synonym for "world." Pantheism should be distinguished from panpsychism *(the view that everything is alive or thinking), and from* pantheism *(the view that the world is god, but god is more than just the world).*

conceivable under different attributes; when conceived under the attribute of extension, we call this substance the World, but when conceived under the attribute of thought, we call it God. (This pantheist view is what led Spinoza to be accused by some of being an atheist, but by others of being "god-intoxicated.") Individual things, then, are temporary modifications of this one substance—like knots in a carpet, or ripples on a lake. Just as the substance as a whole can be conceived under the attributes of thought or extension, so can each of its modifications, so every individual is both a physical thing and a mental thing. For a human being that means that we're both minds and bodies, but these aren't distinct things (as Descartes held)—they're the same thing under different attributes. Spinoza's position is therefore sometimes called *attribute dualism*, as opposed to Descartes' *substance* (or *Cartesian*) *dualism*.

This approach was in part motivated by Spinoza's acceptance of a widely held belief that there was a problem with substance dualism: namely, how two different substances, having none of their properties in common, could causally interact (though in fact it's not at all clear that causation *is* a problem for Cartesian dualism). In Spinoza's system, interaction is not only impossible but would make no sense, for there aren't two things to interact. A modern version of his approach was developed in the twentieth century, known as *Dual-Aspect theory*,

though this was restricted to the mind–body problem rather than being applied to the whole world as in Spinoza's system, and it should be emphasized that for Spinoza attributes are certainly not merely aspects.

EPISTEMOLOGY

There are three kinds of knowledge: perception, reason, and intuition. Perception involves the way our bodies are altered by things outside them; as long as we're careful not to assume that the world really is the way we perceive it, our beliefs will be true, but error results from our carelessness. Reason gives genuine knowledge, because it involves understanding, not simply belief. Intuition is the same, but it works by grasping the connections between things rather than through inference. Only mathematical knowledge is actually achievable through intuition; the rest depends upon reason.

God, being everything that there is, has (or is) complete knowledge; as human beings, our goal should be to increase our knowledge as far as possible, for the more knowledge we gain, the nearer we come to being god, and the freer we are.

Jan de Witt, a close friend of Spinoza, was a Dutch statesman and patron of the sciences. As leader of the Republican party he became a leading opponent of the House of Orange. Popular feeling later turned against him, in favor of William of Orange. De Witt resigned and escaped treason charges, but died at the hands of a mob while visiting his brother, Cornelius de Witt, in prison.

Mind and body are one and the same individual which is conceived now under the attribute of thought, and now under the attribute of extension.

Ethics *II prop.7*

JOHN LOCKE

BORN	1632, Wrington, Somerset	DIED	1704, Oates, Essex

MAIN INTERESTS   Politics, epistemology, science

INFLUENCES   Aristotle, Ockham, Hobbes, Descartes, Gassendi, Malebranche

INFLUENCED   Berkeley, Montesquieu, Reid, Hume, Rousseau, Kant, Rawls

MAJOR WORKS
An Essay concerning Human Understanding, Two Treatises on Government

John Locke was the son of a country lawyer who served as a Captain of Horse in the Parliamentary Army; both his parents died when he was young. He was educated at Westminster School and Christ Church, Oxford, and elected to a studentship in 1659; for three or four years he taught Greek, rhetoric, and moral philosophy there. He hadn't, however, found the conventional, Aristotelian style of philosophy taught at that time to his taste, and went on to study medicine, finally receiving a degree in 1674, and a year later being elected to a medical studentship. Despite not being qualified to practice as a doctor, he did so informally—and this led to an important change in his life, for he operated successfully on Lord Shaftesbury, whose household he joined as adviser, medic, and friend. Shaftesbury, an influential politician, was able to put various government appointments Locke's way. However, Shaftesbury fell from favor, and Locke not only lost a powerful patron but felt threatened enough to leave England for France. His anti-Royalist views certainly made him unpopular in some quarters, and his prudence was probably well founded.

Robert Boyle (1627–91), Locke's scientific mentor, held a mechanistic view of nature. Locke's interactions with Boyle profoundly influenced An Essay concerning Human Understanding.

When Shaftesbury regained his influence briefly, Locke returned to England, but soon felt obliged to leave again, this time for the Netherlands, where he lived for five years, before finally returning to England on the accession of William and Mary. It was during his stay in the Netherlands that he wrote the *Letter on Tolerance*, and finished his two most important works, both published in 1690 after his return to England: *An Essay concerning Human Understanding* and *Two Treatises on Government*.

The new regime in England honored Locke with various government posts. He settled in Essex, at the house of Damaris Masham, where he died at the age of seventy-two, possibly as the result of a journey made to London at the behest of King William.

SCIENCE
Locke's philosophical interests divide roughly into three parts: political, epistemological, and scientific. On the scientific side, he was much influenced by his friend, the Irish scientist Robert Boyle, whom he helped with his experiments, and whose corpuscular theory of matter Locke argued for in the *Essay*. According to this theory, every physical thing is composed of submicroscopic, indivisible particles—corpuscles—and all of an object's properties are the result of the arrangement of its corpuscles. There are two main kinds of property or quality: primary and secondary. They are both the powers of an object to

Christil Church College, Oxford

Christ Church College, Oxford.

produce ideas in us, but whereas the ideas produced by primary qualities resemble the object, the ideas produced by secondary qualities do not.

Primary qualities are spatiotemporal and quantitative (for example, size and shape), whereas secondary qualities are non-spatio-temporal and qualitative (for example, color and taste). The secondary qualities depend upon the primary quality arrangements of the corpuscles of the object, together with the arrangements of corpuscles in the perceiver, and (in the case of sight and hearing) the corpuscles making up the light or the air. Corpuscles themselves, of course, have primary but not secondary qualities. This is a more sophisticated version of a distinction to be found in Galileo and Descartes; they considered the secondary qualities to be subjective, simply in the mind of the observer (and therefore of no interest to science), whereas Locke held all qualities to be objective, genuinely part of the world.

KNOWLEDGE

All knowledge, argues Locke, comes through the senses: there can be no innate ideas, no knowledge placed in us by god from birth. Rather, each of us is born a *tabula rasa*, a blank slate, upon which experience writes. He accepts that we possess innate abilities, such as the ability to reason, but no more. This isn't to say that we can gain knowledge only of what we can actually observe; that would be absurd, as we can certainly use our

reason to go beyond our experience—such as, for example, our knowledge of corpuscles—but not to replace it. The influence of **Gassendi** is clear here, but though he disagrees with Descartes in many respects, Locke is essentially a Cartesian philosopher, studying philosophy in the way that Descartes developed it, and taking as his starting point many of Descartes' ideas.

POLITICS

Locke was very much concerned to oppose the notion of the divine right of kings—the religious defense of absolute monarchy. He set out to show how the political state was established and justified, arguing that in the original, prepolitical state of nature, people find that they need to join together in order to protect their natural rights. That is, there's a need for someone to play the part of an impartial adjudicator and defender of rights, and that adjudicator must have the consent of the people, and in order to gain such protection they must willingly give up their personal right to punish wrongdoing. Society is thus founded on a contract; if the adjudicator breaks the terms of the contract, the people have the right to rebel, and to choose another government.

Experience: In that, all our knowledge is founded; and from that it ultimately derives itself.

An Essay concerning Human Understanding 2,i,2.

In a nutshell:
Knowledge comes from experience; religion and morality are as provable as mathematics.

NICOLAS MALEBRANCHE

BORN	1638, Paris	DIED	1715, Paris

MAIN INTERESTS   Metaphysics, epistemology

INFLUENCES   Plato, Augustine, Descartes

INFLUENCED   Locke, Leibniz, Berkeley, Montesquieu, Hume, Rousseau, Kant

MAJOR WORKS
The Search after Truth, Dialogues on Metaphysics, The Treatise on Nature and Grace

The Index of Prohibited Books was a catalog, published by the Catholic Church, listing books that were considered dangerous to faith and to morality, and that Catholics were forbidden to read on pain of excommunication. It was discontinued in 1966, though it hadn't been published since 1948.

The youngest of a large family, Malebranche suffered from curvature of the spine and a weak constitution, and so was educated at home until he was old enough to attend first the Collège de La Marche, then the Sorbonne, where he studied theology. He disliked the subject (and his teachers thought him mediocre), and though he completed his studies, he didn't graduate. Instead he went on to further studies at the Oratory, and in 1664 was ordained a priest. His career was for the most part one of success and honor: in 1674 he became professor of mathematics at the Oratory; he was elected to the Académie des Sciences in 1699, largely for his *Traité des lois de la communication du mouvement* (1682), though he had produced a number of other successful scientific and mathematical books, including *Réflexions sur la lumière, les couleurs et la génération du feu* (1699).

More important, though, in the year he was ordained he chanced upon **Descartes'** *Treatise on Man* at a bookstall, and it changed his life. Reading Descartes had an effect on Malebranche similar to that described by many religious converts, introducing him to a new world of mathematics and philosophy that his rather reactionary education so far had kept hidden from him. From that time onward he devoted his life to the philosophical task of developing the Cartesian approach in the light of Augustinian ideas, and vice versa. The publication in three volumes of *The*

In a nutshell:
The everyday running of the world, and our perceptions of it, depends upon god.

Search after Truth (1674–1675) set him on this road, and it would be fair to say that the rest of his career was spent developing the ideas and arguments presented in that book, especially in his *Treatise on Nature and Grace* (1680) and *Dialogues on Metaphysics* (1688). He was also motivated by his opposition to Jansenism, and this played a part in the genesis of a long and bitter fight with **Arnauld**, which lasted from about 1680 until Arnauld's death in 1694. That debate was in large part responsible for the placing of his *Treatise on Nature and Grace* on the Index of Prohibited Books in 1690, the *The Search after Truth* following it in 1709.

OCCASIONALISM
There are three main issues of philosophical importance in Malebranche's writing: occasionalism, vision in god, and theodicy. What is now his best-known doctrine, occasionalism, is (like **Spinoza's** attribute dualism) a response to what was widely seen as a problem for Descartes' dualism: how can minds and bodies causally interact when they share no properties? Malebranche's solution is to deny that any finite, created thing—whether mental or physical—has active, causal powers; only god is active, only

God did not create the best possible world because it would have been too complex, and therefore not in keeping with god's nature. God only creates in divine simplicity.

A theodicy *is an attempt to reconcile the notion of god as a benevolent, omnipotent, omniscient creator with the evil that we find in the world. The term was introduced by* **Leibniz** *as the title of one of his books.*

[...] it is only God who is the true cause and who truly has the power to move bodies.

Search after Truth 6,2,iii

god can cause. When a bat hits a ball and the ball flies into the air, their collision is only the *occasion* of the ball's flight, not the *cause*; the causal power is god's. **Al-Ghazālī** defended a very similar view. This point raises problems for the notion of the will, which Malebranche tackles, though not very convincingly. However, his discussion of the notion of cause is penetrating, and anticipates **Hume's** work.

VISION IN GOD

The doctrine of *vision in god* follows from the occasionalist position. Malebranche argues that, as our ideas clearly can't arise from the senses—can't be caused by the world—they must come from god. Thus, though Descartes was right to place ideas at the center of all human perceiving and knowing, those ideas aren't modifications of the mind but essences and archetypes in the mind of god. This account (which has very strong echoes of **Plato's** theory of Forms) is also meant to explain our knowledge of necessary and eternal truths, for though Malebranche was primarily concerned with perception, the theory applies to all our ideas (with a few exceptions, especially the ideas of the self and of god), including the

general concepts that make perception possible. In arguing for his position, Malebranche examines the various alternatives, which leads him to present a detailed and important set of arguments against the notion of innate ideas. It was the doctrine of vision in god that was at the heart of Arnauld's attack on him, though Arnauld's main objection was to Malebranche's account of grace.

THEODICY

Malebranche's *theodicy* involves the claim that, though god could have created the best of all possible worlds (as **Leibniz** argued that he did), god did not do so, as such a world would have been more complex, and thus less in keeping with god's nature. Nor can god interfere in the world in order to improve it, for that would mean that god changed his mind, and god is essentially immutable—what he wills, he wills timelessly. Thus, god does not will, or even *permit*, evil; rather, evil—like good—is an unavoidable consequence of what god wills.

The flight of a ball, after it is hit with a racket is the occasion of the ball's flight, but the cause of the flight is in god's power.

GOTTFRIED WILHELM # LEIBNIZ

BORN	1646, Leipzig	DIED	1716, Hanover

MAIN INTERESTS   Metaphysics, logic, language

INFLUENCES   Ockham, Suárez, Hobbes, Descartes, Arnauld, Malebranche

INFLUENCED   Amo, Kant, Frege, Russell, Iqbāl, Wittgenstein, Strawson, Lewis

MAJOR WORKS
Discourse on Metaphysics, Monadology, New Essays on Human Understanding, Theodicy, New System of Nature

Leibniz was involved in something of a squabble with Newton about who had first developed the infinitesimal calculus; the answer is probably Newton (though the issue is more complicated than that), but it was Leibniz's notation that mathematicians adopted. Indeed, even if he'd done nothing else, his work in mathematics, which also included the development of binary arithmetic, would have ensured that his name was remembered.

The son of a professional philosopher, Leibniz himself became much more: mathematician, jurist, historian, scientist, diplomat, poet, inventor, and courtier. He was educated at the universities of Leipzig, Jena, and Altdorf, where he studied mathematics, philosophy, and law. He turned down an academic career, instead entering into the employ of Baron Boineburg in Frankfurt, while also continuing with his study in the law and pursuing his interest in physics, especially of motion. His work for the baron was varied; Leibniz was at various times secretary, librarian, and even political emissary. This last involved a trip to Paris in 1672, where he made many useful contacts with prominent mathematicians, scientists, and philosophers, including **Arnauld**, **Malebranche**, and Huygens. On a trip to England on a similar mission the next year, Leibniz met Hooke and Boyle, and demonstrated his (incomplete) calculating machine to the Royal Society. He was elected a Fellow of the Society that year (though he failed to complete the calculating machine).

The final stage of Leibniz's life began in 1676, when he took up a post as librarian and counselor to the duke of Hanover. Though he continued to travel, Hanover was his home for the rest of his life, albeit under various employers. His official duties were largely administrative, but he continued to work on a wide range of projects, both practical and academic. On the scientific side, his (failed) attempts to drain mines

In a nutshell:
The world is rationally constructed, so reason can uncover its secrets.

using wind- and water-powered pumps led to influential work in geology; he argued that the Earth started life as a sun whose surface hardened as it cooled, and that fossils were the remains of living things. He also worked on the science of dynamics. Other undertakings included a huge project, for the princes of Brunswick: a history of the Guelf family, which he left unfinished.

Leibniz's non-philosophical work was vast and impressive; and his philosophy is unusual in a number of ways, not least in being scattered over a huge number of small works. Leibniz wrote only two full-sized books: the *New Essays on Human Understanding* (c.1705), and the *Theodicy* (1710). Though important, neither of these texts gives anything like a full account of his system, for which important shorter works are needed—especially the *Discourse on Metaphysics* (1686), the *New System of Nature* (1695), and the *Monadology* (1714)—and also his correspondence. This last is particularly extensive; Leibniz had more than six hundred correspondents, including the foremost scientists, mathematicians, and philosophers of his day. Two sets are of particular importance: that with Arnauld

A rainbow is a well-founded phenomena—It is not an hallucination, and there isn't really a colored arc in the sky, but we experience it. It is our experience that gives the world its order.

(about the material found in the *Discourse on Metaphysics*), and that with Samuel Clarke (on behalf of Newton).

LOGICAL UNDERPINNINGS

Leibniz's philosophical system is founded on a small number of basic principles, of which the best known are the Principle of Sufficient Reason, and the Principle of the Indiscernibility of Identicals (sometimes known as Leibniz's Law). The former says that there is a reason that every fact is as it is and not otherwise; nothing happens without a reason. For example, Leibniz argues that, because there could be no reason for the world to be created at one moment rather than another, then the world couldn't have been created at a particular moment. The latter principle says that if two things are identical, they have all their properties in common. A related principle, the Identity of Indiscernibles (also, confusingly, sometimes called Leibniz's Law), says that if two things have every property in common, they're identical—in other words, there can't be two different things with all the same properties.

MONADS

Leibniz's metaphysics is, at least in its basics, straightforward. Where **Spinoza** held that there is only one substance, Leibniz held that the world is composed of an infinity of simple substances, which he called *monads*. These monads have no causal relations (they "have no windows, by which anything could come in or go out" (*Monadology* §7).

Instead, Leibniz develops a distinctive version of **Malebranche's** occasionalism: the Principle of Pre-established Harmony. This says that god created the monads in such a way that their actions and perceptions harmonize with each other, just as two perfectly made clocks will always tell the same time, even though there's no causal relation between them.

WELL-FOUNDED PHENOMENA

This isn't the only way in which Leibniz reinterprets our normal understanding of the world; there are many examples of what he calls *well-founded phenomena*—appearances that, though founded in the way the world really is, do not represent the world accurately. For example, though a rainbow isn't an hallucination, there isn't really a colored arc in the sky. Similarly, says Leibniz, space, time, bodies, and causes are all well-founded phenomena. The world really is ordered in a way that *corresponds to* our experience of it, but that ordering isn't spatial, temporal, material, or causal. Of course, because there's no causation between monads, we don't really experience the way that they're ordered—each monad contains a complete representation of the whole world, though most of that ordering is too confused and indistinct to count as perception or knowledge. Still, in theory we could gain knowledge of the whole world simply by following the connections between what we find in our minds.

Just as a clockmaker can make two clocks that will tell the same time, without having causal relationship, god created monads in such a way that their actions and perceptions are in tune with one another.

[...] if there were not the best among all possible worlds, God would not have produced any [...]

Theodicy *Book 1 §8*

GEORGE BERKELEY

BORN	1685, Kilcrin, Ireland	DIED	1753, Oxford

MAIN INTERESTS	Metaphysics, epistemology

INFLUENCES	Ockham, Descartes, Malebranche, Locke

INFLUENCED	Reid, Hume, Kant

MAJOR WORKS
Treatise concerning the Principles of Human Knowledge, Three Dialogues between Hylas and Philonous

Upon the whole, I am inclined to think that the far greater part, if not all, of those difficulties which have hitherto amused philosophers, and blocked up the way to knowledge, are entirely owing to our selves. That we have first raised a dust, and then complain, we cannot see.

Treatise concerning the Principles of Human Knowledge, Introduction §3

Born in Kilkenny, Berkeley was first educated at the school there and then at Trinity College, Dublin, where he was elected a Fellow in 1707, and ordained in 1709. His undergraduate philosophical thoughts were first published in 1871 as *Common-Place Book*, later as *Philosophical Commentarie*. This makes clear the influence of **Locke's** *An Essay concerning Human Understanding*; Trinity was at the time dominated by the Cartesian approach to philosophy. Moreover, as Berkeley wrote in his *Commentaries*: "I was distrustful at eight years old and consequently by nature disposed for these new Doctrines." By the age of twenty-five he had published his *Essay towards a New Theory of Vision* (1709) and his best known work, *Treatise concerning the Principles of Human Knowledge* (1710).

In 1713 Berkeley traveled to England, where he published the *Three Dialogues between Hylas and Philonous* and then made two journeys to mainland Europe. In Paris he discussed his philosophy with **Malebranche**.

After a brief return to Ireland, he returned to London in 1724, and for eight years spent much of his time on a project to found a college in the Bermudas. He traveled to Newport, Rhode Island, in 1728, where he lived for four years. When it became clear that the Bermudas venture was doomed, he returned to England, where he published a work written in America—*Alciphron or the Minute Philosopher* (1732)—followed by *The*

In a nutshell:
The world is an idea in the mind of god.

Theory of Vision Vindicated and Explained (1733) and *The Analyst* (1734).

In 1734 he was appointed bishop of Cloyne, and spent the rest of his writing career on largely non-philosophical books, most notoriously *Siris* (1744), a peculiar and tangled work in which he preaches the universal curative properties of tarwater.

Berkeley is best known for his idealism; he held that the world is composed of finite minds and ideas, both ultimately dependent upon the infinite mind of god, and that the belief in the external reality of material things is a philosophical mistake. This is in part a response to the same problem with Cartesian dualism with which Malebranche and **Spinoza** were concerned: the supposed impossibility of a causal connection between minds and bodies. In part, though, it stems from a worry about the so-called "veil of perception": the skeptical claim that, as our experience of the external world isn't direct but always mediated by the senses, we can never be sure that that experience is accurate. By doing away with material bodies, and insisting, in the words of his famous slogan, that *to be is to be perceived*, Berkeley thought he'd solved both problems.

ANTHONY WILLIAM AMO

| **BORN** 1703, Awukenu, Ghana | **DIED** 1784, Ghana |

MAIN INTERESTS Metaphysics, epistemology, logic

INFLUENCES Descartes, Leibniz, Wolff

INFLUENCED Modern African philosophy

MAJOR WORKS
*On the Absence
of Sensation in
the Human Mind,
Treatise on the
Art of
Philosophising
Soberly and
Accurately*

*Whatever feels, lives;
whatever lives, depends
on nourishment;
whatever lives and
depends on nourishment,
grows; whatever is of
this nature is in the end
resolved into its basic
principles; whatever
comes to be resolved into
its basic principles is a
complex; every complex
has its constituent parts;
whatever this is true of is
a divisible body. If
therefore the human
mind feels, it follows that
it is a divisible body.*

Antonius Guilelmus Amo Afer, as he was to call himself, was an Akan of the Nzema people, born in the Axim region of Ghana. His early life is thinly documented, but it seems clear that at age five he was taken to Europe as a slave by the Dutch West India Company, who gave him as a gift to the Duke of Brunswick-Wolfenbüttel in 1707. Upon his arrival at the castle in Lower Saxony, he was baptized and later confirmed in the chapel, then entered the duke's service. He was accepted warmly by the court, treated as a member of the family, and educated, becoming a student at the University of Halle in 1727. After two years, Amo completed his preliminary studies with a disputation: "The Rights of Blacks (Moors) in Europe."

Amo went to the University of Wittenberg for his further studies. There he studied logic, metaphysics, physiology, astronomy, history, law, theology, politics, and medicine. He wrote and spoke six languages: English, French, Dutch, Latin, Greek, and German. In 1734 he successfully defended his inaugural dissertation, which was published under the title *On the Absence of Sensation in the Human Mind and Its Presence in our Organic and Living Body*. This was a critical examination of **Descartes'** dualism, and a defense of a form of modified materialism. His position was that, though there is indeed something that we might call a mind or soul, it is the body, not the mind, that perceives and feels.

In 1735 Amo returned to Halle, where he lectured in philosophy, becoming a professor in 1736. His belief in a close connection between philosophy and the natural sciences, hinted at in his earlier work, was made more explicit in the work compiled from his lectures, the *Treatise on the Art of Philosophising Soberly and Accurately* (1738). In this, Amo presented an epistemology that was very close to that of **Locke** and **Hume**: he argued that there could be nothing in the mind that had not been perceived by the senses. He also examined and presented the case against such intellectual faults as dishonesty, dogmatism, and prejudice.

In 1740 Amo moved to the University of Jena, to lecture in philosophy. However, his life in Jena was unhappy; his patron, the Duke of Brunswick-Wolfenbüttel, had died, and the intellectual and moral climate in Germany was becoming narrower and more illiberal. There are good reasons to hold that the concept of race was invented in eighteenth-century Europe, and with race came racism. Amo returned to Ghana in 1746. What happened next is uncertain, but it is claimed that he was taken to a Dutch fortress in the 1750s, where he later died.

In a nutshell:
Philosophy and science should be our weapons against superstition and slavery.

BARON DE MONTESQUIEU

BORN 1689, Labrède	**DIED** 1755, Paris

MAIN INTERESTS   Politics

INFLUENCES   Aristotle, Hobbes, Descartes, Malebranche, Locke

INFLUENCED   Hume, Burke, Hegel

MAJOR WORKS
The Spirit of the Laws, Persian Letters

It is impossible for us to suppose [African slaves] to be men, because, allowing them to be men, a suspicion would follow that we ourselves are not Christians.

The Spirit of the Laws,
vol.1, book XV, §5

Charles-Louis de Secondat, Baron de Montesquieu, was born at the Chateau de la Brède in Bordeaux, his family's seat. A generally well-liked man (though apparently somewhat overfond of money and position), he was active politically, being president of the Bordeaux parliament from 1716 to 1728, and traveled widely, especially to England, where he spent some time studying the political institutions, attending meetings of parliament, and meeting and corresponding with such eminent figures as **David Hume** and Lord Chesterfield. He was also known for his literary skills, being elected to the Académie Française in 1728, and to the Royal Society in 1730; this was largely the result of his popularly acclaimed book *Persian Letters* (1721), a satire on politics, culture, literature, religion—in fact, of most of contemporary French life. Using the device of foreign travelers trying to understand the strange customs and culture they encounter, it is the ancestor of a long line of similar satirical works, nowadays usually putting extraterrestrial visitors in place of Montesquieu's Persians.

Though his historical book *Thoughts on the Causes of the Grandeur and Decadence of the Romans* (1734) was also well received, his philosophical masterpiece was without a doubt *The Spirit of the Laws* (1748). Despite its tremendous success, it also came in for considerable criticism, with threats to ban it by the Sorbonne and the Assembly of Bishops. Montesquieu wrote a defense of

In a nutshell:

The world, including the political world, proceeds according to regular laws, and to understand any part of it one must learn how it relates to the rest according to those laws.

the book in 1750, and went on to write a couple of shorter works (unpublished in his lifetime), and to extend the *Persian Letters*. He died aged sixty-six of a fever in Paris.

THE FOUNDATION OF STATES

The Spirit of the Laws is one of the acknowledged classics of political philosophy. In it, Montesquieu is influenced by **Locke** (and **Machiavelli**) with regard to his political theories, but by **Descartes** with regard to his methodology, which is scientific (if not terribly systematic); indeed, Durkheim called him the founder of modern sociology. He classifies different systems of government according to their constitutive principles: for a democratic republic, it is virtue; for an aristocratic republic, moderation; for a monarchy, honor; and for a despotism, fear. Each society, its origin, and the changes it undergoes, must be understood in terms of the constitutive principle of its type, its physical situation (climate, geography, and so on), its social conditions (liberty, religion, trade, and so on), and human psychology;

The House of Commons, London, 1742. Montesquieu used the eighteenth-century English constitution as his model for ideal political organization.

these factors are related by causal laws in a wholly natural and mechanical process of development. The laws of each society must be related to its nature and constitutive principle.

THE SEPARATION OF POWERS

Aside from the basic metaphysical background of his political theory, though, Montesquieu's most influential thesis concerns the separation of powers. This is the doctrine that the three functions of the state's power—the legislative (which formulates policy), the executive (which enacts the policy), and the judicial (which applies the law)—must be strictly separate, each being a check on the others. They should be separate, not only legally and in their organizations, but socially; that is, each power is associated with a different social class: the executive was to be the monarch, the legislature, in two houses, represented the aristocracy and the bourgeoisie, and the judiciary represented every class and none. In this way, the powers are naturally balanced, each power checked by a counterpower. His account is modeled in part on the eighteenth-century English constitutional structure, though it has been suggested that his understanding of that structure was somewhat idealized.

Though Montesquieu was in fact concerned at least in part with making a case for strengthening the aristocracy against the encroachment of the monarchy and of the commons, and argued that the best system of government was an aristocratic constitutional monarchy, his ideas had a very strong and direct influence on the framing of the U.S. Constitution.

The reader is often taken aback at the fresh and modern feel of Montesquieu's writing; his attack on the practice of slavery, for example, drips with the sarcasm of outrage. Balancing this is a fault often commented upon by his contemporaries: his tendency to omit argument in favor of fascinating but sometimes dubiously accurate anecdotes about the practices of various peoples around the world or of the ancients—a sort of armchair anthropology.

The U.S. political system and the Constitution were profoundly influenced by Montesquieu's ideas.

OVERVIEW
COMMON SENSE

The notion of common sense has changed significantly over the centuries, as has its relationship with philosophy. For **Aristotle**, and the medieval philosophers such as **Aquinas** who followed him, common sense (*koinē; aisthāsis*, or *sensus communis*) is the mental faculty that unites the information about *common sensibles* that we get from our senses; common sensibles are properties that can be perceived by more than one sense, for example, shape or size. Such properties are perceived as they are in themselves, unlike, for example, color and taste, perceived by only one sense (*special sensibles*). This is the ancestor of **Locke's** distinction between *primary* and *secondary qualities*. But Aristotle's faculty of common sense also has the job of integrating our senses, so that we can judge of a single thing that, for example, it's both round and red.

THE SCOTTISH SCHOOL
A less technical meaning, however, can be found as far back as Roman writers; "common sense" consists of the beliefs of the vulgar mob, against which is set the refined and reasoned beliefs of the philosophers. A rather less negative version of this can be seen as underlying the Scottish school of common-sense philosophy, originating with **Thomas Reid**; here, common sense is taken to be the set of prereflective principles found in all normal human minds. Such principles are basic and, because they originate in god's creation, are also reliable. When philosophy goes against them, it is philosophy that is inevitably mistaken. The trouble here is that different people at different times have very different ideas about what's included in common sense. Moreover, for those who either don't believe in god, or don't believe that god plays the sort of truth-guaranteeing role upon which Reid relies, common-sense beliefs lose their usefulness.

BASIC LIMITING PRINCIPLES
A version of Reid's notion of common-sense beliefs can be found in the work of an early-twentieth-century philosopher, C. D. Broad (1887–1971), in a discussion of what was then called *psychical research*. He introduces the notion of what he calls a *Basic Limiting Principle* (or *BLP*). These are principles that we take for granted in everyday and scientific life; they're either self-evident or based on such overwhelming evidence that it doesn't occur to us to question them.

Another prominent defender of common sense was G. E. Moore (1873–1958), who held that the ordinary person's natural beliefs about the world, based on a straightforward acceptance of what the senses tell us, are more likely to be right than sophisticated skepticism, especially when they concern the existence and contents of the external world.

Common sense has been the subject of much debate, since the very beginnings of philosophical discussion. In Roman times, common sense was considered to be the beliefs of the mob against the rational beliefs of philosophers.

THOMAS REID

BORN 1710, Stachan	DIED 1796, Glasgow

MAIN INTERESTS   Epistemology

INFLUENCES   Arnauld, Locke, Berkeley, Hume

INFLUENCED   Hamilton, Peirce, Moore, Austin

MAJOR WORKS
An Inquiry into the Human Mind on the Principles of Common Sense, Essays on the Intellectual Powers of Man, Essays on the Active Powers of Man

The form of the expression, I feel pain, might seem to imply that the feeling is something distinct from the pain felt; yet, in reality, there is no distinction. As thinking a thought is an expression which could signify no more than thinking, so feeling a pain signifies no more than being pained.

An Inquiry into the
Human Mind, p.183

Reid was educated at Marischal College, Aberdeen, and became a Presbyterian minister. He had accepted **Berkeley's** views until he read **Hume's** *Treatise of Human Nature*; taking Hume's position to be the logical extension of Berkeley's approach, Reid rejected both. His counter to the skepticism he'd found in the *Treatise* and the theories upon which it rested was published as "An Essay on Quantity," in 1748. On the strength of the Essay he became a regent (professor) at King's College, Aberdeen. He wrote *An Inquiry into the Human Mind on the Principles of Common Sense* in 1764 and was elected to a professorship in moral philosophy at the University of Glasgow the same year. Finding that his academic duties interfered with his writing, he resigned and wrote two other books: *Essays on the Intellectual Powers of Man* (1785) and *Essays on the Active Powers of Man* (1788).

Reid traces back to **Locke's** theory of perception the problem that finally surfaces as Hume's skepticism. Locke, followed by Berkeley and Hume, placed ideas between us and the world, and made perception a matter of experiencing ideas rather than the world. Skepticism is then inevitable, for what guarantee do we have that our ideas correspond to the world in the right way? We're also condemned to solipsism, for what seems to be our experience of other people turns out to be simply the experience of our own minds. In place of Locke's approach, Reid develops a version of what is now

known as *direct realism*. The world exists independently of our experience of it, and makes itself known to us through our sensations, which are the direct expression of the world in our minds (this is the case for *primary qualities*; things are more complex and less direct for *secondary qualities*).

Reid's account of common sense is complex. He argues that certain beliefs are imposed upon us by our nature as human beings; these beliefs are held universally, or would be if we weren't sometimes distracted by "the enchantment of words" spun by philosophers such as Locke. Such common-sense beliefs have something of the nature of fundamental principles, so can't be justified by appealing to deeper or more general principles; rather, their justification lies in the fact that our human nature is created by god. Reid is trying to walk a very thin line between making truth a matter of mob rule and resting all our knowledge on the sort of innate beliefs against which Locke had argued.

In a nutshell:
The influence of Reid's thinking spread beyond the Scottish school of common sense, and had a great influence on philosophical thought in European countries, as well as on American pragmatism.

DAVID HUME

BORN	1711, Edinburgh	DIED	1776, Edinburgh

MAIN INTERESTS   Epistemology, ethics

INFLUENCES   Francis Bacon, Descartes, Malebranche, Newton, Locke, Berkeley

INFLUENCED   Everyone who came after him

MAJOR WORKS
A Treatise of Human Nature, Enquiries concerning Human Understanding and concerning the Principles of Morals, Dialogues concerning Natural Religion

What raises the human above the rest of nature is the ability to sympathize. This trait enables us to make moral judgements that are not limited to individuals or cultures.

Hume's early life is relatively poorly documented. Born in Edinburgh, he spent his early years there and on the family estate, Ninewells, near Berwick-upon-Tweed. His father died in 1713, and he was brought up and educated by his mother. He apparently showed intellectual promise very early, and had started his philosophical thinking and writing by the age of sixteen (the year after he graduated from the University of Edinburgh, where he'd matriculated at twelve). Originally destined for a career in the law (his mother's family were lawyers), he instead continued his studies privately, reading a vast range of material—philosophical, mathematical, scientific, historical, and literary.

Between 1726 and 1739 Hume went through a number of significant changes in his thought, before reaching the first stage of his mature position. However, the result of all his efforts, A *Treatise of Human Nature* (1739), whose revolutionary ideas and forthright style he expected to arouse controversy and anger, "fell dead-born from the press," being either ignored or receiving incomprehending sneers.

Hume blamed himself for this, believing that he'd rushed into print too soon. He returned to his work, turning Book I of the *Treatise*

In a nutshell:
One should believe only what one has good reason to believe.

into the *Enquiry concerning Human Understanding* (1748) and Book II into the *Enquiry concerning the Principles of Morals* (1751). The new works differed from the old in a number of ways, not least in leaving out a lot of psychological theorizing about the origins of concepts such as space and time, and including material on the religious implications of his theories. Despite his wish to shock, he had originally been too cautious to include the latter in the *Treatise*.

Hume's only other major philosophical work was the *Dialogues concerning Natural Religion*, which he was again too cautious to publish, and which appeared (in accordance with his instructions) after his death, in 1779. His caution wasn't, in the tolerant atmosphere of eighteenth-century Edinburgh, a matter of fear for his safety but of concern for his social standing; Hume was a popular figure in social and literary circles, both in Scotland and in France, and he thrived in (especially female) company.

Though he published little in the field of philosophy between 1751 and his death, he was far from idle. He never managed to gain an academic position (he was turned down

Edinburgh, during much of the eighteenth century was at the heart of the European Enlightenment movement. It was home to important figures, such as philosopher and economist Adam Smith, scientist and religious sceptic James Hutton, and engineer James Watt, as well as David Hume.

for professorships at Edinburgh and Glasgow), but filled a number of political and diplomatic posts, including undersecretary of state in the Northern Department, private secretary to the British ambassador in Paris, and later *chargé d'affaires* there. He was also keeper of the Advocates Library in Edinburgh, which allowed him to write his six-volume *History of Great Britain* (1754–1762), for which he would be known today even if he hadn't written his philosophical works (he was best known in his own day as an historian). In addition to various shorter essays, Hume produced his *Political Discourse* (1752) and an autobiography that was published posthumously in 1777.

IMPRESSIONS AND IDEAS

Hume divided all the contents of the mind into two categories: impressions and ideas. Impressions are roughly what we should nowadays call "sense perceptions" (though they also included internal impressions such as emotions)—the result of the world *impressing* itself on us via light, air, waves, and so on. We have no control over such perceptions, beyond the crude method of shutting our eyes or blocking our ears. Ideas are faded impressions, the lingering remnants of sense perception. We do have control over these, however, in that we can combine them to form new, complex ideas (such as the idea of a unicorn). It follows that all genuine ideas can be traced back to impressions. This is Hume's central

criterion for the justification of our ideas and beliefs. He applies it to a range of ideas, including causality, miracles, and the self, and in each case finds that there is no relevant impression.

Hume then asks two questions: first, where does the concept come from, if not from experience? Secondly, do we need it? His answers to the first are psychological, appealing to the ways in which our minds work, and especially the imagination. His answers to the second vary—sometimes "yes" (as for causality), sometimes "no" (as for miracles). In all of this Hume is concerned with the epistemological question; he's not arguing, for example, that miracles never happen, only that we have no grounds for believing that they do.

ETHICS

Hume's moral theory is potentially misleading. He seems to be arguing that our moral judgments are subjective, being simply a matter of our feelings of pleasure or displeasure toward actions, events, or people. What raises it above that sort of crude subjectivism is the way that he grounds such feelings in *sympathy*, which is a human trait, not limited to certain individuals or cultures. The statement "Torture is wrong" is no more a subjective claim than "The sky is blue," though seeing that torture is wrong depends, like seeing that the sky is blue, on being a normal human being with normal human faculties.

Next to the ridicule of denying an evident truth, is that of taking much pains to defend it; and no truth appears to me more evident, than that beasts are endow'd with thought and reason as well as men.

A Treatise of Human Nature *I,iii,xvi*

JEAN-JACQUES ROUSSEAU

BORN	1712, Geneva, Switzerland	DIED	1778, Ermenonville, France

MAIN INTERESTS	Education, politics

INFLUENCES	Machiavelli, Hobbes, Descartes, Malebranche, Locke

INFLUENCED	Wollstonecraft, Hegel, Rawls

MAJOR WORKS
The Social Contract, Emile

Man was a "noble savage" when in the state of nature, before the creation of civilization. He has been corrupted by the social interdependence of society.

Brought up first by his father, then less happily by an aunt and uncle, Rousseau ran away from Switzerland at the age of sixteen, becoming the secretary and companion to a wealthy Catholic philanthropist, Louise de Warens. She persuaded him to convert to Catholicism, but more importantly made possible the completion of his education. This allowed him to make a living as a tutor, composer, playwright, musician, and writer—first in Lyon, and then in Paris. Aside from his philosophical writings, Rousseau produced novels, poetry, opera, and works on botany, music, and education.

In 1750 Rousseau won the Academy of Dijon prize for his *Discourse on the Sciences and the Arts*, in which he argued that science and the arts, far from promoting happiness and virtue, in fact serve to corrupt human beings. His *Discourse on the Origin and Foundation of the Inequality among Mankind* (1755), extended his arguments to the ill effects of society on the noble savage in the state of nature. His views provoked an attack from Voltaire, which led to a bitter feud between the two.

In 1762 Rousseau published his two most famous books, a novel, *Emile*, in which he presented his theory of education, and his best-known philosophical work, *The Social Contract*. These aroused great controversy and hostility in both France and Switzerland, and Rousseau moved to Prussia, and then to England. There he stayed with **Hume**, but his mental state had become precarious, and their friendship was destroyed by Rousseau's paranoid accusations. He returned to France, under a false name, in 1768, dying there in 1778, after writing his *Confessions*—an astonishingly honest and revealing autobiographical work, published posthumously in 1782.

THE SOCIAL CONTRACT

Rousseau rejected the view of human nature found in writers such as **Hobbes** and **Locke**, holding that they tried to describe people in the state of nature but ended up describing modern, socialized people transplanted into an imaginary presocial past. He argued that human beings are not naturally selfish, only becoming so as reason begins to affect their lives (and especially when they start to live in communities), stifling their natural sympathy for each other. His account of political society involved people coming together because they found that cooperation was necessary, and making a contract in which they agree to give up all their natural rights to the social whole. When it's passive, this whole is called the State; when it's active, it's called the Sovereign. It forms a sort of political person, with a physical part—the body politic—and a mental part—the *General Will*. This Will concerns what is good for society as a whole, so isn't simply some sort of averaging out or adding up of what each citizen wants (what each thinks is good for herself), but the genuine will of the whole, of which each

This allegorical painting indicates that the French Revolution claimed Jean Jacques Rousseau as its spiritual father.

individual is part, and to which each individual is (voluntarily) subject.

FREEDOM

For Rousseau, only direct, participatory democracy is acceptable; as soon as the people allow themselves to be represented, they lose their freedom. Freedom is indeed at the heart of his political philosophy, but he carefully distinguishes between the low-grade freedom involved in the individual simply doing whatever she wants (being a slave to passions), and the high-grade freedom involved in being part of the social world—the freedom of autonomy, of living by one's own rules rather than without rules. This is in part what he means by the person who tries to go against the General Will being "forced to be free"; unless the Sovereign (the state as active) forces her to follow the rules that she has been part of forming, she'll be back in thrall to her passions. Indeed, she'll suffer from the contradiction of both willing and rejecting what's best for society (the General Will is always right; only individuals fall into error).

It has often been argued that Rousseau's political theory lends itself to justifications of totalitarianism, but this view is ill-conceived. He accepts that, in a national emergency, when swift and decisive action makes the leisurely process of democratic debate and decision-making impractical, it's permissible for there to be a single leader, whose role is somewhat like that of a

totalitarian dictator; however, not only is such a situation temporary, lasting only as long as is strictly necessary, but it is also acceptable only in a state of the sort that Rousseau envisages—he certainly offers no justification for dictatorships in general.

Rousseau's writings were popular and influential with the Jacobins, and so played a part in paving the way for the French Revolution. His educational theories, which advocated a much more permissive approach in emphasizing the senses and physical health rather than intellectual development, had a great influence on later educational theorists and practitioners such as Froebel and Pestalozzi.

Man is born free, yet everywhere is in chains. One thinks himself the master of others, and still remains a greater slave than they.

The Social Contract,
book 1, chap. 1

In a nutshell:
Through society we've lost our freedom and our innate goodness, which we can and should regain.

IMMANUEL KANT

| BORN | 1724, Königsberg | DIED | 1804, Königsberg |

MAIN INTERESTS Epistemology, metaphysics, ethics

INFLUENCES Descartes, Malebranche, Leibniz, Spinoza, Locke, Berkeley, Hume

INFLUENCED Everyone who came after him

MAJOR WORKS
Critique of Pure Reason, Critique of Practical Reason, Prolegomena to Any Future Metaphysics

Two things fill the mind with ever new, and increasing admiration and awe, the more often and steadily we reflect upon them: the starry heavens above me and the moral law within me.

Kant's epitaph (Critique of
Practical Reason 5: 161)

Kant was born into a poor family in Königsberg in eastern Prussia (now Kaliningrad in the Russian Federation). He studied at Königsberg University, and after a few years working as a private tutor, went on to teach there for more than forty years, never traveling more than fifty miles from home. He taught science and mathematics, as well as anthropology and geography (his writings in this field were particularly influential), gradually extending his interests to metaphysics, epistemology, and ethics.

For the next quarter of a century he continued to write on both scientific and philosophical issues, and many of the arguments and positions familiar from his later work first appeared during this period. Kant, though, was struggling with his fundamental approach to philosophy; he swung back and forth between an approach to knowledge that was essentially rationalist in nature, and a skeptical approach to the abilities of reason alone.

It was during this time of uncertainty that he reread **Hume**; this was largely responsible, he later said (with some exaggeration), for wakening him from his dogmatic slumbers. That awakening led to the writing of the monumental *Critique of Pure Reason* (1781), generally known as the First Critique. This was followed by a stream of important works: the *Prolegomena to Any Future Metaphysics* (1783), the *Groundwork of the Metaphysics of Morals* (1785), a thoroughly

In a nutshell:
All human knowledge starts with experience, but knowledge of the world also depends upon the nature of the human mind.

rewritten second edition of the First Critique in 1787, the *Critique of Practical Reason* (1788), known as the Second Critique, the *Critique of Judgement* (1790), known as the Third Critique, *Religion within the Bounds of Reason Alone* (1792–1793), and the *Metaphysics of Morals* (1797). In 1799 ill health forced him to retire from teaching.

METAPHYSICS AND EPISTEMOLOGY
In addressing the question "How is metaphysics possible?" Kant addresses Hume's denial that metaphysics can extend our knowledge because it's concerned with what Hume calls the relations of ideas, and hence can yield only trivial truths. For Kant, if metaphysics can extend our knowledge, as it purports to do, then it must be informative. But metaphysics must be a priori (that is, independent of experience), because the model of knowledge to which we aspire is nonempirical. If it is a priori, then it must also be necessary, for experience "teaches us that a thing is so and so, but not that it cannot be otherwise" (*Critique of Pure Reason* B3). Strict necessity

Kant's categorical imperative is the universal and objective expression of our rational nature. If something is right for one person, it is right for everyone. We debate moral issues and beliefs because we want them to be universally valid.

and universality are the two criteria of a priori*city* for Kant. His most formidable task follows at once: "How are synthetic a priori judgments possible?"

This leads to a question of the possibility of knowledge, and Kant embarks on an examination of its conditions, which involves a distinction between sensible and conceptual conditions. Knowledge must involve both concepts and sensory awareness if it is to be knowledge of objects of possible experience (the outer objects, or phenomenal world). Space and time are the necessary conditions (the pure a priori forms) of our sensibility (sensory awareness), and the pure a priori concepts or categories of the understanding (particularly the concepts of substance and causality) are the conceptually necessary conditions of knowledge. The two kinds of condition compose the Structure of Experience, the former at the level where objects are sensed, the latter at the level where the objects sensed are brought under concepts, and hence can be thought or understood. The nonempirical ground of these concepts is the numerical unity of the self-conscious subject. It is this numerical unity of the self that Hume so desperately needed but was unable to account for, given that his philosophical system allowed him to appeal only to empirical grounds, which can't provide for unity and identity across time; without the numerical unity of the self Hume can't account for one of his central principles: causality.

PHENOMENA AND NOUMENA

Kant further distinguishes the phenomenal world from the world as it is in itself, utterly independent of us: the noumenal world, which is the subject of speculative metaphysics, or pure reason. He doesn't deny that the noumenal world is thinkable or intelligible, but that means that what is intelligible is at best the concept of something in general (not of any particular thing), which is developed purely intellectually, without any spatiotemporal framework. It carries no implication to claims of knowledge, but serves as a limiting concept, that is, setting limits to our sensibility.

ETHICS

Unlike metaphysics, moral deliberation is based on pure practical reason, or the intrinsically Good Will, and the structure of Kant's moral philosophy is built on the interrelated concepts of the self, duty (the recognition of what is good), freedom (at the level of reason), and autonomy (self-governance). We self-legislate the Moral Law, expressed in the unconditional or categorical imperative, which is objective and universal (applicable to all rational beings), because it's an expression of our rational nature. The basic premise is that "ought" implies "can" (that is, one can be morally obliged to do only what one actually can do), thus avoiding prescriptivism.

Without sensibility no object would be given to us, without understanding no object would be thought. Thoughts without content are empty, intuitions without concepts are blind.

Critique of Pure Reason
A51/B75

Just as a camera is a limited piece of equipment which can give us only a visual representation of the world, the world that we see and know through our own physical apparatus is also limited.

JEREMY BENTHAM

BORN 1748, London	**DIED** 1832, London

MAIN INTERESTS Ethics, politics, law

INFLUENCES Epicurus, Hobbes, David Hartley, William Blackstone

INFLUENCED James Mill, J. S. Mill, Peirce, Singer

MAJOR WORKS
An Introduction to the Principles of Morals and Legislation

Nature has placed mankind under the governance of two sovereign masters, pain and pleasure. It is for them alone to point out what we ought to do as well as to determine what we shall do.

An Introduction to the Principles
of Morals and Legislation
chap. I, §1

Bentham was born into a legal family and, like his Utilitarian successor **J. S. Mill**, was an infant prodigy. He was educated at Westminster School and Queen's College, Oxford, where he read law. He completed his legal education at Lincoln's Inn, and was called to the Bar but never practiced. In the course of his studies he had conceived a great dislike for the state of English law, and began working on its reform. His first book—of which part was published in 1776 *A Fragment on Government*—was a criticism of the foremost legal scholar of the time, Sir William Blackstone.

Bentham was also interested in penal reform, going so far as to design a revolutionary form of prison, the *Panopticon*, so called because its design ensured that the prisoners were under constant observation by unseen guards. He spent years campaigning for its use (a few prisons were built around the world with some of its features, but no genuine panopticon ever appeared).

His most important and best-known work is *An Introduction to the Principles of Morals and Legislation* (1789), meant to be the introduction to a work on penal reform but published alone. Here he introduced his Utilitarian theory, according to which the morality of an action is purely a matter of the amount of pleasure or pain that it produces. The precise amount of pleasure or pain could be calculated, he argued, making morality genuinely measurable and scientific.

In their own words:
[Of our moral responsobilities to animals:] The question is not, Can they reason? nor, Can they talk? but, Can they suffer?

An Introduction to the Principles
of Morals and Legislation *VII*

Much of the rest of his life was spent developing this theory and applying it to politics and the law. This largely involved noninterference, for the individual knows best what gives her pleasure and pain, and the good of society is the aggregate of every individual's pleasure and absence of pain.

Though Bentham had a considerable influence on British legal and political reform, as well as on the course of moral and political philosophy, he was even more well known and influential in mainland Europe, and was made an honorary citizen of the French Republic in 1792. He wrote on many important issues, including animal welfare, poor relief, the need for extended suffrage, and the decriminalization of homosexuality.

On his death, Bentham left two relics: a massive hoard of unpublished manuscripts, and his body. Some of the former contain important work in the philosophy of law. The latter is on display in a cabinet in University College, London (which he founded).

MARY WOLLSTONECRAFT

BORN 1759, Spitalfields, London	**DIED** 1797, Somers Town, London

MAIN INTERESTS   Politics, ethics

INFLUENCES   Rousseau

INFLUENCED   J. S. Mill

MAJOR WORKS
*A Vindication
of the Rights
of Men,
A Vindication
of the Rights
of Women*

Men and women must be educated, in a great degree, by the opinions and manners of the society they live in. In every age there has been a stream of popular opinion that has carried all before it, and given a family character, as it were, to the century. It may then be fairly inferred, that, till society be differently constituted, much cannot be expected from education.

A Vindication of the Rights of
Women, p.102

The daughter of a handkerchief weaver and would-be farmer, Wollstonecraft and her family moved around England and Wales a great deal in her eatly life. Her education was presumably therefore also badly disrupted, but she was set on her intellectual career by a neighboring clergyman whom she befriended at age nine when the family lived in Yorkshire. She continued her private study until 1778, when she left home to act as companion to an elderly widow in Bath. After two years, however, her mother's illness called her back. Two years later her mother died and she went to live with her childhood friend Frances Blood; in 1784 they opened a school in Islington, together with Wollstonecraft's two sisters.

It was at this time that Wollstonecraft met Richard Price, a local minister, who with his friend Joseph Priestly was the leader of a group known as the Rational Dissenters. Price was a moral philosopher who had written a defense of a rationalist account of morality—*A Review of the Principal Questions of Morals* (1758)—criticizing those who, like **Hume**, founded morality in the passions (and responding to his argument against belief in miracles). Price was well known at the time, both for his religious views and for his defense of the American and French revolutions.

Wollstonecraft began attending Price's chapel, and also attended meetings at his home, where she met such Radicals as Tom Paine, William Godwin, and the publisher Joseph Johnson, who commissioned from her a pamphlet on education: *Thoughts on the Education of Daughters* (1786). In 1789, in response to an attack by Edmund Burke on Price (about the French Revolution and the divine right of kings), Wollstonecraft wrote *A Vindication of the Rights of Men* (1790). In it she dealt not only with the question of revolution against a bad king, but with wider issues such as the slave trade, the inequalities of society, and the need for reason over prejudice. Then in 1792 she published her most important work, *A Vindication of the Rights of Women*, whose radical content and tone created a storm. In it she argued for the equality of women with men, including female suffrage, and pointed out the ways in which the nature of most women was created by the education chosen for them by men, and perpetuated by the social structures imposed by men (she described marriage as legalized prostitution).

In 1797 Wollstonecraft married fellow Radical William Godwin, but died later that year from complications after the birth of their daughter (who was to become famous as Mary Shelley).

In a nutshell:
*Inequalities are created and sustained
by society, which therefore needs
to be changed.*

Though this is a shorter period than the earlier periods covered in this book, and though in many ways it was merely transitional between the early modern and the modern periods of philosophy, this time saw tremendous advances in three major areas: ethics, politics, and logic and language, together with a philosophical fashion that swept Europe.

The figure who brings the first three areas together in one body of work is the empiricist English philosopher John Stuart Mill, with his development

1770

1806

1813

1818

of Utilitarian moral and political theory, and his groundbreaking and influential work, the *System of Logic*. Mill has been sadly neglected in all his guises except that of the moral and political philosopher, but his thinking had a direct effect on later writers such as Russell (whose godfather he was) and Hempel. The study of logic in particular had been stagnating for some time, and Mill's work had the welcome effect of giving it a much-needed shot in the arm, though the major figure in the field,

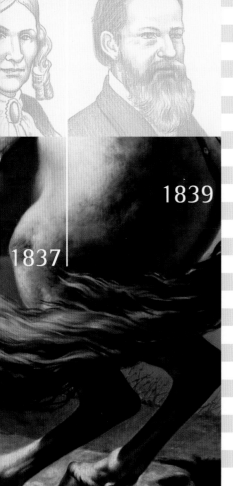

1804	Napoléon becomes emperor of France
1805	Battles of Trafalgar and Austerlitz
1806	End of Holy Roman Empire
1807	Slave trade abolished in the British Empire

NINETEENTH CENTURY
1800–1899

1811	Luddite rising
1812	French retreat from Moscow
1815	Napoléon escapes from Elba; Battle of Waterloo
1819	Peterloo massacre
1821	Death of Napoléon on St. Helena
1825	First railway line opened, Stockton to Darlington
1829	Independence of Greece
1832	Walter Scott and Goethe die. Morse invents wireless telegraphy
1834	Tolpuddle Martyrs
1837	Accession of Queen Victoria
1840	Penny postage instituted. Victoria marries Albert. Start of Opium War
1848	Revolutionary movements sweep across Europe. Gold discovered in California
1850	Start of Taiping Rebellion against Qing Dynasty
1851	Great Exhibition
1853	Perry lands in Japan. Start of Crimean War
1854	Battle of Balaklava; Charge of the Light Brigade

1839

1837

1856	End of Crimean War
1857	Indian Mutiny
1859	*Origin of Species* published. Raid on Harper's Ferry; John Brown hanged
1860	Garibaldi and his Red Shirts take Sicily and Naples
1861	Abraham Lincoln takes office as president. Start of American Civil War; first battle of Bull Run
1863	Polish rising against Russia. Battle of Gettysburg
1864	First Socialist International. Sherman takes Atlanta and Savannah. First Geneva Convention signed
1865	Lee surrenders to Grant. Lincoln assassinated. Slavery abolished in the U.S.A.
1866	Mendel publishes paper on heredity. Russia sells Alaska to the U.S.A.
1868	Japanese Shogunate abolished
1869	Suez Canal opened
1870	Papal infallibility invented. France declares war against Prussia; Siege of Paris
1871	Paris Commune established, then crushed. Trades unions legalized in the U.K.
1876	Bell invents the telephone. Defeat of Custer
1878	Cyprus ceded to Britain by Turkey
1879	Zulu war. Tay Bridge disaster
1881	Revolt of the Mahdi in the Sudan
1886	Geronimo captured. All hostile bands of Native Americans now on reservations
1894	Armenians massacred by Turks (continues for next quarter century)
1895	Discovery of X-rays. Marconi sends wireless message more than a mile
1897	Cretan revolt; Greek-Turkish war. Queen Victoria's Diamond Jubilee
1898	Spanish-American War. Battle of Omdurman. Empress of Austria assassinated. Discovery of radium
1899	Start of Boer War
1900	Relief of Ladysmith. Relief of Mafeking. Boxer Rebellion. Australian Commonwealth proclaimed

beyond a doubt, was **Gottlob Frege**. With regard to his moral and political theories, Mill's brand of Utilitarianism had a profound effect on thinking outside philosophy (though he'd have argued, with some justice, that he was in fact bringing out and refining what was already there).

POLITICAL PHILOSOPHY

Mill, like **Karl Marx**, the other major nineteenth-century political thinker, was very much influenced by the radical thought that had begun to flourish in various forms during the end of the previous century, and that gave rise to a number of political movements, including socialism. Unlike Marx, Mill is also notable (though by no means uniquely so) for resisting—indeed, largely ignoring—the century's main philosophical fashion: Hegelianism, and especially Hegelian idealism. **G. W. F. Hegel's** philosophy rapidly swept across continental Europe (with the major exception of France), becoming the dominant philosophical school, especially in Germany. Then, as its star began to

wane there, it hopped the English Channel and took up residence in the British Isles, making Oxford its center. British Hegelianism was a slightly different animal, modified by various native and non-native influences, especially Kantianism. The British Hegelians, such as Green, **Bradley**, and Collingwood, tended to adopt Hegel's conclusions rather than his philosophical methodology, which is perhaps why they generally resisted the title "Hegelian."

Hegel is important not only for the positive influence that his ideas had on his followers, but also for the way in which resistance to his ideas

The nineteenth century also saw American philosophy come of age, with the birth of Pragmatism. The two major figures associated with the school, **C. S. Peirce** and **William James**, were responsible for the first genuinely distinctive school of American philosophy—a school that many would say held up a mirror to the national character of the United States at the time.

THE FRAGMENTATION OF PHILOSOPHY

This era was the last fling of the system builders—philosophers such as **Spinoza**, **Leibniz**, and **Kant**, who attempted to produce the philosophical

1842   1844   1846   1848

molded thinkers such as Schopenhauer and **Søren Kierkegaard**. Between these two extremes lay thinkers who adopted some of Hegel's approach, but who rejected either his idealism (Marx being an important example) or some of his methodological principles.

A barricade in the Place Vendome, Paris, March 1871. The Paris Commune lasted only two months, but it was the first successful workers' revolution.

equivalent of the scientist's Theory of Everything. Hegel and his followers were opposed not simply by those who disagreed with their conclusions or found flaws in their methods but by philosophers who rejected the systematic approach as either inherently misleading or simply not possible. Philosophy, as with human knowledge systems in general, had become too large to be grasped and unified by a single person; this was the beginning of the full-scale fragmentation of philosophy, which led to more and more specialization during the twentieth century.

GEORG WILHELM FRIEDRICH HEGEL

BORN	1770, Stuttgart	DIED	1831, Berlin

MAIN INTERESTS   Philosophy of history, metaphysics, logic, ethics, politics

INFLUENCES   Parmenides, Plato, Aristotle, Spinoza, Montesquieu, Rousseau

INFLUENCED   Marx, Bradley, Dewey, Sartre, Iqbāl, Radhakrishnan, Singer

MAJOR WORKS
The Phenomenology of Spirit, The Philosophy of Right, The Science of Logic

Hegel held the highest religion to be Christianity, because he claimed that the story of the incarnation symbolizes the manifestation of the infinite Absolute in the finite world.

As the essence of Matter is Gravity, so, on the other hand, we may affirm that the substance, the essence of Mind is Freedom [...]

Reason in History, p.22

Hegel was the eldest of three children, his father a civil servant. After secondary school in Stuttgart (and tutoring in Latin by his mother, who died when he was thirteen), he entered a seminary. Although he studied successfully he wasn't suited to theology, but developed a great interest in philosophy. Despite gaining both his doctorate and his certificate of theology, therefore, he didn't become a minister, but took a job as a private tutor in Berne, hoping to continue his philosophical studies. Hegel was lucky in finding a family that provided him with stimulating discussions, introductions to Bernese intellectual society, and the use of a good library.

From Berne Hegel moved to Frankfurt, still as a private tutor, and then continued his studies at the University of Jena, where he went on to teach logic and metaphysics. In 1806, French troops occupied Jena, forcing Hegel to leave; unable to find an academic job, he took up journalism, then school teaching. Finally he was offered a chair in philosophy at the University of Heidelberg, and from there he went on to teach in Berlin, where he died at the age of sixty-one.

Hegel can be dificult to read. He developed a metaphysical system upon which the rest of his thought depended, so understanding one part of his writings demands that one has grasped the system as a whole. Nevertheless, he had a huge effect on subsequent philosophy, especially in mainland Europe.

In a nutshell:
Reality develops by means of the reconciling (synthesis) of contradictions (between thesis and anti-thesis).

METAPHYSICS AND EPISTEMOLOGY
At the root of Hegel's thought is his account of truth and knowledge, which is bound up with his acceptance, and adaptation, of **Kant's** account of the world and our knowledge of it. Hegel agreed that our experience and knowledge of things in the world is the product of consciousness and, as it obviously can't be the product of the *individual's* consciousness (we don't each create our own world), so the truth about the world must arise out of our *shared* consciousness—out of the whole of human experience, thought, and language. However, there's an interplay between us and the world; while our thought is largely responsible for the creation of truth, there is an important role for the nature of the world, which helps to form our thought.

This also reflects a view that was typical of nineteenth-century Europe—an essential optimism concerning the world and human beings. For Hegel, human history is a process of progress towards freedom. Human thought demands an understanding of earlier thinkers, for without that we can't

For Hegel, the French Revolution symbolized the march toward freedom. It was the principle of the freedom of the will, asserting itself against existing cirmcumstance.

proceed, can't reach understanding of human beings and our place in the world.

HISTORY AND POLITICS

Hegel's account of freedom is grounded in the work of writers such as **Descartes**, **Rousseau**, and **Kant**; he follows them in distinguishing mere absence of external coercion or interference (which is not only the lesser kind of freedom, but is often illusory) from rational thought and choice—a freedom that's achievable by all human beings. In a truly free society we would recognize that our fellow citizens are not an external constraint on our freedom; once we've understood our true nature, we see that our social duties and our self-interest come together (compare Rousseau's account of the ideal state, and the general Will). It's not a simple matter of individuals making choices to come together into society though; for Hegel, it's only through social interaction, through action and choice, that we come to be genuine individuals, true human beings. That is, society comes before the development of individuals, so can't be the result of individual choices.

MASTER AND SLAVE

In a famous section in *The Phenomenology of Spirit* Hegel discusses a social relationship that he characterizes in terms of a master and slave, and that involves a dominance struggle as a result of which one party enslaves the other. The slave does the work while the master enjoys his leisure; thus, the slave is productive, while the master slips into passivity and mere consumption of the slave's produce. Neither party can have any respect for the other, for they are locked into incommensurate mind-sets. However, the active slave inevitably gains a self-consciousness that makes him more powerful than his passive, degenerate master, and the former enslaves the latter, setting the pattern going again. This will continue until the process is resolved—when they come to gain mutual respect, seeing each other as ends rather than as means.

Neither the master nor the slave can be free until they have respect for each other.

This pattern is to be found not only in social structures but in the very structure of reality, or the Absolute. As the Absolute goes through the dialectical process, its development is manifested in Nature (the Absolute manifesting itself in matter) and in human minds and history (the Absolute manifesting itself in consciousness). Hegel traces this latter development from the simplest consciousness of objects, through self-consciousness and rational consciousness, to ethical and religious consciousness, and finally to *absolute knowledge*, in which the subject recognizes itself as identical with the Absolute.

Like most intellectuals of the time, Hegel underwent an unpleasant period of disillusion as the new régime in France turned to the violent and brutal Reign of Terror, though he was unusual in clinging to his revolutionary principles.

JOHN STUART MILL

BORN 1806, London	DIED 1873, Avignon

MAIN INTERESTS   Ethics, politics, logic, science, metaphysics

INFLUENCES   Aristotle, Hobbes, Hume, Bentham, James Mill, Wollstonecraft

INFLUENCED   James, Frege, Russell, Popper, Ayre, Hare, Rawls, Kripke, Singer

MAJOR WORKS
Principles of Political Economy, System of Logic, On Liberty, Utilitarianism

I have been toiling through Stirling's Secret of Hegel. It is right to learn what Hegel is and one learns it only too well from Stirling's book. I say too well because I found by actual experience of Hegel that conversancy with him tends to deprave one's intellect.

Letter to Alexander Bain

J. S. Mill's childhood is famous (some might say infamous) for the extent and precociousness of his early education; his father, the Scottish philosopher and economist James Mill, started him on ancient Greek at the age of three, Hume and Gibbon by six, and Latin and Plato's dialogues at eight, and he studied a wide range of other subjects, including mathematics and chemistry. Perhaps unsurprisingly, he had some sort of nervous breakdown at the age of twenty; his recovery involved a move away from the kind of Utilitarian ethical, political, and economic theory espoused by Bentham and his father, which he had hitherto accepted, toward a more human and realistic version of Utilitarianism (a move often missed or ignored by his critics).

Mill worked for the East India Company, first in his father's office, and finally reaching the post of chief of the examiner's office. When the government took over responsibility for India in 1858, Mill retired and went to live near Avignon. In 1865 he was elected to the House of Commons (as MP for Westminster), but returned to France in 1868 after failing to be reelected. He died there in 1873.

Two crucial parts of Mill's life affected and were affected by his philosophical thinking: his passionate concern for social justice, and particularly the welfare of the working class, and his equally passionate love for Harriet Taylor. The former involved arguments and campaigns for compulsory education for all,

Note:
The explanandum *(pl.* explananda*) is what needs to be explained, the* explanans *(pl.* explanantia*) is what does the explaining.*

women's rights, nationalization of natural resources, and birth control. The latter was complicated by Harriet Taylor being a married woman, though when her husband died in 1849, the couple were able to marry.

Mill is one of the most misrepresented and under-appreciated philosophers in the Western tradition. Not only is his important work in the fields of logic, epistemology, and metaphysics largely ignored, but even his ethical and political theories tend to be represented in terms of crude formulations of Utilitarianism, some of which (such as "the greatest happiness of the greatest number") he explicitly rejected.

SYSTEM OF LOGIC (1843)
This six-book work is astonishing for its breadth and rigor; it goes well beyond what might be expected from its title, covering such areas as epistemology, metaphysics, and social science. In it Mill makes distinctions (such as that between the connotation and denotation of a term), constructs and defends theories (such as the Covering Law model of scientific explanation), and

Mill was in favor of equality for women and campaigned for their voting rights. In this cartoon, Mills' logic; or Franchise for Females (Punch 1867), Mill makes a path for a group of women of varying social classes. The women are taller than the men and some look bitter and unattractive. The image shows that his views on equality for women were not held by everyone.

develops concepts (such as that of causation) that had a huge influence on nineteenth- and early twentieth-century philosophers.

The denotation of a term such as "book" is what it refers to—everything that can be called a book; the connotation is the sense of the term—what it is that justifies us in calling something a book (having pages on which words or images can be printed, written, or drawn, bound along one edge, and so on). Proper names such as "Peter J. King" have only denotation, whereas words such as "unicorn" seem to have only connotation. (Compare **Gottlob Frege**'s distinction between *Sinn* and *Bedeutung*.)

Mill's analysis of scientific explanation is best known via Carl Hempel's (1905–1997) version of it, known as the Covering Law Model. Briefly, a scientific explanation consists of a logical relation between a set of initial conditions—$c1$ to cn—plus a set of covering laws—$L1$ to Ln (which together form the *explanans*) and the *explanandum*, e. A good explanation takes the form of a sound argument:

$L1, L2, L3 \dots Ln$
$c1, c2, c3 \dots cn$
therefore e

Exactly the same model also gives us prediction, so that if we know the laws and the initial conditions, we can predict e.

Mill's account of causation involves taking **Hume's** basic approach and extending it, providing an account that is both less sophisticated than Hume's in its denial that causation is anything more than regular succession, and more sophisticated than Hume's in acknowledging the complexity of causation.

UTILITARIANISM

Mill's ethical and political views, though influenced by various radical theories of the time, including early socialism, were Utilitarian at heart. Utilitarianism is a consequentialist theory; it holds that the morality of an action is a matter simply of its consequences. For Utilitarians, what's important is the utility of an action (that is, the amount of happiness, meaning pleasure and—especially important in the moral context—the absence of pain, produced). Mill rejected Bentham's *felicific calculus* and distinguished between qualities, not merely quantities, of happiness. It is important to note that Mill didn't argue that morality is concerned only with consequences; the morality of an *action* is determined by its consequences, but the morality of a *person* also concerns intentions and motives.

Mill's political theory centers on freedom; he argues that the only grounds for interfering with a person's freedom is to prevent harm to others, and this principle applies to governments as well as to individuals.

It is better to be a human being dissatisfied than a pig satisfied; better to be Socrates dissatisfied than a fool satisfied. And if the fool, or the pig, is of a different opinion, it is because they only know their own side of the question.

Utilitarianism

SØREN AABYE KIERKEGAARD

BORN 1813, Copenhagen		**DIED** 1855, Copenhagen	

MAIN INTERESTS   Religion, metaphysics, epistemology

INFLUENCES   Plato, Kant, Lessing

INFLUENCED   Jaspers, Wittgenstein, Heidegger, Sartre

MAJOR WORKS
The Concept of Irony, Concluding Unscientific Postscript, Either/Or, Fear and Trembling

It is subjectivity that Christianity is concerned with, and it is only in subjectivity that its truth exists, if it exists at all; objectively, Christianity has no existence.

Concluding unscientific Postscript, p.116

Kierkegaard was born into a prosperous Danish family, the youngest of seven children. His upbringing was strict and gloomy, his father, Michael, being burdened by a deep religious guilt and melancholy. Kierkegaard was to say that he had been born old.

He received a good classical education, and generally excelled, especially in Latin, though he seems to have had some difficulty with Danish composition (a weakness that it took him much of his life to overcome). He attended the University of Copenhagen, where he studied theology, philosophy, and literature. After a shaky start, which saw him running up bills and neglecting his studies, his father died, and he resumed his work and finished his degree. He had planned to become a Lutheran pastor, but before he enrolled at a seminary two things happened.

The first was his engagement to Regina Olsen in 1840; the second was the hardening of his resolve to become a writer (a career with which he'd toyed for some years). Writing, however, wouldn't be able to support him and a wife, even with his inheritance; this, together with a mysterious secret that Kierkegaard felt obliged yet unable to tell Regina, caused him to break off their engagement in 1841. This brief passage in his life assumed a disproportionate significance for him, and he constantly returned to it in his writings.

In a nutshell:
People are limited and fallible, and only through recognition of this fact can we hope to develop understanding and to avoid despair.

Kierkegaard's literary career was somewhat fitful, taking some considerable time to take off. Philosophically, he was driven in part by a rejection of Hegelian philosophy, which had become extremely fashionable in Denmark. This was only part of his more general rejection of systematic philosophy, which, he claimed, constitutes an escape from freedom and responsibility into determinism and necessity. His own philosophical output was indeed the very opposite of systematic, not least in that he published under a variety of pseudonyms, often using one pseudonym to attack his own writings under another.

As he established himself as a writer, Kierkegaard became embroiled in more and more controversy, criticizing other writers, the Lutheran Church, and contemporary society in general. Perhaps partly as a result of this constant warfare, as well as of the stress of his heavy schedule of writing, his health suffered, and he collapsed and died at the age of forty-two.

ESTHETIC	ETHICAL	RELIGIOUS
PLEASURE SEEKING	DUTY AND OBLIGATION	SUBMISSION TO GOD
↓	↓	↓
Failure and despair	Loss of autonomy and moral responsibility	True freedom

THE THREE SPHERES OF EXISTENCE

In *Either/Or* (1843), *The Concept of Dread* (1844), *Stages on Life's Way* (1845), and *Fear and Trembling* (1846), Kierkegaard developed an account of human life based upon three spheres of existence between which we have to choose: the esthetic, the ethical, and the religious. Choosing the esthetic sphere lets us in for a hedonistic life of pleasure seeking, for a constant striving for novelty. This choice is motivated by the dread of boredom, and is a flight from despair, but it's doomed to failure—eventually we will fall prey to despair and melancholy. Choosing the ethical sphere lets us in for a life of submission to duty and obligation.

At first Kierkegaard held this to be the right choice, but eventually he recognized that in this submission lies a loss of autonomy, and thus of genuine moral responsibility. He thus developed the notion of the third sphere, which has given us the phrase "leap of faith"; this is the genuinely religious sphere, which involves a submission to god that is somehow consistent with, even necessary for, true freedom. This sphere is beyond rationality, and is typified for Kierkegaard by the story of Abraham and Isaac in the Judeo-Christian Bible.

ABRAHAM AND ISAAC

When god commands Abraham to kill his son Isaac, Kierkegaard points out, unlike the case, for example, of Agamemnon and his daughter Iphigeneia, the action is completely outside common morality. In choosing to obey the command, Abraham neither understands it nor is able to justify his decision except in terms of surrender to god's will. This leap of faith involves what Kierkegaard calls "the suspension of the ethical." It's this leap of faith that is the only way into the religious sphere of existence; there are no rational grounds for religious belief—only the flight from despair and dread.

Kierkegaard's emphasis on the individual's existence, and the need to examine this, led him to refer to his thought as "existential," and paved the way for later existentialist writers.

Kierkegaard envisaged three spheres of existence, each with its consequences. Choosing the religious existence was the only way to attain happiness.

Kierkegaard uses the example of Abraham and Isaac to illustrate how the individual can make a leap of faith, beyond rationality, into the religious sphere of existence. Abraham accepts god's command, surrendering himself to god's will, and in doing so he attains true freedom.

KARL HEINRICH MARX

BORN 1818, Trier (Treves)	**DIED** 1883, London

MAIN INTERESTS   Politics, economics

INFLUENCES   Hobbes, Adam Smith, David Ricardo, James Mill, Hegel, Engels

INFLUENCED   Lenin, Trotsky, Adorno, Gramsci, Singer

MAJOR WORKS
*Communist Manifesto,
Capital,
Grundrisse*

Capitalism centers upon the bourgeoisie and the proletariat. The bourgeoisie (capitalists) own capital, and the proletariat own labor power. Marx contends that the dynamic is exploitative and contradictory, with the interests of the two directly opposed. This contradictory relationship has class conflict within it and class conflict will result in historical change.

Born in the Prussian city of Trier to a middle-class Jewish family (his father, a lawyer, had converted to Christianity for professional reasons), Karl Marx was educated first at the University of Bonn (where he read law, but spent much of his time in beer halls), and then at the University of Berlin, It was at this point that he discovered an interest in philosophy, joining the Young Hegelians. This was a group of thinkers, including theologians and philosophers, who combined an acceptance of secularized versions of **Hegel's** theories with the belief that society (and especially Prussian society) was as yet imperfect. They criticized the church and the Prussian government, and in 1840 Marx found it wise to submit his doctoral thesis (on the ancient Greek atomists) not to the University of Berlin, but to the University of Jena.

In a nutshell:

We're not passively acted upon by the world, but are controllers of it—and we should do so in such a way as to free ourselves and our fellow human beings.

His radical political views made an academic career impossible, however, and Marx went into journalism, becoming the editor of the liberal newspaper the *Rheinische Zeitung*. When the Prussian government closed down the paper, Marx went to live in Paris, where he resumed his philosophical thinking and writing, as well as working as a freelance journalist. It was at this point that he met Friedrich Engels, who alerted Marx to the plight of the working classes, and who pointed him toward the study of economics. The two were to work and write together for the rest of Marx's life.

Political persecution and more dramatic upheavals saw Marx travel from France to Belgium, back to France, and finally to London, where he settled permanently, and where he became heavily involved in the International Working Men's Association (later known as the First International). This last period of his life saw the production of some of the most important of his writings, including *Das Kapital* (*Capital: A Critique of Political Economy*) in three volumes (and a

Marx was not a Marxist

The term "Marxist" is used to refer to those who made use of Marx's vocabulary and basic approach to history and society (and especially to capitalism), and should not be assumed always to accord with what Marx himself actually wrote. Indeed, Marx himself said that he wasn't a Marxist.

Marx and Engels enjoyed a close friendship for over forty years. Engels' industrial interests in the north of England even helped finance Marx and his family, who lived in poverty in London for several years.

projected fourth), the first volume published in 1867, the second two volumes edited by Engels and published posthumously in 1885 and 1894, and the notes for the fourth volume edited by Karl Johann Kautsky and published as *Theories of Surplus Value*, itself in four volumes, from 1905 to 1910.

Marx's health declined badly during the last ten years of his life, and despite his travels to various spas around Europe (he even went to North Africa at one point), it continued to worsen. The deaths of his wife and eldest daughter served to weaken him further; he died in 1883 and was buried in Highgate Cemetery, North London.

Marx's writings are largely concerned with economics, history, and politics. His main philosophical importance lies in the way his theories were developed and used by later political philosophers (his most interesting philosophical work is to be found in the *Grundrisse*, published posthumously in 1941). At the heart of Marx's thought was an acceptance of Hegel's dialectical account of history, together with a rejection of his idealism in favor of materialism.

HUMAN NATURE

Human nature, apart from its fundamental ability and desire to transform the world (labor), depends upon social and economic conditions, and these change over time; human beings, however, have control of these conditions. One of the main elements that needs to be changed is private property, which serves to divide the classes and alienate human beings from their labor, their fundamental power to transform their environment, from their human essence. People become means rather than ends, and by getting rid of private property this is reversed, so that class divisions are dissolved and human beings gain their freedom.

HISTORICAL MATERIALISM

The economic and social conditions are the result of productive forces, and these change through history as human beings gain understanding of and control of their environment. The various social forms, or production relations—such as feudalism, capitalism, socialism, and communism—replace each other in an inevitable pattern. This is the result of irresolvable tension and thus conflict between the productive forces and the production relations, which results in class warfare and revolution: "The history of all hitherto existing society is the history of class struggles" (*Communist Manifesto*, *Marx Engels Werke* 1:88).

The philosophers have only interpreted the world in different ways; the point is to change it.

"Theses on Feuerbach,"
Marx Engels Werke 3:7

From each according to his abilities, to each according to his needs.

"Critique of the Gotha Programme,"
Marx Engels Werke 19:21

THE HON. VICTORIA, LADY WELBY-GREGORY

BORN 1837	DIED 1912

MAIN INTERESTS Language, philosophical logic

INFLUENCES Darwin, Bergson, Schiller, Peirce

INFLUENCED Peirce, Ogden

MAJOR WORKS
Time As Derivative, What Is Meaning?, Significs and Language

[...] every one of us is in one sense a born explorer: our only choice is what world we will explore, our only doubt whether our exploration will be worth the trouble.
[...] And the idlest of us wonders: the stupidest of us stares: the most ignorant of us feels curiosity: while the thief actively explores his neighbour's pocket or breaks into the "world" of his neighbour's house and plate-closet.

"Sense, meaning, and interpretation (I)," Mind N.S. V, 1898

Born to the Hon. Charles and Lady Emmeline Stuart-Wortley, relatively little is known of Welby's early life. She spent much of her time traveling the world and was in Beirut at the time of her parents' death. She also wrote poetry and plays. Her varied activities included founding the Sociological Society of Great Britain and the Royal School of Art Needlework.

In 1863 she married politician Sir William Welby-Gregory, and went to live at Denton Manor in Lincolnshire. Though having little formal education, she mixed and corresponded with prominent thinkers, and educated herself through them. By the late nineteenth century she was publishing papers on meaning in the leading academic journals *Mind* and *The Monist*, and in 1903 she published her book *What Is Meaning?*, followed in 1911 by *Significs and Language*. Also in 1911 she wrote a long article for the *Encyclopedia Britannica* on "significs," the name she'd given to her theory of meaning. She also published papers and a book (*Time As Derivative*) (1907) on the reality of time.

C. S. Peirce reviewed *What Is Meaning?* for *The Nation*, and a six-year correspondence ensued, published as *Semiotics and Significs* (1977). The two philosophers had much in common, both in their approach to the subject and their theories. She had already started a similar correspondence with C. K. Ogden, whose work on meaning was deeply affected by her theories.

Note:
Lady Welby was the goddaughter of Queen Victoria, and served as her Maid of Honor.

Welby's interest in meaning flowed from her original concern with theology, and the interpretation of the Christian scriptures, as brought out in her first book, *Links and Clues* (1881). This developed into a more general worry about the nature of sense in language, including (perhaps especially) the everyday use of language. Much of her work consisted of the development of distinctions between different kinds of sense, and the various relationships between them and ethical, esthetic, pragmatic, and social values. She coined the word "significs" (she'd originally used "sensifics") for her approach; it had the advantage over terms such as "semiotics" and "semantics" of bearing no theoretical baggage, and of indicating the specific area of interest that existing studies had tended to ignore.

She divided sense into three main categories: "sense," "meaning," and "significance," which corresponded to three levels of consciousness, for which she used the astronomical terms "planetary," "solar," and "cosmic" respectively. She explained these distinctions in part by reference to a version of Darwinian evolutionary theory.

CHARLES SANDERS PEIRCE

| BORN | 1839, Cambridge, MA | DIED | 1914, Milford, PA |

MAIN INTERESTS   Metaphysics, logic, epistemology, mathematics, science

INFLUENCES   Duns Scotus, Reid, Hume, Kant, Bentham, Welby

INFLUENCED   Welby, William James, Royce, Dewey, Popper, Wiggins, Haack

MAJOR WORKS
*Studies in Logic,
Collected Papers*

*The opinion which is
fated to be ultimately
agreed to by all who
investigate is what we
mean by truth and the
object represented by this
opinion is the real.*

Collected Papers 5, §407

Peirce's early education was largely provided by his father, Benjamin Peirce, professor of astronomy and mathematics at Harvard. He went on to study chemistry at Harvard in 1855, graduating with a bachelor's degree and then, after a period working for the U.S. Coast and Geodetic Survey, a master's degree, and an Sc.B. in chemistry, despite all of which he managed to obtain only nontenured teaching posts. He gave occasional (badly attended) lectures on the philosophy of science at Harvard for a time while continuing to work for the Coastal Survey. This was very much the pattern of his life for some time: scientific and mathematical work, with part-time or occasional lecturing on philosophy. In 1887 a small inheritance allowed him to retire to Milford in Pennsylvania, where he lived with his second wife, writing in some obscurity (and in constant financial difficulty) until he died of cancer in 1914.

The key part of his life was the founding in Cambridge, in 1871, of the Metaphysical Club—a group of young men, including William James and Oliver Wendell Holmes Jr., who met to discuss philosophical issues. It was at meetings of this club that Pragmatism was born, attributed by James to Peirce, and by Peirce to the lawyer Nicholas St. John Green, another member.

PRAGMATISM

Pragmatism is essentially a theory of meaning and truth, though it is differently formulated by its various proponents; indeed, James' version was so different that Peirce wanted to call his theory "pragmaticism" to distinguish the two. At its heart, Peirce's view was that the meaning of a concept is the sum of its (practical) consequences: "Consider what effects, that might conceivably have practical bearings, we conceive the object of conception to have. Then our conception of these effects is the whole of our conception of the object" (*Collected Papers* 5, §402).

LOGIC

Peirce's logical writings are perhaps his most astonishing and original achievement, though they're fragmentary and scattered across a host of short papers (as with most of his philosophy). He made substantial contributions to quantification theory, propositional calculus, Boolean algebra, and three-valued logic, and is particularly well known for his application of the principles of Boolean algebra to the calculus of relations.

In their own words:
*It is [...] easy to be certain. One has only
to be sufficiently vague.*

Collected Papers 4, §237

WILLIAM JAMES

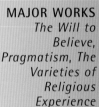

BORN 1842, New York	**DIED** 1910, Chocorua, NH

MAIN INTERESTS   Religion, metaphysics, epistemology, psychology

INFLUENCES   J.S. Mill, Peirce, Bergson

INFLUENCED   Husserl, Dewey, Russell, Wittgenstein, Quine, Putnam

MAJOR WORKS
The Will to Believe, Pragmatism, The Varieties of Religious Experience

Consciousness, then, does not appear to itself chopped up in bits. Such words as "chain" or "train" do not describe it fitly as it presents itself in the first instance. It is nothing jointed; it flows. A "river" or a "stream" are the metaphors by which it is most naturally described.

The Principles of Psychology I,
p.239

James was born to a wealthy and cosmopolitan New York family, and his early education, at home and at various private schools, was expensive, of varying quality, and frequently disrupted by his father's sudden changes of mind. When he was thirteen years old, the family moved to live in England and France for three years, before returning to the United States, where they settled for a year in Newport, Rhode Island, before returning to Europe, this time to Switzerland and Germany. James attended the Geneva Academy, later to become the University of Geneva, where he studied science and mathematics. Again, he stayed only a year before his father took the family back to Newport.

At nineteen he followed his father's wishes by giving up his desire to become an artist and enrolling at Harvard to study medicine. In that same year the Civil War broke out. Two of his brothers enlisted, but he and his brother Henry (who was to become a renowned novelist) were exempt on health grounds. In his second year he took the opportunity to travel to Brazil on an expedition with the naturalist Louis Agassiz, but suffered from appalling homesickness, as well as a mild case of smallpox. Once back at his studies in Harvard, his poor health continued, including depression, and in 1867 he went to France, Germany, and Switzerland for two years. This was primarily for his health, but he also studied physiology, philosophy, and the new psychology.

In a nutshell:
Truth is whatever's useful in thought; morality is whatever's useful in action.

He returned to Harvard, and in 1869 qualified as a doctor, though he never practiced. His depression continued, partly as a result of his lack of any clear direction. Then, in 1872, the president of Harvard, a family friend, offered him a job teaching physiology, which he accepted. Though the first year exhausted him, necessitating another trip abroad, this time mainly in Italy, he continued to teach at Harvard for thirty-five years, rapidly moving from physiology to psychology, and later philosophy. He was, in fact, the first person to teach psychology in the United States. He stayed at Harvard, though occasionally lecturing elsewhere (including Edinburgh and Oxford), until 1907. He died in 1910 with an enlarged heart, after some years of heart trouble.

PRAGMATISM
Though James was, with **Peirce**, the co-founder of Pragmatism, and did more to popularize it as an alternative to Hegelian absolute idealism, his account of it is not as clear as that of Peirce. Indeed, he sometimes exaggerated his position to the point that he brought the pragmatist view into disrepute (as when he claimed that truth and moral

Test every concept by the question "What sensible difference to anybody will its truth make?" and you are in the best possible position for understanding what it means and for discussing its importance.

Pragmatism: A New Way for Some Old Ways of Thinking, *p.60*

For James, the emotion of happiness would be caused by behaviors such as smiling, rather than happiness being the cause of smiling.

rightness were merely whatever was expedient), and Peirce disassociated himself from James' position.

Unlike Peirce, James was particularly concerned to make room for religion in his scheme, and adopted a voluntarist position in the tradition of Pascal and **Kierkegaard**; that is, he argued that though there are no rational grounds for religious belief, there are grounds for wanting to believe. To this he added his version of Pragmatism, arguing that religion is desirable (and true) in that it "works" in some sense. Similarly, scientific theories are to be seen as instruments, their value gauged in terms of their usefulness to us.

PASCAL'S WAGER

Blaise Pascal (1623–1662) argued that if one accepted religious belief, the worst that one risked was being wrong, and so giving up a lifetime of worldly pleasures for no return, whereas the most that one might gain was an eternity of bliss; if, however, one rejected religious belief, the most that one might gain was a lifetime of worldly pleasure, whereas the worst that one risked was an eternity of torment. It thus makes more sense to bet on belief. James argued against the wager in his paper "The Will to Believe."

THE MIND

James' account of mind and body is a form of dual-aspect theory that **Bertrand Russell** later called *neutral monism*. He argues that the mental and physical are in fact different aspects of a single underlying stuff, which he misleadingly calls *pure experience*—misleadingly because in itself it's no more mental than it is physical.

The most distinctive part of James' account of the mental (though independently arrived at by the Danish physiologist Carl Lange, and thus known as the James-Lange theory) is his claim that the subjective feelings associated with emotions are caused by, rather than causing, the relevant physical behavior. That is: "we feel sorry because we cry, angry because we strike, afraid because we tremble" (*The Principles of Psychology* II, p.449).

FRIEDRICH WILHELM NIETZSCHE

BORN 1844, Röcken bei Lützen	**DIED** 1900, Weimar

MAIN INTERESTS   Ethics, metaphysics, epistemology, esthetics, language

INFLUENCES   Machiavelli, Schopenhauer

INFLUENCED   Jaspers, Iqbāl, Heidegger, Sartre

MAJOR WORKS
The Birth of Tragedy,
Thus Spoke Zarathustra,
Beyond Good and Evil,
On the Genealogy of Morals,
Ecce Homo,
The Will to Power

Whatever has value in our world now does not have value in itself, according to its nature—nature is always value-less, but has been given value at some time, as a present—and it was we who gave and bestowed it.

The Gay Science §302

Nietzsche was born in the small Prussian town of Röcken bei Lützen; his father, a Lutheran minister, died when Nietzsche was four, and the family moved to nearby Naumburg an der Saale, where they lived for some years. After secondary education at a good boarding school, he went to the University of Bonn to study theology and philology, the latter being his greater interest. From there he moved to the University of Leipzig, where he discovered the work of Schopenhauer, as well as Kantian-derived critiques of materialist metaphysics.

A riding accident in 1867 disqualified him for military service, and he returned to the University of Leipzig, where he was befriended by Richard Wagner, a friendship that was to have a deep effect on Nietzsche. About this time another friend and teacher recommended Nietzsche to the University of Basel, and in 1869 he took up a position in classical philology. He stayed at Basel for ten years, until failing health—aggravated in diphtheria and dysentery he'd suffered while serving in a field hospital during the Franco-Prussian war—forced him to resign his position.

For ten years he led a nomadic life, made rootless by his having neither renounced his German citizenship nor taken Swiss naturalization. He wandered from country to country, staying in various Swiss, German, French, and Italian towns for a few months

In their own words:
Art makes the sight of life bearable by laying over it the veil of unclear thinking.

Human, All Too Human §151

at a time, though returning regularly to his mother's house in Naumburg. In 1889, in Turin, he collapsed and suffered a mental breakdown (the exact nature and cause of which is unknown). He never recovered, and had spells in clinics and nursing homes, then returned to his mother in Naumburg; when she died in 1897, his sister took him to live in Weimar, where he later died. As executor of his estate, she had sole access to his work, which she distorted to fit her anti-Semitic views, thereby ingratiating herself with Hitler and the Nazi Party.

The doctrine for which Nietzsche is perhaps best known is his rejection of what he called *slave morality*—that is, traditional morality, which he saw as rooted in Christianity, and which he characterized as having been created by the weak mob, whose interests were served by such values as pity, humility, and friendliness. The *Übermensch* ("overman" or "superman") is the strong, creative individual who rises above the slave morality to create new values and to forge new meaning out of the paradox and confusion of the world.

FRANCIS HERBERT **BRADLEY**

BORN 1846, Clapham	**DIED** 1924, Oxford

MAIN INTERESTS History, ethics, metaphysics, logic

INFLUENCES Kant, Hegel, Green

INFLUENCED Collingwood, Russell

MAJOR WORKS
*Ethical Studies,
Principles of
Logic, Appearance
and Reality*

> *In short, the irrational connexion, which the Free-will doctrine fled from in the shape of external necessity, has succeeded only in reasserting in the shape of chance.*
>
> Ethical Studies, p.12

Born in Clapham (then a village in Surrey, now part of London), the son of an Evangelist preacher, Bradley was educated first at Cheltenham College, then at Marlborough, and finally at University College, Oxford, where he read Greats (Classics). In 1870 he was elected to a research fellowship at Merton College, Oxford, where he remained until his death. He was in his day extremely highly regarded, both in the academic world and on the public stage; aside from a long list of honorary degrees and fellowships, he became (three days before his death) the first philosopher to be awarded the Order of Merit.

This high regard didn't last long after his death, partly because he was attacked and misrepresented by philosophers such as G. E. Moore, **Russell**, and **Ayer** (something of an irony, in that his reputation had itself been built in part on similar attacks upon and misrepresentations of **J. S. Mill**).

Bradley was the most prominent of the British Hegelians, a group of philosophers mostly based in Oxford, and including T. H. Green (1836–1882), Bernard Bosanquet (1848–1923), J. McTaggart (1866–1925), and R. G. Collingwood (1889–1943). Though they were heavily influenced by Hegel, their views, and methodologies, were filtered through a variety of other philosophical approaches, especially that of Kant, and they tended to downplay their Hegelianism.

ABSOLUTE (*OR* OBJECTIVE) IDEALISM

Though Bradley avoided or even denied the labels "Hegelian" and "idealist," he clearly falls into both categories. For him, the Absolute—which is to say reality, the totality of existence—transcends our normal understanding and experience of the world, and in particular the categories and relations into which we try to force our understanding, including not only space, time, and cause, but all properties and things. The Absolute is thus a unity—though it's not clear what we're to make of something that contains no relations or differences. Bradley differs from Hegel in offering a nonreligious, if not atheist, account of the Absolute.

In their own words:
The way of taking the world which I have found most tenable is to regard it as a single Experience, superior to relations and containing in the fullest sense everything which is.

Appearance and Reality, p.245

FRIEDRICH LUDWIG GOTTLOB FREGE

BORN	1848, Wismar	DIED	1925, Bad Kleinen, Germany

MAIN INTERESTS Logic, mathematics, language

INFLUENCES Leibniz, J. S. Mill, Lotze

INFLUENCED Husserl, Russell, Wittgenstein, Carnap, Anscombe, Wiggins

*Your discovery of the
contradiction caused me
the greatest surprise
and, I would almost say,
consternation, since it
has shaken the basis on
which I intended to
build arithmetic[...]. It is
all the more serious
since, with the loss of
my rule V, not only the
foundations of my
arithmetic, but also
the sole possible
foundations of
arithmetic, seem
to vanish.*

Letter to Bertrand Russell, in
From Frege to Gödel, ed. J. van
Heijenoort, p.127

Frege's parents taught the girls' school founded by his father. Frege himself attended the local gymnasium, before going on to the University of Jena, where he studied chemistry, philosophy, and mathematics. His father died in 1866, and his mother took over the running of their school, and continued to support Frege financially. After two years at Jena he transferred to the University of Göttingen, where he continued to study mathematics and chemistry, as well as taking courses in physics and the philosophy of religion. He gained his doctorate in 1873, with a thesis on the foundations of geometry.

The following year he was appointed to a lectureship at the University of Jena, and remained there until he retired in 1917. The first five years of his time there was unsalaried (as a *Privatdozent*), and he had to be supported by his mother, who died in 1878. Despite a heavy teaching load, he managed to produce his first important work, *Begriffsschrift, eine der arithmetischen nachgebildete Formelsprache des reinen Denkens* (1879; translated into English as *Conceptual Notation*).

Many of Frege's admirers are disturbed by various facets of his personality, not least by a distasteful bigotry that extended to foreigners in general (and the French in particular), Catholics, and Jews. This is clear from his diaries, though it's not so clear that it made itself known to any great extent in

In a nutshell:

Ambiguity and vagueness may be fine for poetry, but language that deals with truth—and especially the language of science—should be precise and clear.

his behavior; he was quiet and reserved, mixing little with his colleagues.

On his retirement from the University of Jena he moved to Bad Kleinen, where he continued to write until his death. Although he was relatively unknown during his lifetime, he was convinced that his work would eventually gain recognition, and he left his papers to his adopted son, writing: "I believe there are things here which will one day be prized much more highly than they are now. Take care that nothing gets lost." He was right, though unfortunately much of his unpublished work—kept at the University of Münster—was lost when the building was destroyed by Allied bombs during World War II.

LOGICISM AND LOGIC

Frege believed that mathematics, and especially number theory, was part of logic— a view known as *logicism*. On this view, mathematical truths can be deduced from logical axioms. Despite some brilliant and groundbreaking work by Frege, followed by

Frege spent his working life in the mathematics department at the University of Jena. His work, reconceiving the disciplines of logic and language, had a profound influence on twentieth-century philosophy, but was largely ignored until Bertrand Russell came into contact with it.

Bertrand Russell, the best that could be achieved was a reduction of number theory to set theory—but set theory isn't part of logic. Nevertheless, Frege's work in this area gave rise to some important results, though it also led to one of his most important setbacks.

He'd planned to publish the development of his logicist program in *Die Grundgesetze der Arithmetik* (The Foundations of Arithmetic), of which the first volume appeared in 1893, but in 1902—when the second volume was at the printers—Frege received a letter from Russell pointing out that the axiomatic system presented in the first volume was faulty: it could be made to produce a contradiction. Frege included an appendix in the second volume in which he explained the problem and modified one of the axioms, but this meant that some of his theorems could no longer be derived. Despite this setback, which caused him no little distress, Frege's work was of tremendous importance to the philosophy of mathematics and mathematical logic, and its effects can be seen in the work of many mathematicians, perhaps most clearly in Russell and Whitehead's *Principia Mathematica* (3 vols, 1910–1913).

Alhough logic hadn't been neglected in the previous two millennia—for much of the medieval period it was one of the main areas of philosophical interest—Frege was responsible for the first major new approach to the discipline since Aristotle. Alhough the notation that he developed was cumbersome, and is no longer used, modern logic has its origins in Frege's work. In particular he's responsible for the predicate calculus, and for the introduction of quantifiers.

MEANING

Frege's approach to logic was in part informed by his desire to develop a language suitable for the sciences—a language free of ambiguity, vagueness, and all imprecision. Probably his best-known contribution to the philosophy of language is his analysis of meaning into two components: sense (*Sinn*) and reference (*Bedeutung*)—a distinction that is still at the center of modern notions of meaning. The reference of a term is what it picks out, so the reference of "Hesperus" is the planet Venus; the sense of the term is *how* it picks out the reference, how it presents it to the thinker, so the sense of "Hesperus" involves the fact that Venus is thought of as a bright star seen in the evening. This explains why "Hesperus" and "Phosphorus" have different meanings, even though they refer to the same thing, for "Phosphorus" picks out Venus as thought of as a bright star seen in the morning. This isn't a subjective matter; the sense isn't how a particular individual thinks of the reference, but how the linguistic community does so. I might always think of Phosphorus with a shudder, because I connect it with early rising, but that's no part of its *sense*.

The planet Venus is a good example of Frege's idea of two components of meaning in language—sense and reference. Hesperus and Phosphorus refer to one thing—the planet Venus, but they have different meanings. Hesperus makes sense of Venus as a bright evening star whereas Phosphorus makes sense of Venus as a bright morning star.

A proper name (word, sign, sign combination, expression) expresses its sense, stands for or designates its reference. By means of a sign we express its sense and designate its reference.

"On Sense and Reference," in A. W. Moore (ed.) **Meaning and Reference**, p.27

With the twentieth century, the choice of which philosophers to include becomes particularly difficult. As David Hume argued with regard to esthetic judgments, the key factor is the passing of time. Many philosophers, considered to be preeminent in their own lifetimes, are no longer rated very highly, and doubtless history will make the same judgment of some of my choices here.

Moreover, the division of Western philosophy into different traditions—the Anglo-American and the

1859

1859

1872

1889

Continental—has become more firmly established during the last century or so, and though there have been some "crossover stars," it's fair to say that most of those writing in one tradition will have little effect on (and will be little affected by) those writing in the other.

The situation isn't helped by the explosion of philosophical publications, in terms both of books and, more significantly, journals. Academics have to publish to gain and retain jobs, so that where a century ago philosophers published only when they

1902

1905

1901	Queen Victoria dies
1902	End of Boer War
1903	Wright brothers make first flight at Kitty Hawk. Ford Motor Company founded
1904	Russo-Japanese war begins

TWENTIETH CENTURY
1900–2000

1905	Japanese destroy Russian fleet. End of Russo-Japanese war. Separation of Norway from Sweden
1906	Russian general strike; first Duma established. San Francisco destroyed by earthquake and fire. First Labour Members of Parliament in the U.K. Ibsen dies
1909	Union of South Africa formed
1911	Chinese rebellion led by Sun Yat-sen
1912	China becomes republic. Sinking of *Titanic*. Outbreak of Balkan Wars
1913	Treaty of Bucharest; most of European Turkey ceded to Balkan states
1914	Archduke Ferdinand assassinated; outbreak of World War I. Battles of Mons and the Marne, first battle of Ypres
1916	Evacuation of Gallipoli completed. Battle of the Somme. Sinn Fein Easter Rising in Ireland
1917	Russian Revolution. U.S.A. declares war on Germany. Balfour Declaration recognizes Palestine as "national home" for Jews
1917	German kaiser abdicates; Armistice signed by Germans on November 11. British women householders, wives of householders, and university graduates aged above thirty given vote
1916	Paris Peace Conference; Peace Treaty signed at Versailles. Alcock and Brown fly Atlantic. Austrian Empire broken up
1920	First meeting of League of Nations. American women are given the right to vote. Oxford University admits women
1921	Greece invades Turkey. Irish Free State established
1922	Greeks defeated by Turks. Mussolini's Fascist March on Rome. Discovery of Tutankhamen's tomb

1923	Earthquake devastates Tokyo and Yokohama. Turkish Republic proclaimed
1924	Lenin dies. First Labour government in the U.K. Greek Republic declared
1926	British General Strike
1926	Lindbergh flies Atlantic solo
1928	Corinth destroyed by Greek earthquake. Voting age for women in the U.K. lowered to twenty-one
1929	Wall Street crash marks start of Great Depression
1930	Destruction of *R.101* airship
1933	Hindenburg appoints Hitler chancellor of Germany. Burning of Reichstag
1936	Start of Spanish Civil War. Accession and abdication of Edward VIII
1938	Germany annexes Austria. Munich Agreement
1939	Spanish Civil War ends. Hitler invades Poland; UK declares war on Germany
1945	Germany surrenders. United Nations established. US drops atomic bombs on Japan. Japan surrenders
1948	Gandhi assassinated. Nation of Israel proclaimed
1949	NATO established. Communist People's Republic of China proclaimed. South Africa institutionalizes apartheid
1961	Bay of Pigs invasion. East Germany erects the Berlin Wall
1969	Stonewall riot in New York City marks beginning of gay rights movement. Neil Armstrong and Edwin Aldrin walk on the Moon
1973	Vietnam War ends. Arab-Israeli conflict on Yom Kippur. OPEC hikes oil prices in retaliation for Western countries' involvement in Yom Kippur War
1989	Tiananmen Square rally for democracy. Mikhail S. Gorbachev named Soviet President. P. W. Botha quits as South Africa's President Deng Xiaoping resigns from China's leadership. Berlin Wall is open to West
1990	South Africa frees Nelson Mandela, Western Alliance ends Cold War. Germany reunited
1999	Nelson Mandela steps down. War erupts in Kosovo; NATO begins Operation Allied Force. East Timor votes for independence from Indonesia

thought their work was worth making public, now all that matters is that it appear in print. Needless to say, the result is a vast published mass of trivial, emptily technical, and downright shoddy work. It might seem that when one is swamped with quantity, quality would shine out, but unfortunately that isn't the case. Too often the worthwhile work gets lost in the crowd—at least temporarily.

LOGICAL POSITIVISM

The influence of Hegelianism was one of the defining elements of the early twentieth century, in that philosophers were rebelling against it. This

1910   1921

led to different movements on both sides of the divide, but none more extreme than logical positivism—an approach developed in Vienna during the 1920s and 1930s, but with roots that went back to the British Empiricists, especially Hume. This was an extremist empiricism that was self-contradictory, in that it couldn't meet its own central Verifiability Principle: *the meaning of a proposition is its method of verification.* This means that any proposition that can't, in principle, be empirically verified is meaningless. The positivists used this to attack such areas as theology, metaphysics, ethics, and esthetics, but the principle itself is clearly empirically unverifiable, and thus is meaningless (a surprising number of people still hold something like this principle; logical positivism has a peculiar attraction for those who need an excuse not to think about such matters or about ethics and metaphysics).

THE DECLINE OF METAPHYSICAL PHILOSOPHY

On the plus side, the logical positivists had the effect of focusing philosophers' attention on meaning; on the minus side, their attacks on metaphysics and ethics had a long-lasting effect

On the whole, though, the modern period has been a difficult time for philosophy. Both the Continental tradition and Anglo-American philosophy have seen various intellectual fashions come and go, with Continental becoming more wordy and less rigorous while Anglo-American philosophy has grown more arid, substituting technical expertise for genuine depth of thought. Some hold that bringing the two traditions together will revive philosophy's strength and importance, though at present it is difficult to see.

On a practical point: partway through this chapter, the reference to people influenced by the various

1937   1940   1941   1945

(though ethics recovered more quickly). It was no longer acceptable to talk about things, one had to talk about words, or even better, formal patterns of logic. This led to generations of philosophers whose sole aim seemed to be to make philosophy look as much like mathematics as possible, and whose technical cleverness was matched only by the tedium felt by their readers (though, to be fair, the same effect can be achieved without a symbol in sight). Toward the end of the twentieth century this was alleviated a little, and metaphysics began to be rehabilitated.

philosophers is dropped. Living philosophers, and even those who have died recently, form part of the current debate, rather than being clearly marked points in the past by which modern thinkers navigate.

EDMUND GUSTAV ALBERT HUSSERL

BORN	1859, Prostejov	DIED	1938, Freiburg

MAIN INTERESTS   Logic, mathematics, epistemology

INFLUENCES   Descartes, Hume, Fichte, Kant, Brentano, James, Frege

INFLUENCED   Heidegger, Sartre, Merleau-Ponty

MAJOR WORKS
*Logical
Investigations,
Cartesian
Meditations*

*Must not the only fruitful
[philosophical]
renaissance be the one
that reawakens the
impulse of the Cartesian
Meditations.*

Cartesian Meditations, p.5

*Tomáŝ Masaryk was Husserl's
mentor at Leipzig. A former
student of Franz Brentano, it
was Masaryk who suggested
Husserl move to Vienna to
study with Brentano.*

In a nutshell:
*The philosopher must attend to the
essences of things, by examining the
way in which we experience ourselves
and the world.*

Husserl was born in the Moravian town of Prostejov, at that time part of the Austrian Empire (and called Prossnitz), now in the Czech Republic. His family was Jewish, his father a clothing manufacturer who was sufficiently well off to send his son to school, first in Vienna, then closer to home in Olomouc. In 1876 he started his studies in mathematics, physics, and philosophy at the University of Leipzig, where he was taught by Tomáŝ Masaryk (later to be the first president of Czechoslovakia). After two years there he moved on to continue his studies for three years in Berlin before finally going to Vienna, where he completed his doctorate in mathematics in 1883.

After a brief spell teaching in Berlin, he returned to Vienna to study philosophy under Franz Brentano, and there followed a series of teaching posts at Halle (1886–1901), Göttingen (1901–1916), and finally a professorship at Freiburg, where he stayed from 1916 until his retirement in 1928. Each period was marked by philosophical work: at Halle he produced the first volume of his *Philosophy of Arithmetic* and the first two volumes of *Logical Investigations*, as well as finding time to get married; at Göttingen he wrote the first volume of *Ideas Pertaining to a Pure Phenomenology and to a Phenomenological Philosophy*. This period was disrupted by the outbreak of war, and by the death of his eldest son at Verdun.

At Freiburg he entered into the last phase of his professional life, writing among many other works *Cartesian Meditations* (a set of lectures that he gave in Paris in 1929), and the second of two books of *Ideas*. His work continued well after his retirement from teaching, but the last years of his life saw the rise of the Nazi party in Germany. He had experienced anti-Semitism at various stages of his life, in Prostejov and elsewhere, and both he and his wife had been baptized, but this was at a different level; he was professionally humiliated, denied the use of the library at the University of Freiburg, and saw his pupil and successor **Martin Heidegger** become an enthusiastic

Husserl retired from Freiburg in 1928, leaving Martin Heidegger, his former student, as his successor. The rise of Nazism destroyed their relationship, and when Hitler came to power in 1933, Husserl became a victim of anti-Semitism. He was excluded from the university and his work was banned.

collaborator in the Nazification process (Heidegger removed the dedication to Husserl from the 1941 edition of his book *Being and Time*). He died of pleurisy in 1938, his papers rescued by the Franciscan Herman Leo Van Breda, who took them to Belgium, where the first Husserl archive was founded the following year in Leuven.

Husserl's work occupies something of a middle ground between Anglo-American and Continental philosophy. Despite a bad habit of introducing pretentious and often impenetrable jargon, he had a grasp of philosophical (as well as mathematical and scientific) thought and argument that, though it sometimes struggled to free itself from his frequently nebulous style, gave many of his writings sufficient substance to influence later generations of Anglo-American philosophers, and to dominate their Continental counterparts.

MATHEMATICS

In his early writings, Husserl developed a psychologistic account of mathematics, explaining mathematical truths in terms of our psychological processes. This position was severely criticized by **Frege** (using the apt phrase "impenetrable fog"), and Husserl himself went on to repudiate his earlier approach. He didn't, however, accept Frege's position, arguing instead that the truth of, for example, "2+2=4" derives from the essences of 2 and 4. This emphasis on the centrality of essences lies at the heart of his philosophical position, which he called phenomenology.

CONSCIOUSNESS

At the center of Husserl's approach to the nature of thought is a notion that he adapted from one of his teachers, Brentano: *intentionality*. The main characteristic of consciousness (what distinguishes it from nonconsciousness) is that it's always intentional—that is, it's *directed*: we think about, fear, desire, consider, hope for, intend *something*. The conversion of passive sensory information into active consciousness is achieved by what he called *noemata*; as with much of Husserl's writing (and of the writings of his followers), this is a confusing term, with no very clear meaning, though "content of a thought" perhaps comes close. This marks a distinction drawn by Husserl between such content of thought and the act of thinking the thought, mirrored by a distinction between the content of perception and the perceiving of the perception.

When looking at an object, such as a chair, one is aware of the chair and not of oneself; that is, one is not aware of having the experience of looking at the chair. It is the object itself which is the subject of one's awareness. Husserl's philosophical intention was to describe the objects of consciousness without human bias. In doing so he founded phenomenology.

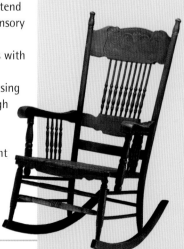

JOHN DEWEY

BORN	1859, Burlington, Vermont	DIED	1952, New York

MAIN INTERESTS Education, epistemology, ethics, psychology

INFLUENCES Hegel, James, Peirce

INFLUENCED Education (especially in the United States and China), Wiredu

MAJOR WORKS
Reconstruction in Philosophy, Experience and Nature, The Quest for Certainty

Dewey campaigned extensively for civil liberties. He was a founding member of the National Association for the Advancement of Colored People and the American Civil Liberties Union. Here, at the annual convention of the League for Independent Political Action, he calls for a liberal third party, as an alternative to the existing capitalist system.

After an unpromising scholastic start, Dewey opted for the recently introduced college preparatory scheme at his local high school, completing the courses so rapidly that he started at the University of Vermont at the age of sixteen. There he received a broad classical education, as well as being introduced to philosophy and to the theory of evolution. After graduating, he taught in a Pennsylvania high school for a couple of years, before returning to Vermont and then moving to Baltimore to enroll for a doctorate at Johns Hopkins University. Dewey was later to write that his ideas owed more to the people he'd known than to the books he'd read; during his time at Johns Hopkins, his three main influences were the psychologist G. Stanley Hall, the Hegelian idealist George Sylvester Morris, and the pragmatist **C. S. Peirce**. It was the Hegelianism that had the most effect on him

In a nutshell:
What matters is practical life, and philosophy's task is to make this easier and richer.

at first, pragmatism replacing it only after many years of striving to reconcile idealism and empirical science.

After receiving his doctorate in 1884, Dewey spent ten years teaching at the University of Michigan (with a brief spell at the University of Minnesota), before moving to the University of Chicago in 1894. While at Michigan he married Alice Chipman, who encouraged his increasing interest in social issues, and encountered two other influences in this regard: the pragmatist philosopher and sociologist George Herbert Mead (1863–1931) and the social philosopher James Hayden Tufts (1862–1942). At Chicago he encountered more important influences— especially on his educational ideas—including the educator Ella Flagg Young (1845–1918), whose Ph.D. he supervised, and who was deeply involved in the University Laboratory School that Dewey founded, and the social reformer (and eventual winner of the Nobel Peace Prize) Jane Addams (1860–1935).

In 1904, after a series of bitter wrangles with the university administration at Chicago, Dewey moved to Columbia, and apart from

The attraction of philosophy

... when it comes to convincing men of the truth of doctrines which are no longer to be accepted upon the say-so of custom and authority, but which are also not capable of empirical verification, there is no recourse save to magnify the signs of rigorous thought and rigid demonstration. Thus arises that appearance of abstract definition and ultra-scientific argumentation which repels so many from philosophy but which has been one of its chief attractions to its devotees.

Reconstruction in Philosophy, *p.20*

the production of books and contributions to academic journals (both in large numbers throughout his professional career), he began to write for a more popular audience; his work appeared in magazines such as *The Nation* and the *New Republic* and he became unusually well known outside the academic world. This fame spread beyond the confines of North America; Dewey traveled to Turkey, Mexico, South Africa, Japan, China, and the Soviet Union, giving lectures, visiting schools, and presenting reports on local educational systems and institutions. His biggest impact was perhaps in China, where his educational theories are still influential today.

Though he retired in 1930, Dewey continued to travel and work until his death in New York in 1952.

INSTRUMENTALISM

Dewey's philosophical position developed from his early Hegelian idealism into a version of pragmatism that he called instrumentalism. The term arose from his view that ideas and judgments are *instruments*, that their nature lies in the way they determine various effects; thus ideas aren't true or false, but are effective and ineffective (judgments might be true or false, but this depends upon their warrantability). His interest in science, and the importance he attached to the experimental method, shows itself especially in his view that ideas (which arise out of experience) lead to judgments, whose

consequences can be tested by further experience. This testing doesn't guarantee truth, but is a pretty good indicator. Thus Dewey's form of pragmatism is considerably less relativist than that of either Peirce or **James**.

EDUCATIONAL THEORY

Dewey held that philosophy could be seen as the theory of education, for he saw education as "the process of forming fundamental disposition, intellectual and emotional, toward nature and fellow-men" ("Democracy and Education," in *Middle Works* 9, p.338). Education shouldn't be simply a Mr. Gradgrind affair of the rote learning of dead facts, but should aim to produce better people, better citizens, by teaching skills and abilities. This involves *practice* more than the learning of theory or facts.

Dewey rejected what he called the spectator theory of education, in favor of active learning. He believed that children should be encouraged to be imaginative and that they could learn more through practical interaction.

BERTRAND ARTHUR WILLIAM RUSSELL

BORN 1872, Trelleck, Wales	**DIED** 1970, Penrhyndeudraeth

MAIN INTERESTS Logic, mathematics, epistemology, metaphysics

INFLUENCES Leibniz, Hume, Kant, Mill, Hegel, Meinong, James, Bradley, Frege

INFLUENCED Carnap, Wittgenstein, Ayer, Popper, Quine, Wiredu, Wiggins

MAJOR WORKS
The Principles of Mathematics, Principia Mathematica (with A. N. Whitehead), The Problems of Philosophy, Our Knowledge of the External World, An Inquiry into Meaning and Truth

Cambridge University calls the examination for final honors in undergraduate degrees the tripos (named after the three-legged stool on which the examiners used to sit).

Russell's parents were prominent freethinkers, his grandfather (the first Earl Russell) had been prime minister and his (nonreligious) godfather was **John Stuart Mill**. His parents both died when he was young, and he and his brother were brought up by their paternal grandparents. After being educated by tutors in a strongly religious and repressive household, he went up to Cambridge to read mathematics at Trinity College, where his interest in philosophy was encouraged; so that after gaining his degree in mathematics he stayed on to read for the second part of the Moral Science Tripos. In 1895 he was elected to a six-year fellowship at Trinity, during which he spent time traveling, and studied philosophy and economics in Berlin. His interest in mathematics and logic was revitalized when he met the Italian mathematician Giuseppe Peano (1858–1932) in Paris in 1900, and he started on a long project to demonstrate that math is reducible to and derivable from logic (logicism), which involved writing, with A. N. Whitehead, the three-volume *Principia Mathematica* (1910, 1912, 1913). This led to his discovery of *Russell's Paradox*, that was the downfall of **Frege's** logicist project.

Russell's life from this point was filled with incident and scandal. In 1916 his antiwar activities lost him his position at Cambridge; he was fined both by his college and the government, and imprisoned for five months. While in prison he wrote his *Introduction to*

In a nutshell:
"Three passions, simple but overwhelmingly strong, have governed my life: the longing for love, the search for knowledge, and unbearable pity for the suffering of mankind."

Mathematical Philosophy (1919). After the war he visited the Soviet Union, whose version and practice of socialism he found extremely disappointing, and the People's Republic of China, where he taught for a time at Beijing University.

Returning to England from China, he founded and ran, with his second wife, a progressive school, then taught at various U.S. universities and colleges. His liberal views on sexual freedom and his criticism of religion, in such works as *What I Believe* (1925) and *Marriage and Morals* (1929), led to intense public disapproval, the revocation of an appointment at the City College, New York, and his dismissal from the Barnes Foundation, Pennsylvania.

In 1944 he was reinstated at Trinity College, and he returned to England. His pacifism was modified by his recognition of the danger posed by Nazism, and he supported the Allied war effort. He was awarded the Order of Merit in 1949, and the Nobel Prize for

Since the H-bomb tests in the early 1950's Russell had actively campaigned against nuclear testing. In 1960 he organized the Committee of 100 out of the main body of CND (Campaign for Nuclear Disarmament). The committee advocated nonviolent direct action, including mass civil disobedience. In 1961 he was one of the many people to be arrested for taking part in a sit-down protest outside the Ministry of Defense in Whitehall.

Literature in 1950. After the war, his pacifist convictions again led him to action, and he campaigned against the nuclear arms race, becoming founder president of the Campaign for Nuclear Disarmament, issuing with Albert Einstein a joint manifesto, and after a public demonstration was imprisoned again, at age eighty-nine. He died after several years living in Wales, for most of that time still active in social campaigns.

Russell is probably best known for three things: *History of Western Philosophy* (1945), logical atomism, and the theory of descriptions. The first of these has introduced many people to philosophy, but of more philosophical importance are the two theories.

LOGICAL ATOMISM
Logical atomism is the theory of meaning laid out in Russell's paper "The Philosophy of Logical Atomism" (1918). It holds that language can be analyzed into fundamental atoms of meaning—building blocks out of which all statements are built. This analysis maps on to an analysis of the world, so that the logical atoms correspond to metaphysical atoms (states of affairs or facts). Such metaphysical atoms, Russell held, would be empirically discoverable, being knowable by direct perceptual acquaintance. A problem that all atomists face is the identification of their atoms. **David Hume** had offered simple ideas of color, shape, and so on; Russell tried objects such as *this patch of red now*;

Ludwig Wittgenstein, whose *Tractatus Logico-Philosophicus* continued and extended Russell's approach, accepted that specifying atoms was impossible. Logical atomism influenced the logical positivists, though both Russell and Wittgenstein eventually abandoned it as a theory.

THEORY OF DESCRIPTIONS
It might be thought that discovering the truth of a statement such as: "Caligula was mad" involves looking for Caligula and then seeing whether or not he was mad. This approach does well enough until we come across a statement such as "The present king of Ohio is mad." We scour the world for the present king of Ohio and don't find one—but then we can't discover if he's mad. In other words, the statement doesn't have a truth value and thus, on Russell's account of meaning, it is meaningless. Yet we do understand the statement, so what's going on? Russell's approach was to analyze such statements so as to bring out their logical (as opposed to grammatical) structure. Thus, "The present king of Ohio is mad" is analyzed as "There is just one thing that has the property of being the present king of Ohio, and that thing has the property of being mad." Now we simply have to scour the world for something that has two properties—being the king of Ohio and being mad—not finding one, we declare the statement to be false, not meaningless.

We all have a tendency to think that the world must conform to our prejudices. The opposite view involves some effort of thought, and most people would sooner die than think—in fact, they do so.

The ABC of Relativity, *p.166*

SIR ALLĀMEH MUHAMMED IQBĀL

| **BORN**   1877, Siālkot, Punjab | **DIED**   1938, Lahore, Punjab |

MAIN INTERESTS   Metaphysics, epistemology

INFLUENCES   Leibniz, Kant, Hegel, Nietzsche, Bergson, Whitehead

INFLUENCED   Modern Islamic philosophy

MAJOR WORKS
The Reconstruction of Religious Thought in Islam

Iqbāl died nine years before the creation of Pakistan, where his birthday is celebrated as a national holiday.

Iqbāl was born in the Punjab (then in India, now a province of Pakistan), and educated at the local school and college in Siālkot, before going on to university in Lahore. He studied Arabic and philosophy, then in 1899 did an M.A. in philosophy. He was appointed Reader in Arabic at the Oriental College in Lahore, and over the next few years became well known as a poet, and wrote his first book (in Urdu), *The Knowledge of Economics* (1903).

In 1905 he traveled to Europe to continue his philosophical studies, first at Cambridge, then at Munich, where he obtained his doctorate with a thesis titled "The Development of Metaphysics in Persia." From 1907 to 1908 he was professor of Arabic at the University of London, and also studied for the bar, becoming a barrister in 1908, when he returned to Lahore to practice law. While an advocate at the Lahore High Court he continued a part-time academic career as professor of philosophy and English literature, being appointed professor of philosophy at the Government College, Lahore, in 1911. He was knighted in 1923.

Despite his law practice, his philosophical work, and his political activities, Iqbāl was best known and respected as a poet. His other activities did bring him some measure of fame, though, especially six lectures that he gave at Madras, Osmania University at Hyderabad, and Aligarh, which were later published as *The Reconstruction of Religious Thought in Islam* (1930). During the early

In their own words:
To exist in pure duration is to be a self, and to be a self is to be able to say "I am."

The Reconstruction of Religious
Thought in Islam, *p.56*

1930s he traveled extensively in the Middle East and Europe, participating in international political conferences, meeting philosophers and politicians, and writing.

He felt that a Muslim state wasn't desirable, as he held to the ideal of a worldwide Muslim community. Nevertheless, he held that, at least in the medium term, the only way for Indian Muslims to live according to the tenets of Islam was in such a state, and he campaigned accordingly (though a recent study based on his correspondence suggests that in fact he had in mind an Islamic Pakistan as part of an Indian federal state).

Iqbāl's philosophical work involved bringing various Western philosophical influences, including **Leibniz**, **Hegel**, and **Nietzsche**, to his Islamic scholarship, thus holding out the promise of a revival of genuine Islamic philosophical thought—a return of Islam to its place in the philosophical world—a promise that has yet to be truly fulfilled.

SARVEPALLI RADHAKRISHNAN

| BORN | 1888, Tiruttani | DIED | 1975, Mylapore, Madras |

MAIN INTERESTS   Religion, ethics, metaphysics

INFLUENCES   Plato, Plotinus, Saṁkara, Kant, Hegel, Bergson

INFLUENCED   India

MAJOR WORKS
*Indian Philosophy,
Eastern Traditions
and Western
Thought*

Religious feeling must establish itself as a rational way of living. If ever the spirit is to be at home in this world, and not merely a prisoner or a fugitive, spiritual foundations must be laid deep and preserved worthily. Religion must express itself in reasonable thought, fruitful action, and right social institutions.

Radhakrishnan was born to a poor Brahmin family in southern India, and went through his early schooling in Tiruttani and Tirupati on various scholarships. At seventeen he went to the Madras Christian College, majoring in philosophy, and graduating with a B.A. and then an M.A. at the age of twenty. Part of the latter involved a thesis on "The Ethics of the Vedanta and Its Metaphysical Presuppositions," which marked the general trend of his future philosophy.

He became assistant lecturer at the Madras Presidency College in 1909, where he continued his study of Hindu sacred and philosophical literature, and extended his knowledge of Western philosophy. He was appointed professor of philosophy at the University of Mysore in 1918, the year he published his first book, *The Philosophy of Rabindranath Tagore*; while there he wrote his second book, *The Reign of Religion in Contemporary Philosophy* (1920). In 1921 he was elected to the prestigious King George V Chair of Mental and Moral Science at the University of Calcutta. Over the next few years he attended various important conferences around the world, as well as writing his best-known work, *Indian Philosophy* (two volumes: 1923 and 1927).

In 1929 Radhakrishnan went to Oxford, where he gave the Upton Lectures on comparative religion, and then the Hibbert Lectures in London and Manchester. On his return to India he spent five years as vice chancellor of Andhra University, until in 1936 he was elected Spalding Professor of Eastern Religions and Ethics at Oxford University—a chair created for him. Over the next three years he lectured on philosophy and campaigned for Indian independence.

In 1939 he was elected a fellow of the British Academy, and returned to India to take up the vice chancellorship of the Benaras Hindu University, whose continued existence and prosperity he secured. In 1947, India finally achieved independence, and Radhakrishnan played a number of important roles in the new state, culminating in the presidency from 1962 to 1967. At seventy-nine he retired from public life.

Radhakrishnan produced a large corpus of philosophical and religious works; though his basic philosophical position was in the *advaita* or non dualist tradition of **Adi Saṁkara**, he departed from that tradition (and much traditional Hindu thought) by arguing for both a personal god and a single, personal self. He developed an idealist position that brought together the European tradition, especially Hegelianism, and the tradition deriving from the *Upaniṣads*.

Note:
Radhakrishnan's birthday is celebrated in India as "Teacher's Day."

LUDWIG WITTGENSTEIN

BORN 1889, Vienna	**DIED** 1951, Cambridge, England

MAIN INTERESTS Mathematics, language, metaphysics, logic

INFLUENCES Augustine, Leibniz, Kierkegaard, James, Frege, Russell, Carnap

INFLUENCED Carnap, Popper, Anscombe, Dummett, Nagel, Kripke

MAJOR WORKS
Tractatus Logico-Philosophicus,
Philosophical Investigations,
On Certainty

The Vienna Circle *was a group of philosophers, mathematicians, and scientists who developed a distinctive philosophical approach known as logical positivism.*

What we cannot speak about we must pass over in silence.

Tractatus Logico-Philosophicus §7

Wittgenstein was the youngest of eight children born to a wealthy Viennese family. He was tutored at home until he was fourteen, then spent three years at Realschule in Linz, before going on to Berlin to study mechanical engineering. In 1908 he moved to England to do a doctorate in aeronautical engineering at Manchester University. This led him to a deeper study of mathematics, and to **Russell's** *Principles of Mathematics.* On his return to Germany he worked briefly under **Frege**, on whose advice he went to Cambridge in 1912 to study the philosophy of mathematics and logic under Russell.

Wittgenstein spent a brief but productive period living in a remote cabin in Norway, where he wrote much of his early masterpiece, the *Tractatus Logico-Philosophicus,* but the Great War broke out and he volunteered for the Austro-Hungarian army. After service in various capacities, including a stint on the Russian front, he was posted to an artillery regiment in Italy, where he was captured and held in a POW camp. He'd continued his philosophical work during the war, and had completed a first draft of the *Tractatus;* he was allowed to send it to Russell in Cambridge, and in 1922 it became the only book that he published during his lifetime.

With the *Tractatus* Wittgenstein considered that all the (genuine) problems of philosophy had been solved, and he returned to Austria.

In a nutshell:
Philosophy's job is simply to analyze our statements in order to expose those that are meaningless (without reference).

He became a primary-school teacher, then a gardener, and finally an architect (designing a house for his sister). During this period he maintained some personal contacts with philosophers, and was introduced to the Vienna Circle by Moritz Schlick. As a result of various discussions, Wittgenstein began to realize that there were problems with the views that he had expressed in the *Tractatus,* and in 1929 he returned to Cambridge to continue his philosophical studies; he became a fellow of Trinity College, and was given a lectureship.

He spent about five years at Cambridge; notes that he dictated to students during that time were collected, and published after his death as *The Blue and Brown Books* (1952). After a brief period in the Soviet Union, he returned to Norway, where he worked on what was to become the *Philosophische Untersuchungen* (*Philosophical Investigations*). He then went back to Cambridge, becoming professor of philosophy in 1939, and taking British citizenship soon afterward. Apart from a period during World War II when he worked

The Cambridge University Moral Sciences, 1913. Cambridge at that time was a place of great intellectual activity. Russell (front, fifth from left) and G. E. Moore (second row, third from right) were extremely influential. Wittgenstein studied under Russell and they became good friends. Wittgenstein became an active member of the Moral Science Club.

as a hospital porter and a laboratory technician, he taught at Cambridge until 1947, when he retired to work on his writing. In 1949 he was found to have prostate cancer; he spent his last two years working in Cambridge, Oxford, and Vienna. The material he'd written up to about 1949 was edited and published after his death as the *Philosophical Investigations* (1953), the work from 1949 until his death as *On Certainty* (1979).

PICTURE THEORY OF MEANING

Wittgenstein's work can be divided into two main periods: the early period is marked by the *Tractatus*, the late period by the *Philosophical Investigations*. The *Tractatus* presents us with seven main numbered propositions, all but the last supplemented by a nested series of supplementary propositions. Its main philosophical position is a version of logical atomism. This is the thesis that our experience and understanding of the world can be analyzed until one reaches bedrock, a set of atomic facts that can be analyzed no further; the world is made up of facts, not of objects. This goes along with Wittgenstein's picture theory of meaning, according to which language succeeds in making claims about the world because of something in common between propositions and what they picture—actual or possible facts. Together they tell us that a statement that can't be analyzed into atomic facts has no reference.

PRIVATE LANGUAGE

In his late period Wittgenstein stuck with the notion of philosophy as a sort of sanitizer of our thoughts and statements, but came to see that he'd been treating language much too simplistically. This led to a shift in approach, from a rather didactic account of how we *should* use language to a more cautious examination of how we in fact *do* use it. One of the best-known parts of the *Philosophical Investigations* is the argument that a logically private language—a language that no one else could *in principle* understand because it referred to its user's private sensations—is impossible. This would have serious repercussions for many areas of philosophy, as it reduces to absurdity the Empiricist attempt to ground knowledge in private experience.

Wittgenstein's work sits uneasily between the Continental and the Anglo-American traditions. Like the Continental philosophers, he tends to offer strings of ideas rather than sustained argument, but the clarity and simplicity of his style, as well as his interest in and mastery of logic, are more Anglo-American. He is claimed by both traditions, though his reputation in Anglo-American philosophy has been on the wane.

Our understanding of the world can be analyzed until we hit bedrock—the facts—and can go no further.

MARTIN HEIDEGGER

| BORN | 1889, Messkirch, Baden | DIED | 1976, Messkirch, Baden |

MAIN INTERESTS   Metaphysics

INFLUENCES   Pre-Socratics, Aristotle, Kant, Kierkegaard, Nietzsche, Husserl

INFLUENCED   Sartre, Ventre, Adorno, Merleau-Ponty

MAJOR WORKS
Being and Time

I saw in [the Nazis] the possibility of an inner recollection and renewal of the people and a path that would allow it to discover its historical vocation in the Western world.

"The Rectorate 1933–34,"
The Review of Metaphysics
(1985), p.483

The nothing itself nihilates.

"What Is Metaphysics?" in Basic
Writings, ed. David Krell, p.105

Heidegger was born into a Catholic family in southwest Germany, and was originally destined for the priesthood, his education being supported by the church—first in Konstanz, then at high school in Freiburg, where he was introduced to philosophy. He attended a Jesuit seminary, but stayed for only a few weeks. He went instead to the University of Freiburg to study theology, but his ill health finally forced him to give up all thoughts of the priesthood, and he switched to courses in philosophy, mathematics, and natural science.

At Freiburg Heidegger received his doctorate in philosophy in 1913; but World War I intervened. He enlisted in the army, though poor health cut short his service, and he returned to his studies, becoming a lecturer at Freiburg in 1915. In the following year **Husserl**, whose work he had studied, arrived at Freiburg; after a brief interruption in 1918, when he was called up to serve on the Western Front, he became Husserl's assistant.

He spent five years, his lectures gaining him a reputation as an interpreter of Aristotle. In 1923 he moved to Marburg as an assistant professor. Although his teaching was highly regarded, his failure to publish held him back, and in 1927 he was pressured into publishing an unfinished version of his book *Sein und Zeit* (*Being and Time*). The book was seen as an important work of metaphysics, and earned him a full professorship at Marburg, though he filled

Note:

*The first edition of **Sein und Zeit** was dedicated to his mentor Husserl. In the second edition, in 1941, Heidegger removed the dedication.*

that post for only a year. In 1928 Husserl retired, and Heidegger returned to Freiburg to take his place.

With the rise of Hitler in the early 1930s, he began to get involved in National Socialist politics, and a month after his election as rector of the University of Freiburg, in 1933, he joined the Nazi Party. He instituted Nazi reforms, and distanced himself from his former mentor, Husserl, who was publicly humiliated by the university. After the war, and despite his protestations of innocence, he was removed from his post and banned from teaching, though the ban was lifted in 1949. He spent the rest of his life traveling, lecturing, and writing, and died in 1976.

Heidegger is perhaps the best symbol of the divide between the Anglo-American and Continental traditions: in the latter he is said to have had enormous influence (one can see aspects of his style in more recent Continental philosophy), while in the former he is accorded little acclaim.

RUDOLF CARNAP

BORN 1891, Ronsdorf	**DIED** 1970, Santa Monica, California

MAIN INTERESTS   Mathematics, physics, logic, epistemology, metaphysics

INFLUENCES   Kant, Frege, Russell, Wittgenstein

INFLUENCED   Wittgenstein, Quine, Popper, Ayer, Putnam

MAJOR WORKS
The Logical Structure of the World, The Logical Syntax of Language, Logical Foundations of Probability

Science is a system of statements based on direct experience, and controlled by experimental verification. Verification in science is not, however, of single statements but of the entire system or a sub-system of such statements.

The Unity of Science, p.42

Born in Ronsdorf in what is now North Rhine–Westphalia, Carnap was seven when his father died, and the family moved to Barmen, where Carnap attended the gymnasium. In 1910 he began studying philosophy, physics, and mathematics at the Universities of Jena and Freiburg (at Jena he studied under **Gottlob Frege**). His academic career (which he then foresaw as being in physics) was interrupted by World War I, and he spent three years in the army, after which he moved to Berlin; there he studied physics, writing his dissertation on a subject that had interested him from the beginning of his studies—space and time. He was advised, however, that his work was more relevant to philosophy, and decided to turn the dissertation in that direction. It was published in 1922 as "Der Raum" ("Space").

From 1923, Carnap began to get to know the members of the Vienna Circle, and in 1926 he moved to Vienna, taking up the post of assistant professor at the university there. He soon became one of the leading members of the circle, and was one of the three authors of its manifesto of 1929. The previous year he had published his first important work, *Der Logische Aufbau der Welt* (*The Logical Structure of the World*), in which he presented a positivist variety of atomism in which every concept, from the most abstract to the most concrete and everyday, was constructed out of our immediate experiences (any that couldn't be were dubbed meaningless).

In 1931 Carnap was appointed professor of natural philosophy at the German University of Prague, where he wrote his next major work, *Logische Syntax der Sprache* (*The Logical Syntax of Language*) (1934). While in Prague he was visited by **Willard van Orman Quine**, who was to be deeply influenced by his work, and who—together with Charles Morris—helped him to move to the United States in 1935 to escape the rise of Nazism.

Carnap spent the next sixteen years as professor at various U.S. universities, in 1941 becoming a U.S. citizen. It was in the 1940s that he became interested in semantics, which led to a number of important books, including *Introduction to Semantics* (1942), *Formalization of Logic* (1943), and *Meaning and Necessity: A Study in Semantics and Modal Logic* (1947). He continued with his interest in the foundations of physics, but his last major work was the *Logical Foundations of Probability* (1950). This presented a rigorously developed account of exactly how scientific theories are *confirmed* (rather than defined, as in his earlier work) by experience. His interest in inductive logic continued, and he was working on it at the time of his death in 1970.

In a nutshell:
Any concept that can't be reduced to the basic expediencies is meaningless.

FENG YOULAN (FUNG YU-LAN)

BORN 1895, Tanghe, Hunan	DIED 1990, Beijing

MAIN INTERESTS   Metaphysics, ethics

INFLUENCES   K'ung fu-zi, Aristotle, Cheng Yi, Zhu Xi

INFLUENCED   –

MAJOR WORKS
History of Chinese Philosophy,
Xin Li-xue,
Xin Yuan-ren

Feng may be best known for his history of Chinese philosophy, but he was one of the most original and influential of the modern Chinese philosophers.

Feng Youlan was born to a moderately well-to-do family, and lived through a series of civil wars and political upheavals. He went to university, first at Shanghai, and then (unable to find anyone to teach him Western philosophy and logic) at Beijing. He graduated in philosophy in 1918, and left on a Boxer Indemnity grant to study at Columbia University, returning to China in 1923, where he finished his dissertation, gaining his Ph.D. from Columbia in 1925.

Over the next ten years he taught at a number of Chinese universities, including Tsinghua University in Beijing. While at Tsinghua, he published his best-known work, the two-volume *History of Chinese Philosophy* in 1934; this applied a Western philosophical approach to Chinese philosophy, and became the standard work of its kind. In 1939 he published his *Xin Li-xue* (*Neo-Lixue*, or *New Rational Philosophy*), in which he developed a rational neo-Confucianism.

The Sino-Japanese War led to Feng fleeing Beijing together with the students and staff from Tsinghua, Beijing, and Nankai Universities. They formed first the Changsha Temporary University in Hengshan, and then the Southwest Associated University in Kunming. In 1946 the universities returned to Beijing, but Feng went to the University of Pennsylvania as a visiting professor. While he was there it became clear that the communists would take power in China. His

Consider this:
It is not necessary that man should be religious, but it is necessary that he should be philosophical. When he is philosophical, he has the very best of the blessings of religion.

more-or-less socialist political views gave him great optimism for China's future, and on his return he studied Marxism-Leninism.

The political climate wasn't what he'd hoped for, however, and by the mid-1950s Feng found his work under attack. He had to rework and repudiate much of his earlier thinking, and rewrote his *History of Chinese Philosophy* to fit the prejudices of the Cultural Revolution. He stayed in China, though, surviving the worst of times, and eventually regained some of his old freedom to think and write, which he did until his death.

Feng took basic metaphysical notions from traditional Chinese thought, and developed and analyzed them using Western philosophy; he was then able to construct a rationalist neo-Confucianist metaphysics, together with an ethical theory that offered an account not only of the nature of morality, but of the structure of human moral development.

JEAN-PAUL SARTRE

BORN 1905, Paris	**DIED** 1980, Paris

MAIN INTERESTS   Metaphysics, epistemology, ethics, politics

INFLUENCES   Kant, Hegel, Kierkegaard, Nietzche, Ventre, Husserl, Heidegger

INFLUENCED   –

MAJOR WORKS
L'Être et le néant,
L'Existentialisme
est un
humanisme

The waiter in the café
can not be immediately
a café waiter in the
sense that this inkwell is
an inkwell, or the glass is
a glass ... It is precisely
this person who I have
to be (if I am the waiter
in question) and who I
am not.

Being and Nothingness, p.59

His father having died when he was young, Sartre grew up in the home of his maternal grandfather. In 1924 he went to the École Normale Supérieure, graduating in 1929. In 1931 he began work as a secondary-school teacher, teaching for various schools, with a year off to study with **Husserl** and **Heidegger** in Berlin. In 1938 he published his first novel, *La Nausée (Nausea)*. In 1939 he was called up for military service in World War II; he was taken prisoner in 1940, but released the following year. Back in France he returned to teaching, and was active in the resistance movement. He continued to write, and in 1943 published his major work, *L'Être et le néant (Being and Nothingness)*.

After the war Sartre gave up teaching, and made his living as a writer. At this time, too, his views found an outlet in political activities; though never a member of the Communist Party, Sartre was very much pro-communist, and considered himself to be a true Marxist. The Soviet crushing of the Hungarian revolution in 1956 disillusioned him, however, and he publicly condemned the French Communist Party for its subservience to Moscow. He continued his political thinking nonetheless, and developed a form of existentialist socialism that was described and developed in his book *Critique de la raison dialectique* (1960).

In 1964 Sartre was offered but turned down the Nobel Prize for Literature, and it could be argued that he was more important for his genuinely literary output than for his philosophy—especially for novels such as *La Nausée*; the three volumes of *Les Chemins de la liberté (The Roads of Freedom)*: *L'Âge de raison (The Age of Reason)*, *Le Sursis (The Reprieve)*, and *La Mort dans l'âme (Iron in the Soul)*; and for plays such as *Les Mouches (The Flies)*, *Huis-clos (The Vicious Circle)*, and *In camera*.

He spent much of the 1960s writing a four-volume work on Flaubert, after which—though he continued to work on various projects—his health deteriorated; he became blind, before dying of a lung tumor in 1980.

Sartre is famous as the chief prophet of existentialism—an attitude toward life or philosophical movement, the origins of which can be traced back to **Søren Kierkegaard**. He saw it as the personal complement to the political approach of Marxism; the former stressed the freedom of the individual self (as well as its responsibility), and the latter set out to enable the expression of that freedom in political liberty.

In their own words:
The For-itself, in fact, is nothing but the pure nihilation of the In-itself; it is like a hole of being at the heart of Being.

Being and Nothingness, p.617

SIR KARL RAIMUND # POPPER

BORN 1902, Vienna	**DIED** 1994, Croydon, England

MAIN INTERESTS   Science, politics, epistemology, philosophy of mind

INFLUENCES   Plato, Hume, Mill, Peirce, Carnap, Schlick, Russell, Wittgenstein

INFLUENCED   –

MAJOR WORKS

The Logic of Scientific Discovery, The Open Society and its Enemies, The Poverty of Historicism, Conjectures and Refutations: The Growth of Scientific Knowledge, The Self and Its Brain

In so far as a scientific statement speaks about reality, it must be falsifiable: and in so far as it is not falsifiable, it does not speak about reality.

The Logic of Scientific Discovery, p.314

Born to a middle-class Viennese Jewish family, his father a lawyer, Popper spent his adolescence in a time of profound turmoil in postwar Austria—an experience that deeply affected his later political thought. Aside from a year at the Vienna Conservatory, where he took courses in piano composition, he studied mathematics, physics, and psychology at the University of Vienna, reading philosophy on his own time; he received his doctorate in philosophy in 1928. He knew and was influenced by the Vienna Circle, and in 1934 they published his first book, *Logik der Forschung* (*The Logic of Scientific Discovery*), but he never wholly accepted their views (indeed, that first book demonstrated his differences from them).

Popper spent the period from 1930 to 1936 as a secondary-school teacher of math and science, but when in 1937 the danger of invasion by Nazi Germany had become clear, he went to New Zealand, where he taught for nine years at Canterbury University College, Christchurch. It was during this period, influenced by the events of World War II, that he wrote one of his best-known works, *The Open Society and Its Enemies* (1945), in which he argued against what he saw as the dangers of various political theories, from **Plato** to **Marx**.

In 1946 Popper moved to England to become a reader at the London School of Economics; he was made Professor of Logic and Scientific Method in 1949, and remained

In a nutshell:

All human knowledge is conjectural, whether scientific, political, or philosophical—generated by the creative mind, and dependent on the context of creation.

there until he retired in 1969. During his time at the L.S.E. he published some of his most important books, including *The Poverty of Historicism* (1957), a return to political philosophy, and *Conjectures and Refutations: The Growth of Scientific Knowledge* (1963), a collection of many of his papers. He was knighted in 1965 and made a Companion of Honor in 1982.

Popper's work did not finish with his retirement, and he not only continued lecturing around the world, but produced striking and well-argued books well into his eighties, some in familiar areas—*Objective Knowledge: An Evolutionary Approach* (1972)—and some on new topics—*The Self and Its Brain: An Argument for Interactionism* (1977), which he co-wrote with Sir John Eccles.

POLITICS

The main target of Popper's political arguments is *historicism*: the view that human history is governed by historical laws

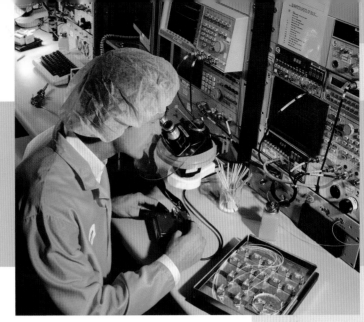

We create theories in order to apprehend the world, but no amount of empirical observation can ever conclusively verify a theory, because just one observation can falsify it. Once a theory is falsified it is replaced by another. Science does not prove theories; it accepts them until they are disproved.

just as the natural world is governed by natural laws. Prediction of any accuracy, he argues, isn't possible when human beings are involved, because their decisions play a crucial role in events, and so causes are mixed with reasons. He argues that historicist theories lead to the setting up of authoritarian, closed societies—that is, societies whose institutions are set in place according to such theories, and that are protected from change. His concern is to defend the notion of the open society, in which the political institutions can be changed by the governed, and in which the greatest possible freedom is given for thought, criticism, and political experiment. Utopian political theories, which try to change society at one time and set up some sort of ideal state, are to be rejected in favor of piecemeal political change.

FALSIFICATIONISM

Popper is best known as a philosopher of science, in which capacity he had an enormous influence, not only on other philosophers, but directly on scientists themselves. At the heart of his approach is the notion of falsification. He argues, with **Hume**, that, though no amount of empirical observation can ever conclusively verify a theory, just one observation can falsify it. Thus science works not by amassing evidence for its theories, but by setting up imaginative and bold conjectures that it then tries to falsify. A theory is corroborated but not verified by its survival of such attempts.

A bold conjecture is one that is very falsifiable—one that makes many predictions that can be tested. This leads to an important corollary: a genuinely scientific theory is one that can be falsified, so any theory that can't be falsified isn't scientific. Popper uses this test to show that such idea systems as astrology, psychoanalysis, and Marxism are pseudo-sciences.

MIND

In *The Self and Its Brain*, Popper joins with Sir John Eccles, a neurobiologist, to present and argue for a dualist theory of mind and body. Popper provides a philosophical account of the main philosophical theories, and presents the philosophical arguments. Eccles explains the neurological side of things, and discusses evidence from the study of the brain, and in a final section they present transcripts of their recorded conversations on the issues.

Popper holds that there are three worlds of experience: World 1 consists of physical objects, World 2 consists of (subjective) mental states, and World 3 consists of the products of the human mind, and is both immaterial and objective. The objects in World 3, though created by the mind, exist independently of them. The world, and especially the person, is a complex interaction of the mental and physical.

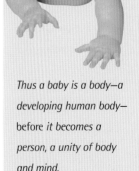

Thus a baby is a body—a developing human body—before it becomes a person, a unity of body and mind.

The Self and Its Brain, p.115; *emphasis in original*

WILLARD VAN ORMAN QUINE

BORN 1908, Akron, Ohio	**DIED** 2000, Boston, Massachusetts

MAIN INTERESTS   Logic, language, science, mathematics, metaphysics

INFLUENCES   James, Russell, Whitehead, Tarski, Carnap

INFLUENCED   –

MAJOR WORKS

From a Logical Point of View, Word and Object, Set Theory and Its Logic, The Ways of Paradox, The Roots of Reference

Manuals for translating one language into another can be set up in divergent ways, all compatible with the totality of speech dispositions, yet incompatible with one another.

Word and Object, p.27

The youngest son of an engineer and a teacher, Quine's early interests were primarily scientific, though while still at school his brother introduced him to the work of William James, and while studying mathematics at Oberlin College in Ohio he encountered **Russell** and Whitehead's *Principia Mathematica*, which led him to take honors courses in mathematical logic. He graduated from Oberlin in 1930, and won a scholarship at Harvard, where he worked on his doctorate under Alfred Whitehead; Whitehead introduced him to the visiting Russell, with whom Quine subsequently carried on a lengthy correspondence. On receiving his Ph.D. in 1932, he spent a year in Europe on a Sheldon Traveling Scholarship from Harvard, and met members of the Vienna Circle: **A. J. Ayer**, Kurt Gödel, and Moritz Schlick, but especially Alfred Tarski and other eminent Polish logicians in Warsaw, and **Rudolf Carnap**, with whom he studied for a short time in Prague.

On his return to the United States he took up a junior fellowship at Harvard, where he worked mainly on logic, becoming an instructor in philosophy in 1936 (teaching for the departments of philosophy and mathematics), and an associate professor in 1941. His academic career was interrupted by the war, which he spent in the decryption division of Naval Intelligence. After the war he returned to Harvard, and was made professor in 1948. In the 1950s he became known for his work on philosophical logic,

In a nutshell:

We should accept as existing only those things that are needed in order for our explanations to work.

marked by his collection of papers *From a Logical Point of View* (1953). This work included his 1951 paper "Two Dogmas of Empiricism" and the newly written "Meaning and Existential Inference." The collection was published during his time in Oxford as Eastman Visiting Professor (1953–1954).

Quine became Edgar Pierce professor of philosophy at Harvard in 1956, and remained in that post until his retirement in 1978, after which he stayed at Harvard as an emeritus professor. He continued working (and traveling widely) until his death.

LOGIC AND SCIENCE

Quine's philosophy had two major influences—pragmatism and positivism—both of which he adapted and altered to fit his own developing views, but the single biggest influence on his thought was Carnap. Nevertheless, the paper that made his name, "Two Dogmas of Empiricism," was in large part a rejection of some of Carnap's central notions, and was in fact concerned to reject two dogmas of logical positivism. The two dogmas were the analytic-synthetic distinction, and scientific reductionism.

Science predicts future experience

As an empiricist I continue to think of the conceptual scheme of science as a tool, ultimately, for predicting future experience in the light of past experience. Physical objects are conceptually imported into the situation as convenient intermediaries—not by definition in terms of experience, but simply as irreducible posits comparable, epistemologically, to the gods of Homer.

"Two Dogmas of Empiricism," in From a Logical Point of View, *p.44*

With regard to the former, Quine argues that there is no acceptable account of analyticity, so that the distinction can't be sustained; this leaves the positivists unable to account for the truth of statements that couldn't be empirically verified, such as mathematical statements. With regard to the latter, he argues that science can't be reduced to individual statements, each testable separately, but that science stands or falls as a whole, a web of statements that touches our experiences at its periphery; it's thus not possible to falsify one statement in isolation from the rest. This "radical holism" was replaced in his later work by a "moderate holism" in which he accepted that observation statements could be tested independently, and that it wasn't the whole of science that rose or fell together, but significant subsets of scientific statements.

LANGUAGE

In *Word and Object* Quine introduces a notion that has been widely discussed: *the indeterminacy of translation*. This is the thesis that, when faced with an unknown language, with no help from bilingual speakers, two linguists could develop two inconsistent accounts of the language that nevertheless accorded perfectly with the observable facts (language use, responses to queries, and so on). Moreover, there would be no grounds for choosing one account over the other; that is, translation is possible. This has implications for our philosophical practices; for example, it rules out the

common view that a statement works by expressing a proposition, so that two sentences used to make statements in the same context such as "it is raining" and "es regnet"—would express the same proposition. Statements can always be correctly interpreted as saying different things (expressing different propositions). Quine's view depends, however, on the assumption that there is no more to meaning than what can be found in the speakers' behavior.

NATURALIZED EPISTEMOLOGY

Perhaps the least attractive of Quine's notions, this naturalized epistemology involves the attempt to reduce our knowledge to the relationship between inputs and outputs—the former being experience, the latter beliefs. The human subject is seen as a physical machine, processing and responding to data. In other words, epistemology is reduced to psychology (and a physicalist, somewhat behaviorist psychology at that).

Whatever the status of his theories, Quine has been enormously influential—both directly, on those he taught (including **Donald Davidson** and **David Lewis**), and indirectly on those who read his work, and the work of his followers (and opponents). Without Quine, modern philosophy would have been very different.

Alfred North Whitehead had a considerable influence on the philosophy of science, logic, and metaphysics, as well as areas such as ethics and education. He taught Bertrand Russell at Cambridge, and later collaborated with him on Principia Mathematica. While teaching at Harvard, Whitehead introduced Quine to Russell, with whom he corresponded for many years.

A statement is said to be analytic if it's true or false solely in virtue of the meanings of the words it contains; it's said to be synthetic if it's true or false in virtue of the way the world is.

For Quine the human is a machine. Our knowledge is a result of us processing experience and forming beliefs.

SIR ALFRED JULES AYER

BORN 1910, London	**DIED** 1989, London

MAIN INTERESTS Logic, metaphysics, epistemology

INFLUENCES Hume, Mill, Russell, Moore, Carnap, Schlick

INFLUENCED –

MAJOR WORKS
Language, Truth, and Logic, The Problem of Knowledge, The Central Questions of Philosophy

The criterion which we use to test the genuineness of apparent statements of fact is the criterion of verifiability. We say that a sentence is factually significant to any given person, if, and only if, he knows how to verify the proposition which it purports to express—that is, if he knows what observations would lead him, under certain conditions, to accept that proposition as being true, or reject it as being false.

Language, Truth, and Logic, p.16

Ayer was educated at Eton College and Christ Church. He graduated in 1932, traveled to Vienna, and met the members of the Vienna Circle—a meeting that set the course of his academic life. Returning to Oxford, he taught at Christ Church until the outbreak of war, when he joined the Welsh Guards, though he spent most of the war in military intelligence. In 1944 he became fellow of Wadham College, Oxford, for two years before taking up the Grote Professorship of the Philosophy of Mind and Logic at University College. He stayed there for thirteen years, but in 1959 was elected Wykeham Professor of Logic, and became a fellow of New College. He was knighted in 1970. In 1978 he retired from his professorship, and was a fellow of Wolfson College until 1983.

Ayer made his name with *Language, Truth, and Logic* (1936), in which he presented logical positivism in a readable and persuasive style. He enthusiastically adopted a hard-line positivism, applying the criterion of verifiability extremely strictly: not only were religious, ethical, esthetic, and many metaphysical statements declared meaningless, but many scientific statements (such as those about fundamental particles) were rescuable only by being reinterpreted as references to observable phenomena.

As Ayer's thinking developed, he realized that the criterion of verifiability was too vague to be a useful text of meaning, and

too strict to allow most human knowledge-gathering activities (indeed, it's a meaningless statement by its own standard). He therefore modified the criterion, for example allowing that a statement be verifiable by a hypothetical observer able to travel anywhere in time and space.

In the end Ayer's position became more a hard-headed, traditional empiricism than logical positivism (although *Language, Truth, and Logic* remains in print, persuading generations of schoolchildren to reject ethics and metaphysics as meaningless). He was in many ways more open-mindedly rational than some of his contemporaries, such as **Quine**; while he rejected beliefs for which there were no good grounds (such as the belief in a god), he kept certain metaphysical beliefs, such as the dualist account of the mind, that he saw as based on experience, and for which physical science had failed to provide workable alternatives (this was unrelated to the near-death experience he had toward the end of his life).

RICHARD MERVYN HARE

BORN 1919, Backwell, Somerset	**DIED** 2002, Ewelme, Oxfordshire

| **MAIN INTERESTS**   Ethics | |

| **INFLUENCES**   Mill, Moore | |

| **INFLUENCED**   – | |

MAJOR WORKS
The Language of Morals, Freedom and Reason, Moral Thinking

In order to bring out the extraordinary nature of the really fanatical Nazi's desires, let us imagine that we are able to perform on him the following trick [...] We say to him "You may not know it, but we have discovered that you are not the son of your supposed parents, but of two pure Jews; and the same is true of your wife" [...] Is he at all likely to say—as he logically can say—"All right then, send me and all my family to Buchenwald!"?

Freedom and Reason, p.171

Hare went to Rugby School, and from there went on, in 1937, to read Classics at Balliol College, Oxford. Despite his pacifist views, he volunteered for service with the Royal Artillery in 1939. He served in the Indian Mountain Artillery until 1942, when he was taken by the Japanese as a prisoner of war for three years, first in Singapore, and then working on the Burma-Thailand railway. This marked him both personally and professionally, strengthening his belief that philosophy, and especially ethics, has a central obligation to help with people's choices, to help them live their lives as moral beings—not only in the relatively benign world of the professional philosopher, but in the much more challenging world outside academia.

Back in England in 1945 Hare finished his degree, and was elected to a fellowship at Balliol College. He remained at Balliol until 1966, when he was elected White's Professor of Moral Philosophy, and moved to Corpus Christi College. In 1983 he retired from his Oxford posts and became graduate research professor at the University of Florida at Gainesville, where he remained until 1994, traveling regularly between Florida and his home at Ewelme in Oxfordshire.

Hare rejected the theory that our moral judgments are simply paraphrases of descriptions of their objects, but he felt dissatisfied with the standard emotivist alternatives, which added only an emotional element. His work was influenced by the ordinary language approach to philosophy, and he took as the foundation of his theorizing the way that moral terms are standardly used. He recognized that the primary role of moral judgments is to prescribe courses of action, and argued that these prescriptions are made distinctively moral largely by being universalizable; that is, they don't refer to a particular individual, but apply to any moral agent. His approach has become known as *prescriptivism*.

Hare is also well known for his defense of a version of Utilitarianism, and for his resulting two-level analysis of moral thinking. He argues that people are capable of two types of moral deliberation: that of act-utilitarian "archangels," thinking critically and making rational decisions using the utilitarian principle directly, and that of rule-utilitarian "proles," thinking intuitively and acting according to their rule-like dispositions. In real life, people are capable of (and need) both, though they are not very good at the former.

Hare's later work included the application of moral theory to questions of practical ethics.

In a nutshell:
Ethical judgments are moral commands that apply to everyone in the relevant situation.

DONALD HERBERT DAVIDSON

BORN 1917, Springfield, Mass.	**DIED** 2003, Berkeley, California

MAIN INTERESTS   Language, logic, epistemology, metaphysics

INFLUENCES   Plato, Aristotle, Spinoza, Kant, Whitehead, Frege, Quine

INFLUENCED   –

MAJOR WORKS
Essays on Actions and Events,
Inquiries into Truth and Interpretation

Davidson began his academic career rather unusually for a philosopher, studying English, comparative literature, and classics at Harvard. However, in his second year he attended two classes in philosophy given by Alfred North Whitehead, and these set him on a different path. After graduating in 1939, he went on to do graduate work in ancient philosophy, gaining his master's in 1941. His doctoral work (on Plato's *Philebus*) was interrupted by World War II, which he spent mainly in the navy in the Mediterranean. On his return, he finished his thesis, receiving his Ph.D. in 1949. One of his most important philosophical influences was **Quine**, who taught him during his time as a graduate student; the immediate result of this was a moving away from Davidson's earlier interest in the literary and history-of-ideas side of things, toward the philosophical and analytic.

Davidson's teaching career started in New York at Queens College, but in 1951 he moved to Stanford University, where he

Jones did it slowly, deliberately, in the bathroom, with a knife, at midnight. What he did was butter a piece of toast. We are too familiar with the language of action to notice at first an anomaly: the "it" of "Jones did it slowly, deliberately, ..." seems to refer to some entity, presumably an action, that is then characterized in a number of ways.

"The Logical Form of Action Sentences," *in* Essays on Actions and Events, *p.105*

In a nutshell:
Mental events are physical events, but this doesn't allow us to apply physical laws to the mental.

stayed until 1967. During the first part of his career at Stanford he worked with Patrick Suppes on decision theory, and this was to have a considerable influence on his later thinking. However, it was during the 1960s that he began to produce the work for which he became famous, starting with his 1963 paper "Actions, Reasons, and Causes."

In 1967 Davidson went to Princeton, where he stayed for three years, followed by six years at Rockefeller and five at the University of Chicago. In 1981 he took up a position at the University of California, Berkeley, and stayed there until his sudden death (after surgery on his knee) in 2003.

MIND AND ACTION: "ANOMALOUS MONISM"
Davidson's account of the mental is difficult to follow, and he put a great deal of effort into grappling with its deep inconsistencies (these inconsistencies he tended to attribute to the subject matter rather than to his theories). He was a devout physicalist, holding that causation holds only between physical events. Unlike his mentor Quine, however, he tried to combine this view with

in order for us to learn to communicate through language, that language must be constructed of a finite number of elements, even if the potential number of expressions of that language is infinite.

is an event that's intentional under some description: the contracting of certain muscles, the moving of a knife, the buttering of a slice of toast—these are all the same event, described differently, and insofar as they are intentional under those descriptions, they are all the same action.

LANGUAGE

Davidson's writings on mind and action form what's probably the most influential part of his work, but they're closely connected to his philosophy of language. He argued that natural languages had to be constructed out of a finite number of elements, in order for their users to master them; the task of the philosopher of language is thus to show how the meanings of well-formed sentences depend upon their parts. His approach to this task involves two main parts: a theory of truth (drawing on the work of Polish logician Alfred Tarski, whose definition of truth in formal logical languages Davidson adapted to natural languages), and a theory of radical interpretation (that is, a theory of how to assign meanings to a hitherto completely unknown language). The former part develops **Frege's** notion that the meaning of a statement is given by its truth conditions. The latter part involves a principle of charity, which says that our interpretation of a language should maximize the number of statements in that language that are true.

the claim that mental terms can't be reduced to physical terms. This means that if what is described as a mental event is involved in a causal relation, the event must in fact be physical, though its mental description can't be reduced to a physical description. This led him to argue that mental descriptions can't figure in scientific laws, and that there are no scientific laws on the basis of which mental events (that is, events described as mental) can be explained and predicted. On the other hand, such events are subject to the constraints of rationality, consistency, and coherence; otherwise they fail to constitute the mental. Because Davidson accepts that only one kind of thing really exists, he calls his theory *monism*, and because the mental descriptions can't be explained in terms of laws, he calls his monism *anomalous*.

For Davidson, reasons for acting are the causes of our actions; after all, he argued, what could we mean by saying that someone acted for certain reasons if not that those reasons are what caused him or her to act in the way he or she did? This is slightly complicated by his view of actions. An action

Alfred Tarski studied and taught logic and philosophy in Warsaw, moving to the University of California, Berkeley in 1942. He had considerable influence in the field of logic. Davidson adapted his theory of truth in formal logical languages to argue that natural languages are constructed of a limited number of elements.

There is no such thing as a language, not if a language is anything like what many philosophers and linguists have supposed.

"A Nice Derangement of Epitaphs," in **Truth and Interpretation**, ed. LePore, p.446

SIR PETER FREDERICK STRAWSON

BORN	1919, London	DIED	–

MAIN INTERESTS	Logic, language, metaphysics, epistemology, ethics

INFLUENCES	Aristotle, Leibniz, Hume, Kant, Wittgenstein, Russell, Ryle, Ayer

INFLUENCED	–

MAJOR WORKS

Introduction to Logical Theory, Individuals, Freedom and Resentment, Skepticism and Naturalism, Entity and Identity, The Bounds of Sense

The concept of a person is logically prior to that of an individual consciousness. The concept of a person is not to be analyzed as that of an animated body or an embodied anima.

Individuals, p.103

Born in Ealing in west London, the son of a headmaster, Strawson's early education was at Christ's College, Finchley. He won a scholarship to St. John's College, Oxford, and this (together with a state scholarship and the help of an anonymous benefactor) allowed him to go on to undergraduate study. He originally intended to read English, but changed his mind before he started his degree (partly as a result of reading **Rousseau's** *Social Contract*), and switched to Philosophy, Politics, and Economics (P.P.E.).

He graduated in 1940, when he was called up for military service in the Royal Artillery. He served his war years on the home front, though he spent time in Italy and Austria as part of the army of occupation until his demobilization in 1946. On his return he spent a year as assistant lecturer in philosophy at the University College of North Wales, Bangor, and during his time there he applied for, and won, Oxford's John Locke Scholarship. His work for this led Gilbert Ryle to recommend him for a post as college lecturer at University College, Oxford, and he was elected to a fellowship there the following year.

Strawson remained at Oxford from 1948 until 1968. In 1950 he published his first important paper, which is still influential today; in "On Referring" he presented a critical discussion of **Russell's** theory of descriptions, and in so doing challenged widely held beliefs about the way meaning

In a nutshell:

Philosophy should be concerned with things as we know them, not with some abstruse and abstract world beyond our experience or with some artificial formal theory.

and truth are related. In 1968 he was elected Waynflete Professor of Metaphysical Philosophy in the University of Oxford, which took him to a fellowship at Magdalen College. He was knighted in 1977.

LOGIC AND LANGUAGE

Strawson's early work was primarily concerned with issues of logic and language. He was very much in the *ordinary language* tradition that centered on Oxford at the time. In this view, many philosophical problems arise when one takes terms and constructions out of their normal linguistic contexts, and these problems can be solved by careful analysis of everyday usage of language. Thus, in his early paper "On Referring," Strawson argued that Russell had misunderstood the use of referring expressions such as "the present king of France," trying to make them fit a certain philosophical theory, and so being forced to paraphrase. Similarly, albeit on a wider scale, in his book *Introduction to Logical Theory* (1952) and elsewhere Strawson

Nuremburg trial 1945. Strawson's philosophical approach claimed that our concepts of responsibility and blame are compatible with the determinist hypothesis; he held that even if our behavior is predetermined, our ethical relationships would not change, we would still hold people responsible for their actions.

argued that the logical connectives of formal logic were too far removed from ordinary linguistic usage to allow philosophers to understand and explain language from a formal standpoint.

METAPHYSICS

Strawson's 1959 book *Individuals: An Essay in Descriptive Metaphysics* was one of the most important factors in bringing metaphysics back into mainstream philosophy, from which it had been partly exiled by the logical positivists and their followers. Strawson calls what he is doing in the book *descriptive* metaphysics, to distinguish it from what he calls *revisionary* metaphysics; the latter tries to *revise* the way that we think about the world, arguing that appearances mislead us as to the true nature of reality (he places **Descartes**, **Leibniz**, and **Berkeley** in this camp), whereas the former merely tries to describe the *way* that we think about the world, the structure of our thought concerning such things as material bodies and people (in this camp he places **Aristotle** and **Kant**). Thus, Strawson's metaphysical writing isn't a complete departure from his earlier work, as he explains: "It doesn't differ in kind of intention [from philosophical, or logical, or conceptual analysis], but only in scope and generality" (*Individuals*, p.9).

By "individuals" Strawson means primary, basic particulars that are identifiable and re-identifiable. This, he thinks, means that they

must exist in space-time, which rules out Descartes' minds and Leibniz's monads. On the other hand, some of them—people—have mental as well as physical properties, and this leads him to a property dualism: a person isn't made up of two substances, as in Descartes' scheme—it's one thing with two kinds of property.

Strawson's interest in metaphysics of what he conceived as being of a Kantian kind led to his writing on Kant's *Critique of Pure Reason* in one of his most important books, *The Bounds of Sense* (1966). This was far more than a mere commentary; it offered a philosophical discussion that took Kant's work as its starting point and focus.

ETHICS

In his extremely influential paper "Freedom and Resentment" (1962; reprinted in his 1974 book of the same name), Strawson argues that the fact that we hold people responsible for their actions is a natural part of human life that we can't give up. Thus, metaphysical claims that all our actions are wholly determined by preceding causes are irrelevant to ethical behavior; even if (*per impossibile*) such claims were to be proved true, our interpersonal relationships wouldn't—*couldn't*—change. This is a new and unusual version of a position known as compatibilism; that is, it sets out to show that our notions of responsibility, of praise, blame, and resentment, are compatible with the determinist hypothesis.

GERTRUDE ELIZABETH MARGARET ANSCOMBE

BORN	1919, Limerick, Ireland	DIED	2001, Cambridge, England

MAIN INTERESTS   Ethics, action, religion

INFLUENCES   Aristotle, Anselm, Aquinas, Hume, Frege, Russell, Wittgenstein

INFLUENCED   –

MAJOR WORKS
Intention, An Introduction to Wittgenstein's Tractatus

...the government's professed intentions are [...] unlimited. They have not said: "When justice is done on points A, B, and C, then we will stop fighting." They have talked about "sweeping away everything that Hitlerism stands for" and about "building a new order in Europe." What does this mean but that our intentions are so unlimited that there is no point at which we or the Germans could say to our government: "Stop fighting; for your conditions are satisfied."

The Justice of the Present War Examined, p.10

Anscombe was born the youngest of three children, whose father was a science teacher in London. She was educated at Sydenham school in London, and went up to Oxford in 1937 to read classics at St. Hugh's College; in her first year there she became a Catholic. She graduated in 1941, and went to Newnham College, Cambridge, to do graduate work.

While at Cambridge Anscombe attended lectures by **Wittgenstein**, and was very much influenced by his approach to philosophy. When, in 1946, she returned to Oxford to take up a research fellowship at Somerville College, she stayed in contact with Wittgenstein, and they formed a close friendship until his death in 1951. Together with G. H. von Wright and Rush Rhees, she was Wittgenstein's literary executor, and played a leading role in editing and translating his work into English; her translation of *Philosophische Untersuchungen* was published in 1953 as *Philosophical Investigations*, and she followed this with a number of other translations, as well as writing about Wittgenstein's work. She also translated, with Geach, an edition of Descartes' philosophical writings.

Aside from her work on other thinkers—who also included such major figures as Aristotle, Anselm, Aquinas, Hume, and Frege—Anscombe was an original philosopher in her own right, and her book *Intention* (1957)

In their own words:
...if someone really thinks, in advance, that it is open to question whether such an action as procuring the judicial execution of the innocent should be quite excluded from consideration—I do not want to argue with him; he shows a corrupt mind.

"Modern moral philosophy ..."
Philosophy (1958), p.16

was widely regarded as a seminal work in the philosophy of action. Similarly her work in moral philosophy led to a revival of virtue ethics (as well as introducing the term "consequentialism"). In fact her moral thinking was at the root of much of her philosophical work—even the writing of *Intention* was prompted in large part by her view that President Truman (whose receipt of an honorary degree from Oxford she'd recently protested) was guilty of war crimes in his use of atomic weapons against Japanese civilians.

In 1967 Anscombe was elected a fellow of the British Academy, and in 1970 she returned to Cambridge as professor of philosophy, a position she held until her retirement in 1986. Much of her time was spent traveling around the world, teaching and lecturing.

JOHN BORDLEY RAWLS

BORN	1921, Baltimore, Maryland	DIED	2002, Lexington, Massachusetts

MAIN INTERESTS Politics, ethics

INFLUENCES Hobbes, Locke, Rousseau, Mill, Kant, Sidgwick, Berlin, Hart

INFLUENCED –

MAJOR WORKS
A Theory of Justice, Political Liberalism, Justice as Fairness: A Restatement

My aim is to present a conception of justice which generalizes and carries to a higher level of abstraction the familiar theory of the social contract as found, say, in Locke, Rousseau, and Kant.

A Theory of Justice, p.11

Born in Maryland, Rawls' early education was at Kent School, Connecticut. He went to Princeton in 1939, graduating in 1943, and immediately joining the U.S. Army, serving in the infantry in the Pacific. He saw the aftermath of the use of atomic weapons (and later published a condemnation of the U.S. government's actions). Perhaps as a result of this he turned down a commission, and left the army as a private.

Rawls returned to Princeton in 1946, and completed a doctorate in moral philosophy in 1950. After two years teaching at Princeton he spent a fruitful year on a Fulbright fellowship at Christ Church, Oxford. On his return he became first assistant, then associate professor at Cornell University. During his time there he published a paper entitled "Justice as Fairness," based on thinking that he'd done at Princeton, Oxford, and Cornell; this formed the basis of much that came later.

In 1960 he became a professor at M.I.T. He spent only two years there, however, before moving to Harvard, where he was to remain for forty years. He had been working on the ideas that informed his *magnum opus* since he was at Cornell. When he finally published *A Theory of Justice* in 1971 it was an almost immediate success, catapulting him into the forefront of political philosophy—however many papers and books he published, Rawls was always known as the author of *A Theory of Justice*. In his later work, however, he

modified his views, moving toward the left (insofar as such a simplistic label can be applied to a complex thinker like Rawls).

Rawls' account of justice is extensive and complex, but at its heart are two principles: a principle of equal basic liberties, and a principle about social and economic inequalities. This latter states, first, that such inequalities should be allowed only if they serve to benefit those who are worst off in society, and second, that there should be equality of *opportunity*. The fairness of these principles, argues Rawls, is brought out by the fact that we would choose them even if we were in what he calls "the original position" of being behind a "veil of ignorance." That is, if we were faced with choosing the kind of society in which we were to live, but without knowing who we'd be in that society—if we were ignorant of our sex, social background, value system, talents, and so on—we would choose a society that was maximally fair. Thus, we would choose Rawls' two principles.

In their own words:
Each person possesses an inviolability founded on justice that even the welfare of society as a whole cannot override.

A Theory of Justice, p.3

THOMAS SAMUEL KUHN

BORN	1922, Cincinnati, Ohio	DIED	1996, Cambridge, Mass.

MAIN INTERESTS   Science

INFLUENCES   Koyré, Bachelard, Popper, Quine, Fleck

INFLUENCED   –

MAJOR WORKS
The Copernican Revolution, The Structure of Scientific Revolutions, The Essential Tension

In a sense that I am unable to explicate further, the proponents of competing paradigms practice their trades in different worlds. [And in doing so,] the two groups of scientists see different things when they look from the same point in the same direction.

The Structure of Scientific
Revolutions, p.149

Kuhn studied physics at Harvard, graduating in 1943. He spent World War II employed at Harvard, and then attached to the U.S. Office of Scientific Research and Development in Europe. After the war he returned to his studies in theoretical physics at Harvard. While working on his doctorate he taught a class of nonscientists, for which he did research into scientific history; this so undermined his views of the nature of science that he moved into the field of the history and philosophy of science. He eventually became assistant professor in general education and the history of science.

In 1956 Kuhn moved to the University of California at Berkeley, where he published his first book, *The Copernican Revolution* (1957), a study of the development of heliocentric cosmology. He became a professor of the history of science in 1961, and published his most famous and influential book *The Structure of Scientific Revolutions* (1962). He became the M. Taylor Pyne Professor of Philosophy and History of Science at Princeton, in 1964. While there he produced *The Essential Tension* (1977), and his last book, *The Black-Body Theory and the Quantum Discontinuity* (1978). In 1983, after a year as a fellow at the New York Institute for the Humanities, he went to M.I.T., becoming the Laurence S. Rockefeller Professor of Philosophy until 1991.

In *The Structure of Scientific Revolutions*, Kuhn presented an account of how science

Note:
The notion of a paradigm is one of the most misunderstood in philosophy, being misapplied in all sorts of nonscientific (especially artistic) areas, where it makes little sense but looks impressively intellectual.

develops rather than how it *should* be done. Normal science, he argued, consists of solving problems, and this is carried on by scientists working within a shared framework of background theories, assumptions, techniques, and typical models—a paradigm. Problems that can't be solved—anomalies—build up, and the resulting tension leads to a scientific revolution, a shift to a new paradigm. Normal science continues within this new paradigm until the next shift.

Though illuminating in many ways, one problem with Kuhn's account was that the term "paradigm" was made to do too much work, so that it had no clear meaning. In his paper "Second Thoughts on Paradigms," Kuhn corrected this, using the term "disciplinary matrix" for the broad sense of "paradigm" (the values, beliefs, techniques, shared by the scientific community), and "exemplar" for the narrower sense (standard, exemplary theories giving an accepted pattern for solutions to problems).

OVERVIEW
PHILOSOPHY OF SCIENCE

For more than two thousand years, philosophy included what we now call the physical sciences, the two disciplines only really beginning to divide during the early modern period. That division, however, was never total. The relationship between science, philosophy, and the philosophy of science is still a complex one, with no clear, nonarbitrary, dividing lines. A sign (or, perhaps, one of the causes) of their closeness is the fact that many philosophers of science started life as scientists.

We can distinguish the methods of science from those of philosophy in various ways. The most obvious is that science is concerned with the empirical, with knowledge gained from careful use of observation. What is known as the *naïve empiricist* view of science is that scientists start by making observations of the world, generalize from those observations to create theories, and then test those theories by making fresh observations. This view is naïve in that it fails to notice that the distinction between observation and theory is far from clear-cut; all observations are at least bound up with and dependent upon concepts and skills, at worst laden with theory. Moreover, what exactly is to count as an observation? The use of the unaided senses, or may we use devices? Is the use of a telescope observation? A radio telescope? An optical microscope? A scanning electron microscope?

Many modern scientists dismiss philosophy as irrelevant to science. Most of them do so on the basis of their acceptance of some variant of logical positivism's "Criterion of Verifiability" (that only what can be empirically verified is meaningful); that is, they dismiss philosophy on the basis of their unreflective acceptance of a philosophical theory that has long been discredited (and that rules out much of science, as well as itself). Nevertheless many, if not most, of the great scientists have either seen themselves as being as much philosophers as scientists (for example, Darwin and Einstein), or have at least acknowledged the effect of philosophy on their work (**Popper** is a philosopher often cited in this respect).

There are a great many central questions with which the philosophy of science is concerned: What is the nature of science? How does it differ from the nonsciences, and what is its relationship with them? Do such disciplines as history, economics, sociology, and psychology count as genuine sciences? What is required of a good scientific explanation? What constitutes scientific progress? What is the status of scientific theory? In addition to these, there are questions that arise from individual branches of the sciences, especially physics and, more recently, biology: What is the nature of space and time? What metaphysical implications does quantum theory have? What is life? Are species natural or human-created divisions of the living world?

The modern philosophy of science has tended to concentrate on one central question: What exactly is the status of scientific theories? Are they attempts to describe the world, or are they simply predictive tools? That is, is science trying to reach the truth about the way the world (and especially the unobservable world) is, or is it concerned only to produce testable (and usable) consequences? The former sort of position is known as realism, the latter as instrumentalism. Instrumentalism in particular comes in a number of forms, from the crude logical positivism that denies meaning to statements about the unobservable, to the more sophisticated "constructive empiricism" that allows that theories do genuinely try to describe the world, but that only the testable consequences matter to science.

One of the main realist responses to instrumentalism is known as the *no miracle* argument (associated especially with the early writings of **Putnam**): given that scientific theories do produce much successful prediction, this would be an astonishing coincidence if the theories weren't at least partly true descriptions of the nature of the world.

DUMMETT
SIR MICHAEL ANTHONY EARDLEY

BORN	1925, London	DIED	–

MAIN INTERESTS	Logic, language, mathematics, epistemology, metaphysics

INFLUENCES	Brouwer, Frege, Wittgenstein

INFLUENCED	–

MAJOR WORKS
Frege: Philosophy of Language, Truth and Other Enigmas, Origins of Analytic Philosophy, The Logical Basis of Metaphysics, The Seas of Language

Born in London, Dummett attended Sandroyd School in Wiltshire and Winchester College, after which he served in the armed forces from 1943 to 1947. On his return after the war, he went up to read P.P.E. at Christ Church, Oxford, graduating in 1950, when he won a fellowship at All Souls College, Oxford. He also taught philosophy part-time at Birmingham University for a year (1950–1951), and in 1962 was appointed Reader in the Philosophy of Mathematics at Oxford. In 1979 he was elected Wykeham Professor of Logic at Oxford, and he held the chair until his retirement in 1992. Over the years he has held visiting positions at universities around the world. He and his wife, Ann, have involved themselves in social causes, especially the fight against racism and the issue of immigration, both topics on which he has written. He has also found time to publish a number of works on the tarot.

Dummett has made significant contributions to many areas of philosophy, especially the philosophy of language, philosophical logic, and metaphysics, but his first important work was *Frege: Philosophy of Language* (1973). He has continued to work and write on **Frege** throughout his career, and is one of the most important and influential Fregean scholars in the world; we owe it to Dummett, in fact, that Frege's work is available to English-speaking philosophy in the way that it is now.

In a nutshell:
What's true is what's proved; what's false is what's disproved.

LANGUAGE
Language is at the heart of Dummett's philosophical work. Indeed, he claims that philosophy before Frege was flawed by its insistence on the primacy of epistemology, instead of grounding itself in the study of language. This is a controversial view on many counts, not least because Frege himself seems not to have noticed that he was concerned with language (he believed that he was dealing with logic and thought).

For Dummett, the debate between realists and antirealists is in fact a debate about semantics—about how language gets its meaning. The realist holds that all meaningful statements are either true or false (this is the *Principle of Bivalence*), and that this is independent of us. Thus, a realist about the past will hold that "Ethelred the Unready had indigestion on his twenty-first birthday" is either true or false, even though there's no way to tell which is correct. The antirealist, however, holds that the truth of a statement is a matter of the evidence for or against it—the conditions under which the statement would be assertible or deniable. Because we can't offer any evidence for or against the statement about Ethelred, it is

The conflict between realism and antirealism is a conflict about the kind of meaning possessed by statements of the disputed class.

Truth and Other Enigmas, p.155

neither true nor false. This denial of the principle of bivalence links Dummett's views on language and truth to his account of mathematics.

MATHEMATICS

Dummett is largely responsible for the continuing interest in a certain antirealist account of mathematics: *intuitionism*. This was first put forward by the Dutch mathematician L. E. J. Brouwer (1881–1966), and holds that mathematical objects are not real or independent of us, as Platonist realists hold, but are constructed by mathematicians. Thus, a mathematical statement is simply the report by a mathematician of what she constructed, and is true or false just in case there's either a proof or disproof of it. In cases where no such proof or disproof exists, the statement has no truth value—it is neither true nor false.

In fact Dummett didn't accept Brouwer's version of intuitionism, because it relied upon the private objects and operations in the minds of mathematicians. Rather, he took over the basic approach, but argued that what counts for the truth of a mathematical statement is that there be a proof of it; it then becomes the mathematician's job to construct such a proof.

This disagreement between realists and antirealists has direct and practical implications for mathematics and logic. For example, given a proof that the truth of some statement p implies the truth of another statement q, and a proof that the falsity of p also implies the truth of q, the realist can conclude that q is true even if she has no proof or disproof of p, because the principle of bivalence tells us that p must be either true or false, and both possibilities imply q (is true). The antirealist, however, rejects the principle, and so has more work to do; she has to prove either that p is true or that it is false.

Dummett popularized the term antirealism as part of his work toward a principle for resolving a number of debates. Each debate has a common form but the subject matter varies widely. In each debate, there is a realist, and an antirealist position. The positions apply a different logical method to the statement. In this debate on a statement about the past, a realist would contend that the statement "Ethelred the Unready had indigestion on his twenty-first birthday" must be true or false. The antirealist would contend that the truth of the statement is a matter of evidence for or against it.

Learning language involves learning what justifications are required for sentences of different kinds. In its initial stages, it requires the child to respond to the assertions of others; but later, also to question what may be asserted, even as a matter of common agreement.

Frege: Philosophy of Language, *p.622*

JACQUES DERRIDA

BORN	1930, El-Biar, Algeria	**DIED**	2004, Paris

MAIN INTERESTS Language, linguistics, politics, epistemology

INFLUENCES Marx, Rousseau, Saussure, Lévi-Strauss, Heidegger

INFLUENCED Most post-structuralist thought

MAJOR WORKS
De la Grammatologie,
L'Écriture et la Différence,
La Dissémination,
Spectres de Marx

Jacques Derrida was born July 15, 1930, into an indigenous Jewish family in Algeria, which was at that time a French colony. He was expelled from school under anti-Semitic Vichy laws in 1941, and was more interested in football than education for a time, failing his baccalauréat in 1947 and only making it into the École Normale Supérieure in Paris at the third attempt in 1954. After his degree, he spent four years teaching at the Sorbonne before returning to the École Normale, where he spent much of his professional life. Derrida was most lionized, however, in the English departments of American universities, and he lectured regularly in California and New York. He died on October 8, 2004.

In a nutshell:
By breaking down the assumptions and processes behind writing and speaking, we can go beyond them and find new ways of thinking about the world.

as his detractors, and as with all ideas, Derrida's theories have to be understood in the social and intellectual context of their time. French philosophy in the 1960s was dominated by the linguistics of the Swiss theorist Ferdinand de Saussure. Saussure argued that language was a system, in which the key to understanding was not the words themselves but the *differences* between them. An individual word, or sign, has meaning not in itself, but in the way it differs from other signs, both in sound/mark (the *signifier*) and in concept (the *signified,* the meaning of the word). An arbitrary shift in signifiers, say from "cat" to "mat," produces a fundamental change in meaning.

Thus Saussure's interest was in the deep-level structures that govern this meaning, rather than the superficial language itself. Inspired by scientific revelations such as the

Real meaning comes in the differences between signs, and those differences themselves become new signs

LANGUAGE AND DIFFERENCE
Few thinkers have been as misused and abused as Derrida, by his followers as much

Metaphysical closure

I think that all concepts hitherto proposed, in order to think the articulation of a discourse and of a historical totality, are caught within the metaphysical closure that I question here, as we do not know of any other concepts and cannot produce any others, and indeed shall not produce so long as this closure limits our discourse ... [Therefore our work] consists in questioning the internal structures of these texts as symptoms.

De la Grammatologie, p.147-8

decoding of DNA, other thinkers like the anthropologist Claude Lévi-Strauss extended Saussure's analysis of language to other social systems such as family and political structures, arguing that they too could be read as language-like systems. This "structuralism" was the theoretical framework against which Derrida was reacting.

Derrida's innovation was to show that the differences in signifiers *never end*: each new meaning itself becomes a new signifier, creating what Derrida called "infinite play." There is no stable halting point in language, yet at the same time, because we need words to have specific meanings, we treat them as if they do and hold back the process of infinite play in everyday life. This tension between the dynamic movement of change and the restraint of change in language Derrida called "*différance*," playing on the French for both difference and deferment.

DECONSTRUCTION

Importantly, Derrida did this not merely for academic debate but to destabilize what he saw in the works of thinkers such as Lévi-Strauss and Rousseau as a division of the world into crass binaries of innocence/guilt or authenticity/artifice. The authors themselves are not necessarily aware of these divisions, which they use to make points about the relative worth of certain cultures or ideas versus others. By close textual analysis of these authors' works,

Derrida tried to reveal the hidden assumptions and objectives in their writing, and in doing so, work through or "deconstruct" the rigid frameworks within which they operated, opening our minds to the possibility of new and less constrained ways of thinking.

Derrida was often excoriated by the right for allegedly denying the possibility of truth and hijacked by liberal graduate students to justify ever more arcane analyses of game shows and children's toys. While his fondness for wordplay and his opaque writing style undermined Derrida's desire to reach out to ordinary people beyond the universities, the radicalism of his efforts to move beyond the clumsy polarities of good and bad that bedevil contemporary politics cannot be denied.

Deconstruction: breaking down the walls to open up new spaces.

OVERVIEW
AFRICAN PHILOSOPHY

The Kenyan philosopher Henry Odera Oruka distinguishes what he calls four trends in African philosophy: ethnophilosophy, philosophic sagacity, nationalistic-ideological philosophy, and professional philosophy. In fact it would be more realistic to call them candidates for the position of African philosophy, with the understanding that more than one of them might fit the bill.

Ethnophilosophy involves the recording of the beliefs found in African cultures. Such an approach treats African philosophy as consisting of a set of shared beliefs, a shared world view—an item of communal property rather than an activity for the individual.

Philosophic sagacity is a sort of individualist version of ethnophilosophy, in which one records the beliefs of certain special members of a community. The premise here is that, though most societies demand some degree of conformity of belief and behavior from their members, a certain few of those members reach a particularly high level of knowledge and understanding of their cultures' world view; such people are known as sages. In some cases, the sage goes beyond mere knowledge and understanding to reflection and questioning—these become the targets of philosophic sagacity.

An immediate worry is that not all reflection and questioning is philosophical; besides, if African philosophy were to be defined purely in terms of philosophic sagacity, then the thoughts of the sages couldn't be African philosophy, for they didn't record them from other sages. Also, in this view the only difference between non-African anthropology or ethnology and African philosophy seems to be the nationality of the researcher.

The problem with both ethnophilosophy and philosophical sagacity is that there is surely an important distinction between philosophy and the history of ideas. No matter how interesting the beliefs of a people such as the Akan or the Yorúba may be to the philosopher, they remain beliefs, not philosophy. To call them philosophy is to use a secondary sense of that term, as in "my philosophy is live and let live."

Nationalistic–ideological philosophy might be seen as a special case of philosophic sagacity, in which not sages but ideologues are the subjects. Alternatively, we might see it as a case of professional political philosophy. In either case, the same sort of problem arises: we have to retain a distinction between ideology and philosophy, between sets of ideas and a special way of reasoning.

Professional philosophy is the view that philosophy is a particular way of thinking, reflecting, and reasoning; that such a way is relatively new to (most of) Africa; and that African philosophy must grow in terms of the philosophical work carried out by Africans and applied to (perhaps not exclusively) African concerns. This sort of view would be the intuitive answer of most Western philosophers (whether of Continental or analytic persuasion) to the question, "What is African philosophy?"

Ethnophilosophers attempt to show that African philosophy is distinctive by treading heavily on the "African" and almost losing the "philosophy." Their main rivals are the professional philosophers, who hold that African philosophy must grow out of philosophical work carried out by Africans, and therefore tread heavily on the "philosophy," but risk losing the "African"; this risk, however, is by no means unavoidable, and many African philosophers have indeed successfully avoided it, including Kwame Anthony Appiah, Kwame Gyekye, **Kwasi Wiredu**, Oshita O. Oshita, Lansana Keita, Peter Bodunrin, and Chukwudum B. Okolo.

KWASI WIREDU

BORN　1931, Kumasi, Ghana	**DIED**　–

MAIN INTERESTS　Philosophical logic, epistemology, metaphysics, politics

INFLUENCES　Plato, Hume, Kant, Russell, Dewey, Ryle, Hampshire, Strawson

INFLUENCED　–

MAJOR WORKS

Philosophy and an African Culture, Cultural Universals and Particulars: An African Perspective

For a body of thought to be legitimately associated with a given race, people, region, or nation, it is sufficient that it should be, or should become, a living tradition therein. It is indifferent whether it is home brewed or borrowed wholly or partially from other peoples.

"On Defining African Philosophy," in African Philosophy: The Essential Readings, ed. T. Serequeberhan, p.106

Wiredu attended Adisadel secondary school from 1948 to 1952; it was here that he encountered philosophy—first **Plato's** dialogues, then the work of **Bertrand Russell**. He was an undergraduate at the University of Ghana in Legon, graduating in 1958, before going on to study at University College, Oxford, gaining the B.Phil. in 1960. At Oxford he was taught by Gilbert Ryle, **Peter Strawson**, and Stuart Hampshire, and wrote his thesis on "Knowledge, Truth, and Reason." He taught philosophy at the University of Keele (at that time University College of North Staffordshire) for a year, before returning to the University of Ghana in 1961. He taught there for twenty-three years, became head of department in 1971 and professor in 1981, the latter a year after the publication of his first book, *Philosophy and an African Culture*.

He has held visiting professorships at U.C.L.A. (1979–1980), the University of Ibadan, Nigeria (1984), the University of Richmond, Virginia (1985), Carleton College, Minnesota (1986), and Duke University, North Carolina (1994–1995 and again 1999–2001). He has also held fellowships at the Woodrow Wilson International Center for Scholars (1985) and the National Humanities Center, North Carolina (1986). Since 1987 he has held the position of professor of philosophy at the University of South Florida, Tampa.

Wiredu argues that it is important to distinguish between the folk beliefs and world views that can be found in and are distinctive to all cultures, and philosophy. He is thus opposed to the ethnophilosophy and philosophic sagacity approaches to African philosophy; such "folk philosophy," as he calls it, can form part of genuine philosophy (indeed, he has said of his own work that he is "indebted to the thought of unnamed metaphysicians who left Akan culture [my culture] cosmological riddles in drum language"), but only with the addition of rigorous argument and critical analysis. His own philosophy is thus firmly in the professional philosophy camp, and he is one of the most accomplished in this field in modern African philosophy.

In accordance with his understanding of the nature of philosophy, Wiredu's methodology involves applying methods of analysis and argument (influenced especially by the pragmatist thought of **Dewey** and the concern with language of Ryle and **Strawson**) to the rich linguistic and cultural resources of his own people (the Akan), in areas such as truth and human rights. The result is wholly philosophical, and of interest to any philosopher of whatever cultural background; at the same time, however, it is centrally and essentially African.

In a nutshell:

Wiredu represents African philosophy, but his philosophy is not solely relevant to Africa.

DAVID WIGGINS

BORN 1933, London	DIED –

MAIN INTERESTS   Metaphysics, logic, ethics

INFLUENCES   Aristotle, Leibniz, Hume, Frege, Peirce, Russell, Quine, Davidson

INFLUENCED   –

MAJOR WORKS
*Identity and Spatio-Temporal Continuity,
Sameness and Substance, Needs, Values, and Truth,
Sameness and Substance Renewed*

...what sortal concepts we apply to experience determines what we can find there, [but this] is to be understood in the unexciting way in which one understands the statement that the size and mesh of a net determine not what fish are in the sea but which ones we shall catch.

"On singling out an object determinately,"
in P. Pettit and J. McDowell [ed.], **Subject, Thought, and Context**, p.171

Born in London, Wiggins went to St. Paul's School, and read classics at Brasenose College, Oxford. He approached philosophy reluctantly, but was soon excited and enthralled. In 1957 he joined the civil service, but left after a year to take up a scholarship at Princeton. In 1959 he became a philosophy lecturer at New College, Oxford, and was elected a fellow the following year; he stayed there until 1967, when he became professor of philosophy at Bedford College, London. In 1981 he returned to Oxford for eight years as a fellow of University College before moving back to London as professor of philosophy at Birkbeck College. In 1993 he was elected Wykeham Professor of Logic at Oxford, and returned to New College until his retirement in 2000.

Wiggins has never followed philosophical fashion; at times, he has been noteworthy for the steadfast way that, as teacher and philosopher, he has plowed his furrow in relative obscurity, while a succession of stars have flared in the philosophical firmament. Once their brightness has died away, however, he is to be found still stubbornly following the argument where it leads him. The feature that characterizes his philosophical work across various topics is a concern with the nature of things, the world, and us—the metaphysical question of the way that objects "are articulated or isolated or found or drawn or formed or carved out in the world."

In their own words:
The larger the obstacles nature or other people put in our way, and the more truly hopeless the prospect, the less point most of us will feel anything has. [...] In the end, point is partly dependent upon expectation of outcome; and expectation is dependent upon past outcomes.

Needs, Values, and Truth, *p.98*

Wiggins offers a combination of nominalism (or conceptualism) and realism: a sort of conceptualist realism. He argues that, though we choose how to conceptualize reality, we don't choose what's there to be conceptualized; although we impose the lines of demarcation between kinds of thing, we don't do so arbitrarily—there are right and wrong ways to do it. In ethics he offers a similar combination of elements of subjectivism and realism, giving an objectivist moral theory according to which moral judgments are subjectively conditioned with respect to their sense, but aim at truth. For example, when we work through everything that's involved in slavery, it becomes evident that there's nothing else to think but that slavery is intolerable and wrong.

THOMAS NAGEL

BORN	1937, Belgrade	DIED	–

MAIN INTERESTS   Mind, epistemology, ethics, politics

INFLUENCES   Kant, Wittgenstein, Strawson, Rawls, Wiggins, Williams, Kripke

INFLUENCED   –

MAJOR WORKS

The Possibility of Altruism, Mortal Questions, The View from Nowhere, Equality and Partiality

Nagel has also written an introduction to philosophy, aimed at younger readers, titled **What Does It All Mean?** *(1987).*

Nagel graduated from Cornell University in 1958. He went on to Corpus Christi College, Oxford, where he did the B.Phil., and then to Harvard for his Ph.D., which he received in 1963. He first taught at the University of California at Berkeley from 1963, then at Princeton University from 1966 to 1980, working his way up from assistant professor to full professor. It was while associate professor there that he published his first book, *The Possibility of Altruism* (1970); his second work—*Mortal Questions* (1979)— came out a year before he moved to New York University, where he is professor of philosophy and Fiorello La Guardia Professor of Law.

Nagel's work is perhaps the most powerful defense found in modern philosophy against any physicalist, functionalist, neurobiologically reductive, or eliminative theory of consciousness. He defends the irreducibility, not only of mental concepts but, more important, of the reality of subjective facts and their inseparability from a subject who experiences the world from a particular point of view; he sees this point of view as the essence of consciousness, not merely a reflection on it. Thus, consciousness essentially entails that there is something it is like to be a particular conscious being. It is this undeniable fact that poses the greatest challenge to the claims of any monistic, or reductionist, theoretical account, that marks the important difference between physical phenomena, for which reduction is possible, and subjective phenomena, where reductive attempts are impossible. Without the fact that there is something it is like to be a conscious being, monistic theories are less interesting and self-obliterating; with it, such theories are hopeless. Nagel's central thought is captured in his most influential paper, "What Is It Like To Be A Bat?" (1974), reprinted in *Mortal Questions*.

Nagel's work in moral and political philosophy is also realistic and Kantian in approach, finding in the facts of self-consciousness at least the necessary conditions for the possibility and nature of morality and altruism, of equality and political commitment. Self-conscious beings have the capacity to step back and reflect on themselves, their actions, their lives, and the world. Nagel's main interest in these areas is with practical rationality and autonomy—the ability to think and choose under the guidance of practical rational requirements. Also like Kant, he opposes any relativist and reductive accounts of morality and political theory.

In their own words:

Just as there are rational requirements on thought, there are rational requirements on action, and altruism is one of them.

The Possibility of Altruism, p.3

SAUL AARON KRIPKE

BORN	1940, New York	DIED	—

MAIN INTERESTS	Philosophical logic, language, metaphysics, epistemology

INFLUENCES	Mill, Frege, Russell, Wittgenstein, Wiggins

INFLUENCED	—

MAJOR WORKS
Naming and Necessity,
Wittgenstein on Rules and Private Language

If pain is brain process it cannot exist without being felt as pain.

Born in New York, Kripke grew up in Omaha, Nebraska. He studied at Harvard, from which he graduated in 1962. He was something of a youth prodigy, publishing papers on logic while still in his teens, and on graduation he was appointed a junior fellow at Harvard until 1966 (while also teaching as lecturer and then assistant professor at Princeton), then became a lecturer at Harvard from 1966 to 1968. He left to take up a post as associate professor at Rockefeller University in 1968, becoming professor in 1972, but moved to Princeton in 1976, where he remains, having transferred to emeritus status in 1997. He is also Distinguished Professor of Philosophy at the City University of New York Graduate Center, and a fellow of both the American Academy of Arts and Sciences and the British Academy.

Kripke's philosophical importance lies mainly with his work in three areas: meaning, metaphysics, and modality, though his iconoclastic discussion of some of **Wittgenstein's** ideas has also been influential. He is unusual among modern philosophers in that much of his work is unpublished, some of it existing only in the form of tape-recordings or transcripts.

MEANING, MODALITY, AND MIND

In *Naming and Necessity* (1980), based on lectures he'd given at Princeton, Kripke criticized the descriptivist theory of reference of philosophers such as **Frege** and **Russell**—that is, the view that a name works by association with descriptions that are satisfied by the object to which the name refers. Like **J. S. Mill** he denies that proper names have meanings at all. He offers instead a causal theory of reference, which holds that a name picks out or refers to an object because of a chain of causes linking the use of the name through communities of speakers back to an initial baptism. The initial baptism might itself have involved a description, but that's generally lost as the name is passed on from user to user.

Kripke also introduces the notion of rigid designation. A referring expression is a rigid designator if it picks out the same object in every possible world at which that object exists; it's a nonrigid or weak designator if it picks out different objects at different worlds. Definite descriptions are generally weak designators, whereas names (including terms such as "pain" and "brain state") are generally rigid designators. The expressions "the writer of 'Scrapple from the Apple'" and "Charlie Parker" actually both refer to the same man, but Parker mightn't have written "Scrapple from the Apple"—so whereas "Charlie Parker" always picks out the same person, "the writer of 'Scrapple from the Apple'" picks out Dizzy Gillespie at some possible worlds, Thelonious Monk at others, and even a precocious Saul Kripke at some bizarre worlds.

Now, Charlie Parker was billed as "Charlie Chan" for the recording of *Jazz at Massey*

Hall in 1953, so it's true that Charlie Chan *is* (i.e. is the same person as, is identical with) Charlie Parker. Any true identity statement is necessarily true, yet we could know that Charlie Chan was Charlie Parker only by experience. There are, then, necessary truths knowable only empirically.

There are two main approaches to the notion that an object has an essence: first, that the essence is a matter of how we choose to describe the object, not a feature of the object itself (this is the position adopted by **Quine**), and second, the view held by Kripke, that the essence is some property or set of properties of the object that can be empirically discovered. Whereas the essence of a kind of stuff will be something like its molecular structure, the essence of an individual is its origin; for example, the essential nature of water is to be H_2O, whereas the essential nature of a human being is the fertilization of a particular egg by a particular sperm.

Kripke argues that states such as pain also have essences; for example, the essence of pain, what constitutes pain, is the sensation of pain—is painfulness. Connecting metaphysics and language, if "pain" and "brain state" are rigid designators, then if pain and brain states are identical, they're necessarily identical. But if it's possible that there is the relevant brain state without painfulness, or vice versa, they're not necessarily identical, and so not identical at all. Physicalism, which identifies pain with some physical or functional state, is therefore false.

WITTGENSTEIN

Kripke has published material from a series of lectures he gave at Princeton as *Wittgenstein on Rules and Private Language* (1982). This isn't so much a commentary on (the later work of) **Wittgenstein** as a philosophical work that takes as its starting point and focus some of Wittgenstein's positions and arguments—though Kripke does offer a somewhat unusual account of what he takes to have been the shape of Wittgenstein's concerns. He takes the central focus of Wittgenstein's arguments to have been the issue of rule following, and tries to show that the private-language argument is a specific application of those general ideas. This is so different from the standard view that critics have dubbed the subject of his book "Kripkenstein."

[The cluster concept theory of names] really is a nice theory. The only defect I think it has is probably common to all philosophical theories. It's wrong.

Naming and Necessity, p.64

In a nutshell:
The essence of a thing is its origin.

DAVID KELLOGG LEWIS

BORN 1941, Oberlin, Ohio	**DIED** 2001, Princeton, New Jersey

MAIN INTERESTS   Logic, language, metaphysics, epistemology, ethics

INFLUENCES   Leibniz, Hume, Ryle, Quine, Strawson

INFLUENCED   –

MAJOR WORKS
*Convention,
Counterfactuals,
On the Plurality
of Worlds, Parts
of Classes*

...every world is actual at itself, and thereby all worlds are on a par. This is not to say that all worlds are actual—there's no world at which that's true, any more than there's ever a time when all times are present.

On the Plurality of Worlds, p.93

Lewis' parents were both academics, one a professor of government, the other a medieval historian. His early education was at Oberlin High School, where he developed an interest in chemistry, and in fact he initially went as an undergraduate to Swarthmore College to study chemistry. After spending a year abroad at the University of Oxford (1959–1960), where he attended lectures by such figures as Ryle, Grice, **Strawson**, and Austin, he switched to philosophy on his return to Swarthmore. After graduating in 1964 he went on to Harvard to work on his Ph.D. under **Quine**.

In 1966 he went to U.C.L.A. as an assistant professor, and published his doctoral thesis as *Convention: A Philosophical Study*, in which he used game-theoretical concepts to analyze linguistic conventions. In 1970 he moved to Princeton as an associate professor, becoming a full professor in 1973. This was also the year in which he published one of his most important books: in *Counterfactuals* he presented a novel and extremely influential analysis of counterfactual conditionals in terms of possible-world theory, and introduced the theory with which he was to be closely associated for the rest of his life—modal realism. In *On the Plurality of Worlds* (1986), part of which he'd given as the John Locke Lectures at Oxford in 1984, he extended his account of modal realism, and provided a detailed defense of it. He stayed at Princeton until his death in 2001 of complications

In a nutshell:

"Humean supervenience: [...] the doctrine that all there is to the world is a vast mosaic of local matters of particular fact, just one little thing and then another."

Introduction to **Philosophical Papers**,
Vol. II, p.ix

attendant upon the diabetes from which he'd suffered all his life.

He was an enthusiastic traveler, especially enjoying railway journeys, and reserved his greatest affection for Australia, which became something of a second home to him.

Lewis' philosophical interests were broad, as evidenced by the contents of the five volumes of his collected papers published so far: ethics, politics, metaphysics, epistemology, philosophical logic, language—he wrote on a vast range of subjects, from holes to worlds, from **Anselm** to **Mill**, from the mind to time travel. In everything he wrote he was rigorous, committed, and clear, but perhaps the most distinctive thing about him was his attitude toward other philosophers, and especially toward criticism: one can scarcely find a book or paper attacking Lewis' views that doesn't

Philosophy and the man on the street

It is not to be demanded that a philosophical theory should agree with anything that the man on the street would insist on offhand, uninformed, and therefore uninfluenced by any theoretical gains to be had by changing his mind. (Especially not if, like many men on the streets nowadays, he would rise to the occasion and wax wildly philosophical at the slightest provocation.)

On the Plurality of Worlds, p.134

A philosophical theory should not be accountable to the average man in the street because he is uninformed and as such is unlikely to change his mind as a result of theoretical argument.

contain an acknowledgment to him for his help. What mattered to him—what he loved—was the ideas, the arguments, the philosophy, not winning or being right. He was the ideal, the model philosopher; he is also (and this is a very different matter) widely regarded as being the best philosopher of his generation—perhaps of the twentieth century.

POSSIBLE WORLDS

Lewis is perhaps best known for his modal realism. As he emphasizes in the preface to *On the Plurality of Worlds*, this isn't realism in the common modern sense of a claim about semantics or truth or the limits of knowledge or the principle of bivalence; it's simply a claim about what exists. It's the view that our talk about possible worlds ("Could this be the best of all possible worlds?" "There's a possible world in which kangaroos have no tails," and so on) isn't about a set of mental or linguistic or otherwise constructed objects, but about worlds just as real as this one. Our world is special to us because we live here (in other words, it's the actual world), but otherwise it's no more real than any other world. The inhabitants of other worlds call their own worlds actual, too, and they're right to do so; "actual" is an indexical term like "here" or "now."

Although statements such as "I might have been a contender" are to be explained in terms of what the case is at other possible

worlds, that's not to say that we (or anything else) exist in more than one world; rather, we have *counterparts* in other worlds—people who are very like us and who correspond to us in those worlds (rather as someone might correspond to me in a computer simulation). Not only do we not exist in other worlds, but they're completely closed to us—they're spatiotemporally and causally isolated from each other, so inter-world travel makes no sense.

When philosophers and other academics talk about the world, or about possible worlds, they mean "the universe" or possible "universes" rather than this or any other planet.

SUSAN HAACK

BORN	1945, Burnham, England	DIED	—

MAIN INTERESTS   Logic, language, epistemology, metaphysics, science, law

INFLUENCES   Francis Bacon, Peirce, Russell, Strawson, Quine, Austin

INFLUENCED   —

MAJOR WORKS

Deviant Logic, Philosophy of Logics, Evidence and Inquiry, Manifesto of a Passionate Moderate, Defending Science—Within Reason

Tempting as it is to overreact to Churchland's unseemly rush from the nonpropositional workings of the ganglia of the sea slug to his vulgar pragmatism about the goal of inquiry, I acknowledge that it might be desirable for epistemologists to pay more attention than they mostly have to the pre-propositional, to knowing how, and to tacit knowledge.

Evidence and Inquiry, p.169

Haack read P.P.E. at St. Hilda's College, Oxford, graduating in 1966, and went on to do the B.Phil. She then took up a fellowship for three years at New Hall, Cambridge, where she also earned her Ph.D. In 1971 she went to the University of Warwick as a lecturer, becoming a reader in 1976, and professor in 1982. Since 1990 she has taught at the University of Miami, where she is Cooper Senior Scholar in Arts and Sciences, professor of philosophy, and professor of law.

Haack's forte is clear, incisive, often wryly humorous writing. She is deeply attached to the philosophical ideal of honest inquiry, and impatient both with the vacuities of intellectual fashions (though not so impatient that she can't find the time to slice off their fancy icing to reveal the dried-out sponge cake beneath) and with the aridity of much academic philosophy. Though she made her name with her first two books, both on logic—*Deviant Logic* (1974) and *Philosophy of Logics* (1978)—her contributions to philosophy have perhaps been most important in the field of epistemology, starting with the work that she presented in *Evidence and Inquiry* (1993).

Haack's contributions to epistemology center on and start with what she calls, somewhat inelegantly, "foundherentism": a double-aspect theory combining elements of foundationalism and coherentism. Having assessed each of these two traditional (and

In their own words:

Headlines in the Official Newsletter of the University of Warwick, I recall, announced "Major Research Success for Physics at Warwick"; the text told us, not of some breakthrough achieved by our physicists, but of their landing major research funding.

Manifesto of a Passionate Moderate, p.194

traditionally opposed) approaches to epistemology, she concludes that each approach has its strengths, and tries to develop a view that allows for the importance both of empirical experience and of the mutual support between beliefs. Her central explanatory analogy is with crossword puzzles: one's degree of certainty that the answer to a particular clue is correct is often dependent upon the support given to the answer by intersecting answers or potential answers. This analogy is developed and articulated so as to present a rich and sophisticated theory of knowledge.

OVERVIEW
MORAL
PHILOSOPHY

Moral philosophy can be divided into two areas: metaethics and normative ethics. The latter further divides into two main areas: practical ethics and an area for which there's no traditional label, but which lies between the very abstract reasoning of metaethics and the concern with individual problems of practical ethics. In Western philosophy especially, the main areas of interest have traditionally been metaethics and the more abstract normative ethics. Practical ethics became important about the middle of the twentieth century, but is now one of the largest areas of philosophy in terms of funding and (partly as a result of this) the amount of research carried out and published, and the number of courses taught at universities.

METAETHICS

"The examination and analysis of questions about the meaning of moral terms (conceptual analysis) or about the nature, status, and knowability of moral values (metaphysics and epistemology)." An example of the former is **R. M. Hare's** argument that it's part of the meaning of moral statements that they be *universalizable*; that is, a specific judgment such as "Mary shouldn't have robbed that bank" is only moral if it implies the general judgment: "No-one (in Mary's position) should rob banks." An example of the latter is **Plato's** argument that there are genuine moral values for us to discover. An example of a combination of the two approaches is **David Wiggins'** argument that we discover moral values, though our understanding isn't completely independent of our conceptual capacities and sensitivity.

The central debate in metaethics is between those who take moral values to be objective and those who take them to be subjective. Each general position further subdivides, however, making the debate a large and complex one. For the record, my own view is a version of *objectivism*: moral values are objective, and applicable to any sentient, sapient, empathic being that shares our sensitivity and sensibility. Such beings share the same basic moral responses and cognitive capacities, which grow out of our knowledge of what it is to feel (for example, pain or fear), our grasp of what it is for others to feel (not simply an intellectual but an emotional grasp), and our ability to reason (for example, to extend our empathy beyond what is immediate or obvious, and to act appropriately).

ABSTRACT NORMATIVE ETHICS

The development of a general way of making moral choices, for example, Do what God tells you! or, Act so as to avoid causing unnecessary suffering! Typical positions include **J. S. Mill's** utilitarian principle: "actions are right in proportion as they tend to promote happiness, wrong as they tend to produce the reverse of happiness" (*Utilitarianism*, Chapter 2). This doesn't tell us what "right" *means*, as in metaethics, nor does it tell us how to act in a certain situation as in practice ethics; rather it gives a general methodology for performing right actions and avoiding wrong ones.

PRACTICAL OR APPLIED ETHICS

The attempt to answer specific questions about how we should act, such as: Are abortion, euthanasia, or suicide morally wrong? How should we treat nonhuman animals? Could there be a genuinely just war? Is there any moral issue with regard to human cloning? Typical conclusions in practical ethics include **Peter Singer's** claims that we shouldn't kill animals for food, and that affluent nations should shelter far more refugees than they in fact do. Here, although he gives extensive arguments for these conclusions, and considers and argues against opposing views, Singer isn't concerned about investigating the nature of morality. The answers to questions in practical ethics must presuppose some metaethical position, and perhaps some position from abstract normative ethics too (in Singer's case, for example, he argues from a Utilitarian position), and much disagreement and confusion in this area can be traced to people's failure to examine their metaethical positions. Practical ethics tends to shade into areas such as political and social philosophy.

PETER SINGER

BORN	1946, Melbourne
DIED	—
MAIN INTERESTS	Ethics, politics
INFLUENCES	Hegel, Bentham, Mill, Marx, Hare
INFLUENCED	—

MAJOR WORKS
Democracy and Disobedience, Animal Liberation, Practical Ethics, The Expanding Circle, How Are We to Live?, Rethinking Life and Death, One World: Ethics and Globalization

Speciesism—the word is not an attractive one, but I can think of no better term—is a prejudice or attitude of bias in favor of the interests of members of one species and against those of members of another species.

Animal Liberation, p.6

Singer's parents were Viennese Jews who fled to Australia in 1938. His father became a successful importer of coffee and tea, and his mother practiced medicine. Singer went to Melbourne University, where he studied law, history, and philosophy, graduating in 1967. Having received an M.A. in 1969 (with a thesis on "Why Should I Be Moral?"), he went on a scholarship to University College, Oxford, to do the B.Phil., which he took in 1971. He was Radcliffe Lecturer at University College from 1971 to 1973, during which time he worked on a thesis on civil disobedience under **R. M. Hare** (published as *Democracy and Disobedience*, in 1973).

From Oxford he went to teach at New York University for sixteen months, during which time he researched and wrote his second book, *Animal Liberation* (1975). He then returned to Melbourne, where, apart from numerous visiting appointments round the world, he has remained—first as senior lecturer at La Trobe University, then from 1977 as professor of philosophy at Monash University. Since 1999 he has also been Ira W. DeCamp Professor of Bioethics at the University Center for Human Values, Princeton.

Not only are Singer's philosophical interests confined largely to the fields of ethics and politics, but even within those fields he's almost solely interested in practical problems such as our treatment of animals, abortion, and euthanasia. Despite this (or perhaps

In a nutshell:
To live a life of compassion and consideration for others is not only morally right, but personally rewarding.

because of it), Singer is one of the best-known modern philosophers, and certainly the most controversial. His greatest influence has been in the field of animal ethics.

ANIMALS
Singer's 1975 book *Animal Liberation* sets out his agenda. In it he argues that though human beings have a long history of mistreating animals, there is no moral justification for such behavior. At the heart of morality is the wrongness of causing unnecessary suffering, but suffering doesn't come in different qualities, only some of which are morally relevant—we can't condemn the pain caused to members of one species while condoning the pain caused to members of another, any more than we can do so for different races or sexes. The fact (insofar as it is a fact) that nonhuman animals lack our intellect and our moral understanding is irrelevant here; it is no more right to make a dog suffer than it is to do the same to a newborn baby.

Animal Liberation contains not only philosophical argument, but also a great deal of evidence about such issues as animal

The rights of animals

If a being suffers there can be no moral justification for refusing to take that suffering into consideration. No matter what the nature of the being, the principle of equality requires that its suffering be counted equally with the like suffering—insofar as rough comparisons can be made—of any other being.

Animal Liberation, *p.8*

Humans have no moral justification for cruelty to animals.

experimentation and factory farming. What it doesn't enter into is the theoretical basis of Singer's moral position, though his references to and quotations from **Jeremy Bentham** indicate the relevance of Utilitarianism; that is, what makes an action morally wrong is its harmful consequences, the pain that it causes. Singer makes this Utilitarian foundation of his views more explicit in later works.

Singer's book has had tremendous impact, not only on individuals—bringing many people, philosophers and nonphilosophers alike, to vegetarianism—but also on society. We now take the notion of animal liberation for granted as a respectable moral cause; when Singer was writing, it was widely seen as the concern of eccentrics and little old ladies with too many cats.

LIFE AND DEATH

Singer's notoriety stems mainly from his conclusions about abortion, euthanasia, and infanticide. He argues that, though they can suffer, the unborn, infants, and severely disabled people lack the ability to plan and anticipate their future; it is therefore morally

permissible, *under certain circumstances*, to end their lives. The proviso is important, as is his careful distinction between what should be said about voluntary and involuntary euthanasia. Singer offers full and rigorous arguments for his various moral positions, but instead of debating the issues with him, many of his opponents (including, unhappily, some philosophers) prefer rhetoric, polemic, and even physical abuse. He has been accused of holding Nazi or near-Nazi views, and campaigners have tried to have his lectures and even academic appointments canceled (and have sometimes succeeded; see, for example, "On Being Silenced In Germany," the appendix to his 1993 edition of *Practical Ethics*).

When opponents do address Singer's arguments, they often do so on the basis of distorted and oversimplified versions—which is especially odd, given that he is one of the clearest of philosophical writers, with much of his work being aimed specifically at a lay readership.

The "pro-choice" stance on abortion argues from a position of individual liberty thereby avoiding the moral status of the fetus. Singer claims abortion cannot be simply about a right to choose, we have to establish that the fetus is not worthy of protection. His controversial stance is that in some circumstances the fetus is indeed not worthy of protection.

SUGGESTED READING

GENERAL BOOKS
Dictionaries
Simon Blackburn, *Oxford Dictionary of Philosophy* (Oxford University Press, 1996)
Nicholas Bunnin & Jiyuan Yu (eds.), *The Blackwell Dictionary of Western Philosophy* (Blackwell, 2004)
Antony Flew & Stephen Priest (eds.), *A Dictionary of Philosophy* (Pan Books, 2002)

Introductions, Companions, and Readers
Kwame Anthony Appiah, *Thinking it Through: An Introduction to Contemporary Philosophy* (Oxford University Press, 2003)
Robert L. Arrington (ed.), *A Companion to the Philosophers* (Blackwell, 1999)
Nicholas Bunnin & Eric Tsui-James (eds.), *The Blackwell Companion to Philosophy* (Blackwell, 2002)
John Cottingham (ed.), *Western Philosophy: An Anthology* (Blackwell, 1996)
Alexander Lyon Macfie (ed.), *Eastern Influences on Western Philosophy: A Reader* (Edinburgh University Press, 2003)
William McNeil & Karen Feldman (eds.), *Continental Philosophy: An Anthology* (Blackwell, 1998)
A. P. Martinich (ed.), *A Companion to Analytic Philosophy* (Blackwell, 2001)
Thomas Nagel, *What Does It All Mean? A Very Short Introduction to Philosophy* (Oxford University Press, 1987)
Ruth J. Sample, Charles W. Mills, James P. Sterba (eds.), *Philosophy: The Big Questions* (Blackwell, 2003)

SPECIFIC AREAS
Metaphysics
Richard Gale (ed.), *The Blackwell Guide to Metaphysics* (Blackwell, 2002)
Peter van Inwagen, *Metaphysics* (Oxford University Press, 1993)
Peter van Inwagen & Dean W. Zimmerman (eds.), *Metaphysics: The Big Questions* (Blackwell, 1998)
Michael Jubien, *Contemporary Metaphysics* (Blackwell, 1997)
Jaegwon Kim (ed.), *Metaphysics: An Anthology* (Blackwell, 1999)
Jaegwon Kim & Ernest Sosa (eds.), *A Companion to Metaphysics* (Blackwell, 1995)

Epistemology
Linda Martin Alcoff (ed.), *Epistemology: The Big Questions* (Blackwell, 1998)
Jonathan Dancy, *Introduction to Contemporary Epistemology* (Blackwell, 1985)
Jonathan Dancy & Ernest Sosa (eds.), *A Companion to Epistemology* (Blackwell, 1992)
Jaegwon Kim (ed.), *Epistemology: An Anthology* (Blackwell, 1999)
Charles Landesman, *An Introduction to Epistemology* (Blackwell, 1997)
Adam Morton, *A Guide through the Theory of Knowledge* (Blackwell, 1997)

Logic and Language
Bob Hale & Crispin Wright (eds.), *A Companion to Philosophy of Language* (Blackwell, 1997)
Dale Jacquette (ed.), *A Companion to Philosophical Logic* (Blackwell, 2002), *Philosophical Logic: An Anthology* (Blackwell, 2001)
Andrea Nye (ed.), *Philosophy of Language: The Big Questions* (Blackwell, 1998)
Stephen Read, *Thinking about Logic* (Oxford University Press, 1995)
Patrick Shaw, *Logic and Its Limits* (Oxford University Press, 1997)

Moral and Political Philosophy
R. G. Frey (ed.), *A Companion to Applied Ethics* (Blackwell, 2003)
Robert E. Goodin & Philip Pettit (eds.), *Contemporary Political Philosophy: An Anthology* (Blackwell, 1997)
Brad Hooker (ed.), *Truth in Ethics* (Blackwell, 1996)
Hugh LaFollette (ed.), *Ethics in Practice: An Anthology* (Blackwell, 1997)
D. McNaughton, *Moral Vision* (Blackwell, 1988)
Robert L. Simon (ed.), *The Blackwell Guide to Social and Political Philosophy* (Blackwell, 2002)
Peter Singer, *Practical Ethics* (Cambridge University Press, 1993)
Peter Singer (ed.), *A Companion to Ethics* (Blackwell, 1993)
James P. Sterba (ed.), *Ethics: The Big Questions* (Blackwell, 1998)
Leo Strauss & Joseph Cropsey (eds.), *History of Political Philosophy* (University of Chicago Press, 1987)
Adam Swift, *Political Philosophy: A Beginners' Guide for Students and Politicians* (Polity Press, 2001)
Bernard Williams, *Morality: An Introduction to Ethics* (Cambridge University Press, 1993)

Philosophy of Mind
Samuel Guttenplan (ed.), *A Companion to Philosophy of Mind* (Blackwell, 1994)
Jaegwon Kim, *Philosophy of Mind* (Oxford University Press, 1996)
Colin McGinn, *The Character of Mind* (Oxford University Press, 1982)
Thomas Nagel, *The View from Nowhere* (Oxford University Press, 1986)
Georges Rey, *Contemporary Philosophy of Mind* (Blackwell, 1996)
Bernard Williams, *Problems of the Self* (Cambridge University Press, 1973)

Philosophy of Religion
Brian Davies, *An Introduction to the Philosophy of Religion* (Oxford University Press, 1993)

J. L. Mackie, *The Miracle of Theism* (Oxford University Press, 1982)
Philip Quinn & Charles Taliaferro (eds.), *A Companion to Philosophy of Religion* (Blackwell, 1999)
Eleonore Stump & Michael J. Murray (eds.), *Philosophy of Religion: The Big Questions* (Blackwell, 1999)
Charles Taliaferro, *Contemporary Philosophy of Religion* (Blackwell, 1998)

Philosophy of Science

David L. Hull, *Philosophy of the Biological Sciences* (Prentice-Hall, 1974)
Peter Machamer & Michael Silberstein (eds.), *The Blackwell Guide to the Philosophy of Science* (Blackwell, 2002)
W. H. Newton-Smith (eds.), *A Companion to the Philosophy of Science* (Blackwell, 2000)
Lawrence Sklar, *Philosophy of Physics* (Oxford University Press, 1992)
Elliott Sober, *Philosophy of Biology* (Oxford University Press, 1993)

SPECIFIC PERIODS

Steven M. Emmanuel (ed.), *The Blackwell Guide to the Modern Philosophers* (Blackwell, 2000)
Patrick Gardiner (ed.), *Nineteenth-Century Philosophy* (Free Press, 1969)
Jorge J. E. Gracia & Timothy Noone (eds.), *A Companion to Philosophy in the Middle Ages* (Blackwell, 2002)
Steven Nadler (ed.), *A Companion to Early Modern Philosophy* (Blackwell, 2002)
Terry Pinkard, *German Philosophy, 1760–1860 : The Legacy of Idealism* (Cambridge University Press, 2002)
Christopher C. Shields, *The Blackwell Guide to Ancient Philosophy* (Blackwell, 2002)

NON-WESTERN TRADITIONS

Ray Billington, *Understanding Eastern Philosophy* (Routledge, 1997)
Brian Carr & Indira Mahalingam (eds.), *Companion Encyclopedia of Asian Philosophy* (Routledge, 1997)
Eliot Deutsch & Ron Bontekof (eds.), *A Companion to World Philosophies* (Blackwell, 1997)
Robert & Kathleen Higgins Solomon (eds.), *From Africa to Zen: An Invitation to World Philosophy* (Rowan & Littlefield, 2003)

African

Kwame Gyekye, *An Essay on African Philosophical Thought: The Akan Conceptual Scheme* (Temple University Press, 1995)
Paulin Hountondji, *African Philosophy: Myth and Reality* (Indiana University Press, 1983)

Samuel Oluoch Imbo, *An Introduction to African Philosophy* (Rowan & Littlefield, 1998)
Tsenay Serequeberhan (ed.), *African Philosophy: The Essential Readings* (Paragon House, 1991)
Kwasi Wiredu, *Philosophy and an African Culture* (Cambridge University Press, 1990)
Kwasi Wiredu (ed.), *A Companion to African Philosophy* (Blackwell, 2004)

Chinese

Chung-Ying Cheng & Nicholas Bunnin (eds.), *Contemporary Chinese Philosophy* (Blackwell, 2002)
Feng Yu-lan (trans. Derek Bodde), *A History of Chinese Philosophy* (Princeton University Press, 1983)
Fung Yu-Lan, *A Short History of Chinese Philosophy* (Free Press, 1997)
Philip J. Ivanhoe and Bryan W. Van Norden (eds.), *Readings in Classical Chinese Philosophy* (Seven Bridges Press, 2001)
Wing-Tsit Chan (ed.), *Sourcebook in Chinese Philosophy* (Princeton University Press, 1992)

Indian

Sue Hamilton, *Indian Philosophy: A Very Short Introduction* (Oxford University Press, 2001)
Richard King, *Indian Philosophy: An Introduction to Hindu and Buddhist Thought* (Edinburgh University Press, 1999)
J. N. Mohanty, *Classical Indian Philosophy* (Rowan & Littlefield, 2000)
Sarvepalli Radhakrishnan and Charles A. Moore (eds.), *A Source Book in Indian Philosophy* (Princeton University Press, 1967)

GLOSSARY

A POSTERIORI Knowledge is *a posteriori* (or *empirical*) if it can only be gained through experience. (*see* a priori)

A PRIORI Knowledge is *a priori* if it can be gained without experience. (*see* a posteriori, empirical)

ANALYTIC A statement is said to be analytic if it's true or false solely by virtue of the meanings in the words it contains. (*see* synthetic)

ANTIREALISM There are many kinds of antirealism, some applying to everything, some only to certain categories (such as moral values or the future). The antirealist generally holds either that statements of the relevant kind are neither true nor false, or that objects or events of the relevant kind don't actually exist. (*see* realism)

ATOMISM Literally, the view that the (physical) world is made up of atoms—tiny, indivisible, fundamental particles—in various arrangements. The term can be applied to other areas, as for example *logical atomism*, according to which language is explained in terms of simple, fundamental units of meaning, which correspond to the simple, fundamental facts that make up the world.

CARTESIAN "Of Descartes." Applied either to Descartes' arguments, positions, and methods, or (sometimes misleadingly) to those of his followers.

COGNITIVE Of the mental, processes involving or related to understanding, belief, knowledge (as opposed, for example, to willing). Of utterances those that can be true or false (as opposed, for example, to commands or questions).

COHERENTISM The coherentist holds that our knowledge of a set of propositions is founded in the strength of their coherence—in the way that they fit together and support each other. (*see* foundationalism)

COMPATIBILISM The position, also known as *soft determinism*, that moral responsibility, praise, and blame are compatible with the view that the world is wholly determined—that every event, whether physical or mental, has a wholly determining cause.

CONCEPTUALISM The theory that the meaning of general and abstract terms rests on them referring to concepts. (*see* nominalism, realism)

CONTINGENT Something is contingent if it depends upon something else for its existence, occurrence, or nature, or if it might not have existed. A proposition is contingently true or false if it might have been otherwise.

DUALISM The view that there are two kinds of thing. The most common dualism is the view that the world consists of mental and physical objects (minds and bodies). (*see* monism, physicalism, idealism)

EMOTIVISM The metaethical theory that what appear to be moral statements are in fact expressions of the speakers' emotions, and thus not true or false. (*see* subjectivism)

EMPIRICAL An empirical belief is one whose justification depends upon experience. (*see* a priori, a posteriori)

EMPIRICISM The view that all knowledge (or all knowledge apart from that of the nature of relations between concepts, as in logic) is based on experience—usually, though not always, sense experience.

EPISTEMOLOGY The view that what justifies beliefs needn't be known to the justified believer.

EXTERNALISM Philosophy of mind and language: the view that the contents of our mental states and the meanings of our words derive, not from within us, but from the external world.

FOUNDATIONALISM The foundationalist holds that the possibility of knowledge rests ultimately on a set of beliefs, which don't themselves need justification in terms of further beliefs; such foundational beliefs may be *a priori* or *a posteriori*. (*see* coherentism, positivism)

FUNCTIONALISM The *physicalist* thesis that mental states are defined by what causes them and by their effects (on behavior).

IDEALISM The *monistic* metaphysical thesis that the world is fundamentally (the product of the) mental. This basic thesis comes in very different forms, including those of **Leibniz**, **Berkeley**, and **Hegel**. (*see* physicalism)

LINGUISTIC TURN refers to a switch in interest by many philosophers in the Anglo-American tradition from talking about what there is, how we know about it, how we ought to behave, and so on, to talking about the words we use.

MATERIALISM In the philosophy of mind. (*see* physicalism)

MODALITY The modality of a proposition *p* is the way (the mode) in which *p* is true; we might say for example that *p* is necessary, or possible, or past, or future, or permissible, or obligatory. Philosophers—and especially logicians and philosophers of logic—have tended to concentrate on the "logical modalities" such as necessity and possibility.

MONISM Any theory that argues that there is only one kind of thing in a given domain. With regard to the nature of the world, the main monistic approaches are *idealism* and *physicalism*.

NECESSARY Something is necessary if it depends upon nothing else for its existence, or if its non-existence is impossible. A proposition is necessarily true or false if it couldn't have been otherwise. (*see* contingent)

NOMINALISM In medieval philosophy, the view that only individuals exist, *universals* being merely names. (*see* realism)

PARADOX A paradox occurs when a valid argument with premises thought to be true has a conclusion that contradicts either itself or some other proposition thought to be true. Paradoxes are important because they indicate the existence of a mistake of some sort—usually with one or more of the premises of the argument in question.

PHYSICALISM The *monistic* metaphysical thesis that there is nothing but the physical. Specifically, there is no non-physical mental substance, there are no minds; every genuine matter of fact can be explained in terms of

physical things and their relationships.

POSITIVISM The *foundationalist* view (essentially a radical *empiricism*) that either all genuine knowledge or the highest form of knowledge comes from our sensory experience of the world; such knowledge is positive in that it is given in experience and needs no further (metaphysical or theological) justification. Logical positivism was an even more extreme version, drawing on modern advances in formal logic, and extending positivist claims to meaning.

PRAGMATISM American philosophical school centered on a theory of meaning (and, among later pragmatists, truth): the meaning of a concept, or the truth of a proposition, is exhausted by its practical implications.

PROPOSITION We can distinguish between sentences, which are linguistic items used to make statements, which express propositions. A proposition is what is stated, believed, implied, understood; to understand a statement is to grasp the proposition that it expresses.

REALISM In medieval philosophy, the view (opposed to *nominalism*) that *universals* exist independently of our thought. More generally, realism in any area is the view, either that a certain sort of object (or property, or state of affairs) really exists, or that a certain sort of statement can be true or false. (*see* antirealism, physicalism, relativism, subjectivism)

RELATIVISM The view that, at least in some areas, truth is relative

to a culture, society, or other relevant idea-system.

SUBJECTIVISM A general approach to morality according to which moral judgments are in some way an expression of the individual's tastes or feelings. Subjectivist theories range from crude *emotivism*, according to which "murder is wrong" says no more than "murder—boo!" to the claim that moral judgments are universal (because all or most human beings have the same basic emotional reactions to the same actions and events), but that this universality is contingent and liable to change.

SUBSTANCE Traditionally, one of the main concerns of metaphysics; thus, many accounts of substance have been argued for. The three main (and interlinked) notions are: whatever it is that underlies properties but can't itself be a property (substance as **substratum**); whatever exists independently of anything else; the essence or real nature of a thing.

SYNTHETIC A statement is said to be synthetic if it's true or false in virtue of the way the world is. (*see* analytic)

UTILITARIANISM Moral and political theory according to which the morality of an action is purely a function of the amount of happiness or unhappiness that it produces for others (our judgment of the morality of a person, on the other hand, must take motives into account).

WORLD Everything that exists; thus, the world isn't a separate object, but simply the totality of objects (or, on some accounts, the totality of facts or of events).

INDEX

CREDITS

Quarto would like to thank and acknowledge the following for supplying illustrations and photographs reproduced in this book:

(Key: l left, r right, c center, t top, b bottom, b/g background)

6, 7, 61t, 63t, 85, 131t, 142b Bettmann / CORBIS; 8 Science Museum, London/HIP / TOPFOTO; 9 The Image Works / TOPFOTO; 10b/g Wolfgang Kaehler / CORBIS; 13t CM Dixon / HIP / TOPFOTO; 24b Ted Spiegel / CORBIS; 26b Stock Montage / GETTY IMAGES; 27 Araldo de Luca / CORBIS; 39tl, 51b, 53l, 78b/g, 116b/g Archivo Iconografico, S.A. / CORBIS; 42b/g, 113t, 169t The British Library/HIP / TOPFOTO; 51t Christine Osborne / CORBIS 55, 67, 69, 73, 83t, 109, 111, 118, 127, 179 TOPFOTO; 65 Otto Rogge / CORBIS; 71t Gianni Dagli Orti / CORBIS; 89 Stapleton Collection / CORBIS; 95, 96b, 99t, 105t, 121b, 135t, 136b/g Hulton Archive / GETTY IMAGES; 97 Karen Huntt / CORBIS; 121t Fotomas / TOPFOTO; 123t HIP / TOPFOTO; 139cr, 178 Robert P. Matthews, Princeton University; 140b Scheufler Collection / CORBIS; 141t Austrian Archives / CORBIS; 143 Todd Pearson / CORBIS; 145 Jimmy Sime / Central Press / GETTY IMAGES; 149t Trinity College Library, Cambridge; 157t Hulton-Deutsch Collection / CORBIS; 163t Yevgeny Khaldei / CORBIS; 170b Peter Stubbs www.edinphoto.org.uk; 177 Herman Leonard / ArenaPAL; 183t Les Stone / CORBIS; 183b David Reed / CORBIS

All other illustrations and photographs are the copyright of Quarto Publishing plc. While every effort has been made to credit contributors, Quarto would like to apologize should there have been any omissions or errors—and would be pleased to make the appropriate correction for future editions of the book.

AUTHOR ACKNOWLEDGMENTS
My thanks to those philosophers who supplied me with information and suggestions, and especially to Andrea Christofidou for her help and support.